DEDICATION

·

*To every preacher who is guided by the words
of the Holy Spirit in proclaiming the gospel
as God's power to save, and who honors the church as "the temple of
God" in which the Holy Spirit
dwells, is this volume in-
scribed by the
author*

Books by

H. Leo Boles

———————

ELAM'S NOTES (FOUR VOLUMES, 1928-1931)

IS INSTRUMENTAL MUSIC IN CHRISTIAN WORSHIP SCRIPTURAL?

UNFULFILLED PROPHECY

BIOGRAPHICAL SKETCHES OF GOSPEL PREACHERS

BOLES' BIBLE QUESTIONS

COMMENTARY ON MATTHEW

COMMENTARY ON LUKE

COMMENTARY ON ACTS OF APOSTLES

THE HOLY SPIRIT

The Holy Spirit

His Personality, Nature, Works

By

H. LEO BOLES

GOSPEL ADVOCATE COMPANY
Nashville, Tennessee

Published by Gospel Advocate Co.
P.O. Box 150
Nashville, TN 37202
www.gospeladvocate.com

First Published: 1942

ISBN 0-89225-501-3

PREFACE

The author of this book gave a series of lectures during the month of January, 1938, on "The Holy Spirit" at Freed-Hardeman College, Henderson, Tennessee. Many gospel preachers heard these lectures and suggested that a book should be written on the subject. Encouraged by so many to write the book, the author has kept the subject in mind and on his heart for these five years; special research work for three years was made and the entire field of books available on the Holy Spirit has been studied; this work represents two years of intensive study on the subject.

A sermon preached or an article written and published may be remembered for only a few days or months and then fade from the memory and be lost, but a book on such an important subject as one member of the Godhead may live for centuries, and be read by thousands in each generation. This reminds one forcibly of the weighty responsibility that rests upon an author of a book. Eternity alone can reveal the good or evil that a book may do. The author of this book lays just claim to at least one merit of it: *it is written in the language of "the common people."* It is free from the theological terms that usually burden a book on such a theme; it is hoped that it may be read with ease and profit. There will be found some repetitions of arguments which have purposely been made that certain truths may be impressed on the reader.

No claim is made to absolute perfection for this book; however, it is claimed that the revealed truth of the Bible is expressed on its pages. A word in vindication of the treatment of this subject should be made. So far as the author knows, there is no book on the Holy Spirit that discusses so many phases of this important subject in such a simple way as presented in this work. There are many books on the work of the Holy Spirit, but these do not present the truth as is here discussed. The Scriptures throughout are let to be the exponents of the Holy Spirit himself and his work. The Bible is the words of God through the Holy Spirit, and it has seemed wise and best to let the Holy Spirit explain his own works. Many treatments of this great theme have gone into the field of theology and cumbered the discussions with traditional vagaries that confuse the reader. So the aim in the following pages has been to bring together the Scriptures, and to present them in a coherent way to enable the reader to grasp easily divine thought. Many aspects of the Holy Spirit and his work had to be touched upon lightly, or not at all, as space would not permit such a full discussion that some of the subjects seem to demand.

Many long-cherished theories and oft-repeated traditions about the Holy Spirit which have been made respectable by age and popularity have been exposed and refuted. No apology is made for a vigorous refutation of the·errors which have long clustered around "The Holy Ghost." No subject of such importance to the salvation of man is more confused in the minds of the common people than the work of the Holy Spirit; hence, the need of a frank and clear discussion on the subject. It is a frequent and just complaint among the common people that the doctrine of the Holy Spirit has been strangely neglected. Even preachers are not clear on this subject; many of them have preached one or two sermons on the subject, and that is about all that is usually done in the study of this question. Sometimes an article may have appeared in some religious journal on the subject, and that is about the extent of the teaching or study that has been given to this subject. It is hoped that the present study with all its limitations may contribute something to the reader and lead him into a fuller and more accurate understanding of the Holy Spirit.

The Scripture text at the head of each chapter expresses the theme of the chapter. There is a progressive development in the arrangement of the chapters on the personality, nature, and work of the Holy Spirit. The brief outline at the beginning of each chapter will aid the reader in studying the chapter; moreover, this outline may serve as the foundation of a sermon. Hence, the book may be considered as a series of sermons on thirty-six phases of the Holy Spirit and his work. No display of knowledge or attainment by the author has been sought, but a plain, practical, and scriptural presentation of the simple truth is here presented on *The Holy Spirit*.

H. Leo Boles.

March 4, 1942.

CONTENTS

PART ONE

PART TWO

CONTENTS

INTRODUCTION

Perhaps the average reader thinks of the introduction to a book as unnecessary and uninteresting matter. Sometimes he is right. The writer will not inflict on the readers of this volume a long one.

The subject of this book is one about which there is much false teaching and popular misunderstanding. Is the Holy Spirit an influence, a mere energy, or a person? Does he operate directly upon the sinner in conversion or through means and instrumentalities? Does he operate only through the Word of God? How does he dwell in the church? These are a few of the many phases of the subject discussed in this treatise. This is by far the most thorough and comprehensive treatment of the Holy Spirit to be found among the churches of Christ. It is an indispensable contribution to the literature on the subject.

In the preparation of this work Brother Boles has given us a rare volume. Some books are rare because of their age; others, because of their scarcity; others, by reason of their associations; and, still others, by reason of their intrinsic value. Someone has said that the rarest kind of a book is one to be read—one really worth reading. This is a book worth reading and re-reading. It is a book, as Bacon would say, "to be chewed and digested—to be read wholly and with diligence and attention." We predict for it just this treatment from Bible students and scholars.

"A great book that comes from a great thinker, it is a ship of thought, deep-freighted with truth, with beauty too. It sails the ocean, driven by the winds of heaven, breaking the level sea of life into beauty where it goes, leaving behind it a train of sparkling loveliness, widening as the ship goes on. And what a treasure it brings to every land, scattering the seeds of truth, justice, love, and piety to bless the world in ages yet to come."

For this volume we predict a wide circulation and a period of usefulness that will extend to generations yet unborn.

B. C. GOODPASTURE.

PART ONE

CHAPTER I

THE HOLY SPIRIT

INTRODUCTION.

Every Bible subject to be studied; some to be studied more than others; some are more practical than others.

I. THIS A NEGLECTED BIBLE THEME.

    1. Why neglected.

    2. Is a prominent Bible subject.

    3. Why given a subordinate place in Christian thinking.

    4. Holy Spirit left in obscurity too long.

    5. Must be restored to proper place.

II. HISTORY OF CHRISTIAN THOUGHT.

    1. Eighteenth century placed emphasis on God the Father.

    2. Nineteenth century placed stress on Christ the Savior.

    3. Twentieth century should accentuate equally the Holy Spirit.

    4. Work of Holy Spirit overshadowed by salvation in Christ.

III. IGNORANCE ABOUT THE HOLY SPIRIT.

    1. More superstition than on other subjects.

    2. Many minds cluttered with useless traditions.

    3. Few think of Holy Spirit as a divine person.

IV. BIBLE ONLY SOURCE OF INFORMATION.

    1. May learn of God in nature. (Psalm 19: 1.)

    2. His wisdom and power declared in nature.

    3. Cannot learn of Christ from nature.

    4. Cannot learn about Holy Spirit from nature.

    5. Must go to the Bible.

    6. Holy Spirit doctrine deeply imbedded in Bible.

THE HOLY SPIRIT

"But the Comforter, even the Holy Spirit, . . . he shall teach you all things." (John 14: 26.)

All things that God has revealed to man and preserved for man in the Bible should be studied diligently and prayerfully. The fact that God has spoken to man and recorded that message by inspiration, and preserved to the present time this message, carries with it sufficient importance to impel man to study it. There are some phases of Bible teaching that are of more practical value today than others. That which God has spoken to Christians is of more practical value than some of the messages found in Old Testament Scripture. That which was spoken to Abraham was highly important to him, but is not as urgent on us as some of the lessons on Christian living. While everything in the Bible has its value in the edification of God's people today, yet there are different degrees of appraisement on various teachings; hence, the study of some subjects is of greater essentiality than some others. However, no phase of Bible teaching is to be willfully neglected in our study. We should study what the Bible teaches about the Holy Spirit.

I. THIS A NEGLECTED BIBLE THEME

The Bible teachings about the Holy Spirit and his works are among the most neglected phases and aspects of our teaching. The subject of the Holy Spirit is so sublime and so far beyond the knowledge of the ordinary person that it has been neglected, if it is not the most forgotten phase of Bible teaching. It is difficult to understand why this Bible theme freighted with such importance should be so long neglected. No subject that is so vitally connected with man's redemption has been neglected as the study of the Holy Spirit. It is a prominent Bible subject; it stands out as emphatically as the subject of faith. The doctrine of the Holy Spirit is a cardinal and unmistakable teaching of Christ and receives in the Bible a large place.

This subject has been given a subordinate place in Christian thinking. Religious leaders have not studied the subject and, hence, have not been stressing the teaching of the Bible about the Holy Spirit; the religious leaders have been ignorant of this phase of Bible teaching and have emphasized other teachings until the subject has been almost lost or enshrouded in superstition. There is needed today a thorough scriptural examination and exposition of the great truths revealed in the Bible concerning the third member of the Godhead. Even those who have been doing some teaching on this subject need to re-examine the truth of the Holy Spirit as taught in the Bible. Not only should teachers restudy this subject, but all lovers of Bible truth, in the sphere of practical piety, need a fresh study of the Holy Spirit. It is hoped that some light may be thrown on different aspects of this subject, both in its relation to Christian thinking and to practical Christian living. This study of the person, work, and ministry of the Holy Spirit is undertaken with great humility; an approach to the subject is made with a consciousness of the need for reverence, wisdom, and guidance by him of whom these things are now written.

An endeavor is here made to lift this challenging theme from obscurity in Christian thought to the hilltops of clarity in our thinking. Of all the theological problems that have ever engaged the mind of man, probably none have presented so much difficulty; it is to be hoped that this study will not lead the student to any dizzy heights of metaphysical speculations. It is true that this great theme has its difficulties and that the subject still bristles with vexing questions and unsolved problems; however, there is the simple side of the teachings of God's Word on this theme, and we may comprehend easily much of the Bible teaching on the Holy Spirit. This subject must be restored to its proper place in the plan of salvation; it must be brought into the fore of Christian thinking and living.

II. HISTORY OF CHRISTIAN THOUGHT

Much may be gained by reviewing the history of Christian thought; there may be gleaned from this history some facts that will enable one to make a study of the Holy Spirit with greater enthusiasm. One needs but to go back to the eighteenth century to get the trend of thought on great Bible themes. During the eighteenth century great emphasis was put on the study of God as the Father. During this time many different phases of Bible teaching on God were made; his nature, his relation to the universe, his power, wisdom, and love, all received due emphasis. Many intricate and complex questions were raised at that time concerning the foreordination and predestination of God; profound theories were advanced about his providence; and indubitable and unquestionable facts were collated of the works of God, His love for his people and his Fatherly care over them received much attention. No one would claim that undue emphasis was placed upon God or any of his characteristics, nature, or works; however, not enough stress was placed upon other subjects. That field was cultivated to the neglect of other fields of thought and Bible teaching.

As is prone with human thinking, the pendulum swung to another extreme; so in the nineteenth century theologians began to neglect the study of God and placed emphasis on the study of Christ. Before the nineteenth century closed, great emphasis had been placed on the study of Christ. There was a great hunger for knowledge concerning Christ as the Savior. There were more treatises on the doctrine of Christ than ever before; more lives of Christ were written in the nineteenth century than all the other centuries put together. Many impractical questions were raised and discussed. What is the relation between God and Christ? How could divinity become humanity? How could the Son of God, if divine, die? How can his blood cleanse from sin? What were the mysteries of the atonement? Why was it necessary for Christ to die? Such profound questions were studied and answers were attempted during the nineteenth century. Many foolish questions were also asked and considered. Why was Jesus a man and not a woman found a place in the discussion of theologians. All through the nineteenth century study was made of the historical Christ. They wanted to know what he was like; what he really taught; what he actually did; whether his miracles were real. There was a deep feeling that the creeds had obscured the real Bible teaching concerning the Savior of man. Like the eighteenth century, not too much emphasis was placed on Christ as the Savior of man, but other teachings of the Bible were neglected.

The twentieth century should place equal emphasis on the third member of the Godhead. A plea is here made, not that God should receive less emphasis, neither that Christ should not be made as prominent in Christian thinking, but that the Holy Spirit should receive due emphasis in the revelation of God to man, and be brought out of the fog and obscurity into the sunlight of Bible truth as revealed in the book of God. It seems that everywhere men and women are found groping and hungering for more definite knowledge of the Holy Spirit. In many circles of religious people may be found people who want to break through the barriers of circumstance and the limitations of present-day doctrines and launch out into a larger freedom of thought on the subject of the Holy Spirit. It is now time to help those whose hearts are yearning for a fuller knowledge of Bible truth on this subject; it is time to break the shackles of tradition and liberate souls from the bondage of ignorance about the Holy Spirit. The work of the Holy Spirit has been overshadowed by our salvation in Christ; hence we do not appreciate the fact that the Holy Spirit has such an important part in man's salvation.

III. Ignorance About the Holy Spirit

People know something about God; they know more about Christ. They know that God is a Spirit, or a spiritual being; they know something of his characteristics and attributes; they know his omnipresence and his omniscience; they know his love and mercy. They know the personality of Christ and his advent to earth; they know that he came in the flesh, lived in a body like ours, was crucified, buried, raised from the dead, and ascended back to God. But they know very little about the Holy Spirit. There has clustered around this member of the Godhead so many superstitions and traditions that people know very little of the Holy Spirit and his ministry. So many mistakes have been made under the influence of tradition about the Holy Spirit, and such disastrous results have come from errors in teaching about the Holy Spirit, that it is difficult to clear the mind so that the truth of God can guide them in their study. There should be no partial teaching on this subject, no teaching without a full and comprehensive knowledge of all the Scriptures on this subject; a partial truth is often the source of the gravest error. No other subject mentioned in the Bible is surrounded with such unwarranted opinions, false practices, and abominable customs as that of the Holy Spirit.

So many minds are cluttered with the useless plunder of traditions and superstitions which prevent their accepting the truth that it is almost impossible for some people to get a correct understanding of the Holy Spirit and his work. People must come to the Bible free from any predisposition to the particular tradition or any special interpretation or peculiar emphasis that may be biased by religious superstition. One must come to the subject with no textbook but the Bible and with a complete willingness to let the Bible say what it says, and to make such interpretations and applications as come evidently from a careful and prayerful study of the entire Bible on this sublime theme.

Very few people have learned to think of the Holy Spirit as a divine person. If people would learn to think of the Holy Spirit as they do God and Christ, much of the confusion would clear away. The Holy Spirit must be regarded as a member of the Godhead, and as a divine being. Any other conception does injustice to the subject. Let all attempt to clear their minds of the jumble of chaos on the subject and "receive with meekness the implanted word" on this very important subject. The light of divine truth can dispel the darkness that has surrounded many with respect to the simple teaching of the Bible.

IV. BIBLE ONLY SOURCE OF INFORMATION

God's "elder scriptures," the book of nature, reveal much about God. No one can study nature without studying God. Everything in the earth, on the earth, or above the earth reveals something about God. The laws of the natural realm are the thoughts of God. "The heavens declare the glory of God; and the firmament showeth his handiwork. Day unto day uttereth speech, and night unto night showeth knowledge." (Psalm 19: 1, 2.) The most insignificant thing in nature, if studied intelligently, will reveal something about God. Much may be learned from nature about the power, wisdom, and existence of God. When the heavens "declare the glory of God," they at the same time declare the existence of God. Nothing could declare the glory of anyone or anything without at the same time declaring the existence of that one.

> "God moves in a mysterious way
>   His wonders to perform;
> He plants his footsteps in the sea
>   And rides upon the storm."

We cannot learn of Christ from nature. We must come to revelation in order to learn of Christ. No matter how close a student of nature may observe, he cannot see Christ in nature; no matter how profound may be one's research in nature, he cannot find Christ. The same is true with respect to the Holy Spirit. While the Holy Spirit and Christ were present at the creation of the universe and had something to do with creation, yet the study of the material universe does not reveal anything about the nature or work of the Holy Spirit in the redemption of man. The only source to which we can go to learn of the Holy Spirit is the Bible. The teaching concerning the Holy Spirit is deeply imbedded in the Bible. From the first of Genesis to the last of Revelation do we find something about the Holy Spirit. All that man has ever known or can know about the Holy Spirit must be learned from the Bible. We honor the Bible as the authority for all information on this important and sublime theme. If the study of the Bible on this question is neglected, man must forever remain in the eclipse of the darkness of ignorance. "But unto us God revealed them through the Spirit: for the Spirit searcheth all things, yea, the deep things of God." (1 Cor. 2: 10.)

As we can learn of Christ only through revelation and a record of his work, so we can learn of the Holy Spirit only through his work. The Bible is a work of the Holy Spirit; in it he reveals himself as fully as man can know him. There is no need for man to look into nature to learn about the Holy Spirit; there is no use for man to look at the experiences and traditions of men to learn of the Holy Spirit. The only true source of information is the Bible—a product of the Holy Spirit. It is true that many have failed to study the Bible to learn of the work of the Holy Spirit; they have sought to learn of his work by looking into the hearts of men and hearing them relate their experiences. There is need to reiterate that the Bible is our only authority for all that we may know about the Holy Spirit. It has been neglected as a book that teaches much about the Holy Spirit. It matters not how man may have overlooked the study of the Bible, the fact remains that the Bible only can teach us of the Holy Spirit. The Holy Spirit has been overlooked in the writings, discourses, sermons, conversations, prayers, meditations of men, and only traditions which have been handed down have found a place in the teachings of many about the Holy Spirit. Throughout the Bible sentences, verses, and paragraphs are sown broadcast on many pages about the Holy Spirit; it is easy to collect what the Bible reveals about the Holy Spirit; hence, the task of collating material for meditation is easy enough. The teachings of the Bible concerning the Holy Spirit have occupied a comparatively small place in the public teachings of many preachers. Let us honor the Bible as the Book that reveals to us the Holy Spirit, his nature, works and part in the redemption of the race.

Chapter II

THE GODHEAD

Introduction.

"Godhead," same as "Godhood." Godhood and manhood used in a similar way.

I. Godhead Composed of Three Members.

1. God the Creator, Father.
2. The Word, Son of God, Christ.
3. The Holy Spirit, Comforter.

II. Other Names for Godhead.

1. The divine family.
2. Trinity.
3. The sacred three.
4. The divinity.
5. The deity.

III. Holy Spirit Coeternal with God and Christ.

1. "God" (Gen. 1: 1) plural in the Hebrew.
2. "Let *us* make man in *our* image." (Gen. 1: 26; 3: 22.)
3. Baptism in the name of the three. (Matt. 28: 19.)
4. Entreaty to God by Christ and the Holy Spirit. (Rom. 15: 30.)
5. Benediction in name of three. (2 Cor. 13: 14.)

IV. Need to Know Holy Spirit.

1. Must study the Bible.
2. Doctrine of Godhead lies at the heart of revealed truth.
3. Wrong views of Holy Spirit lead to confusion.
4. False theories.
5. Must accept only what is revealed.

CHAPTER II

THE GODHEAD

"We ought not to think that the Godhead is like unto gold, or silver, or stone, graven by art and device of man." (Acts 17 : 29.)
"For in him dwelleth all the fulness of the Godhead bodily." (Col. 2 : 9.)

In a complete study of the Holy Spirit we must study the Godhead. "Godhead" is another form of "Godhood"; in many ancient forms these two words stand side by side; both have survived until today, though not in equally common use. "Godhead" is more frequently used now than "Godhood." "The Godhead" is frequently used merely as a stronger synonym of "God," although it is used with more or less emphasis upon that in God which makes him God. The fundamental meaning of "Godhead" is the same as that of "Godhood"; these terms express the state, dignity, condition, quality of Jehovah. As manhood is used to express that which makes a man a man, and childhood that which makes a child a child, so Godhead is that which makes God God. When Godhead is applied to a being, we affirm that all that enters into the idea of God belongs to him. In this use of the term "Godhead" is equivalent to the Latin "Divinity"; it also means the same as "Deity."

The term "Godhead" is found but few times in the New Testament. In the Authorized Version it is found three times. (Acts 17 : 29; Rom. 1 : 20; Col. 2 : 9.) There are three different Greek words in each of these passages; they are "theion" (Acts 17 : 29), "theiotes" (Rom. 1 : 20), and "theotes" (Col. 2 : 9). "Theion" means that which is divine, concretely, "the deity." In Acts 17 : 29 Paul uses this term in addressing a heathen audience; it throws emphasis on the idea of God as contrasted with that which is made by the hand of man. "Divinity" and "Deity" are not found in the King James Version of the New Testament. The Revised Version translates "theiotes" "Divinity" in Rom. 1 : 20. Paul says in Rom. 1 : 20 that the "everlasting power and divinity" are clearly seen by the works of God. Here "theiotes" means the whole of that by which God is constituted what we mean by "God." "Theotes" in Col. 2 : 9 means that in Christ is seen the

Father and the Holy Spirit; the whole plenitude of the Godhead dwells in Christ.

I. Godhead Composed of Three Members

There are three members of the Godhead. Standing first always in the triune divinity is God. He is the Creator, Jehovah, the Almighty, Lord God, and Father. He is revealed to us in the Bible as supreme in wisdom, power, love, mercy, and justice; he is the Creator of the universe; he is the great Planner and Designer of the universe; he is supreme in authority and the Sovereign Ruler of the universe. In the spiritual realm he is the Father of our spirits. We are taught to address him as "our Father who art in heaven." He stands related to us as the God and Father of his people. He is a Spirit, or spiritual being; it is in him, or by his grace and mercy, that we live and have our being. He is always placed at the head of the list of the divine family. God is not only a being; he is a spiritual being; he is a divine personality; he is a divine, speaking personality with all power and wisdom. He must be regarded as such. He is always referred to in the masculine gender and with a personal pronoun.

Christ is placed as the second member of the Godhead; he is given many names and titles in the Bible. Some of the names given to God are also applied to Christ. In his relation to man he is said to be the "Son of man"; in his relation to God he is called "the Son of God." He is the only member of the Godhead that has been clothed in the flesh. He was born of Mary of the tribe of Judah in the flesh; he lived in this body and accomplished the will of God; he became "obedient even unto death, yea, the death of the cross." He was buried and was raised from the dead for our justification. Before he came to earth he existed "in the form of God, counted not the being on an equality with God a thing to be grasped, but emptied himself, taking the form of a servant, being made in the likeness of men." (Phil. 2: 6, 7.) He is the Savior of man, the Redeemer of our race.

The third member of the Godhead is the Holy Spirit. This member is of the same nature and essence as God and Christ; the Godhead is thus composed of three coeternal and coequal persons;

they are the same in nature and essence, but are distinct personalities. The Holy Spirit is always put third when spoken of in the Bible; as God is placed first in the Trinity, so the Holy Spirit is put third; Christ, when spoken of in connection with the other two members, is thus put between them. The Holy Spirit is called the Comforter, and other titles are given to him in the Bible. It is enough now to think of the Holy Spirit in his coordinated relation to the other members of the Godhead. When spoken of in relation to the other members, the Bible refers to the Holy Spirit in terms of personality. Christ spoke of the Holy Spirit as a person distinct from himself.

II. Other Names for Godhead

It is wise to speak of things as the Bible speaks of them; it is right to speak of the divine persons as the Bible speaks of them; then, and only then, can we know that we are using the correct terms. However, man has coined other words as synonyms, titles, and names for some of the persons and things that belong to God. In a complete study of the Holy Spirit and the Godhead, it is necessary to notice some of the names that man has given to the Godhead. One of the phrases that man has coined is "the Divine Family." This name suggests the close relation that exists between the members of the Godhead, and also that they constitute a family; it suggests that they are closely related, that they are akin. This term expresses an interest in each other and a cooperation in activities.

"The Trinity" is another term that man has given to the Godhead. This term is given because of the fact that there are *three* members of the Godhead; it expresses in a very emphatic way that the Godhead is composed of *three*. In nearly all heathen religions there are triads of supposed divinities; man has given this name to the Godhead in keeping with terms used in other religions. "The Trinity" expresses in a very definite way the number of members closely related as composing the Godhead.

"The Sacred Three" is a term that expresses the same idea as "Trinity." The term "sacred" carries with it the reverence and respect that should be given to the Godhead. There is but little use for this term as applied to the Godhead; it only enriches the vocabulary of theology without adding any new idea; it does not express any new phase of the Godhead and may be discarded.

"The Divinity" is another name given to the Godhead. It has some divine authority. The term in the Greek is translated "divinity" in Rom. 1: 20 in the Standard Version; it is variously translated "divine character," "divine nature," and "Godhead" in different versions. This term expresses a different shade of meaning from that of other names given.

The "Deity" is another term that is sometimes applied to the Godhead. It expresses more of the divine nature than some of the other terms; it carries with it the idea of the eternal, the everlasting, the immortal, the never-dying idea. These terms are mentioned that the reader may have an understanding of the theology of the Godhead. There are a few other names given, but these are so rare that they are omitted here.

III. Holy Spirit Coeternal with God and Christ

The Holy Spirit was present in the creation. "In the beginning God created the heaven and the earth." (Gen. 1: 1.) Here "God" in the original is in the plural; this means that there was a plurality of divine beings "in the beginning" when the "heaven and the earth" were created; it means that the Godhead was present and participated in the creation. God the Creator was present, the Word or Christ was present, and the Holy Spirit was present. God was there planning the creative work. "In the beginning was the Word, and the Word was with God, and the Word was God. The same was in the beginning with God. All things were made through him; and without him was not anything made that hath been made." (John 1: 1-3.) "And the Word became flesh, and dwelt among us." (Verse 14.) This shows that Christ, the second member of the Godhead, was present at the creation. While God, the first member of the Godhead, was present and planning creation, the Word or Christ was the agent through whom all things were created. The Holy Spirit was present at the creation; the third member of the Godhead was included in the term "God" in Gen. 1: 1.

"And the earth was waste and void; and darkness was upon the face of the deep: and the Spirit of God moved upon the face of the waters." (Gen. 1: 2.) So the Holy Spirit or "Spirit of God" was present and participated in the creation of the universe, and was the organizer of the things created by God through the Word. Hence, there was a plurality of persons in the creation.

After creating the material universe, God created man. He said: "Let us make man in our image, after our likeness." (Gen. 1: 26.) Here, again, the plural form is used; God said let *"us"* make man in *"our"* image. Here we see the Godhead cooperating in the creation of man. After man had sinned, we have God speaking again and saying, "Behold, the man is become as one of us, to know good and evil." (Gen. 3: 22.) Here we have the plural pronoun *"us"* used; again emphasizing the fact that the Godhead was present "in the beginning" of creation and the making of man. Man is the product or creature of the divine plurality, the Godhead. Man, the masterpiece of God's creation, is a product of all the persons in the Godhead.

The New Testament also brings together the divinity and names them as composing the Godhead. Jesus, after his resurrection and just before his ascension, gave his commission to his apostles, and said: "Go ye therefore, and make disciples of all the nations, baptizing them into the name of the Father and of the Son and of the Holy Spirit." (Matt. 28: 19.) Here we have the sublime act of baptism as commanded to be done in the name of the Godhead, or into the name of the Godhead, the Father, Son, and Holy Spirit. This brings one into the covenant relation of the Father, Son, and Holy Spirit. The Holy Spirit is associated here with the Father and the Son; the Holy Spirit is thus connected with the salvation of man.

Again, Paul makes an earnest entreaty to the brethren who are at Rome. He says: "Now I beseech you, brethren, by our Lord Jesus Christ, and by the love of the Spirit, that ye strive together with me in your prayers to God for me." (Rom. 15: 30.) Here God is mentioned last in the text, but he is first in the thought expressed by the apostles. The prayer is to God; it is made through Christ, and aroused by the Spirit in the hearts of these Christians. A prominent place is given to the Holy Spirit.

It is similar to the benediction given by Paul to the church at Corinth. "The grace of the Lord Jesus Christ, and the love of God, and the communion of the Holy Spirit, be with you all." (2 Cor. 13: 14.) The emphasis in this benediction is placed upon "the grace of the Lord Jesus Christ" and "the love of God," and "the communion of the Holy Spirit." Emphasis is placed upon "grace," "love," and "communion"; however, the three members of the Godhead are mentioned. Christ is mentioned first since it was through him that the grace came to man; his name has been made prominent in man's redemption; "wherefore also God highly exalted him, and gave unto him the name which is above every name; that in the name of Jesus every knee should bow, of things in heaven and things on earth and things under the earth, and that every tongue should confess that Jesus Christ is Lord, to the glory of God the Father." (Phil. 2: 9-11.) The Holy Spirit is mentioned last, as is usually the case, and shows that this follows the order of placing the third member of the Godhead last.

IV. NEED TO KNOW HOLY SPIRIT

The doctrine of the Godhead is revealed only in the Bible; no one can learn of Christ the Savior or the Holy Spirit from nature. Only those who will patiently study the Bible with a desire to know its teachings concerning the Holy Spirit will ever know the exact position of the Holy Spirit in the Bible and the Godhead. The teachings of the Godhead lie at the very heart of revealed truth; this teaching is the center from which all other tenets of faith radiate. The doctrine concerning the Godhead embodies truth which never has been discovered, and is indiscoverable by natural reason; we are dependent upon revealed truth for all that we may know about it. With all the searching that man has been able to do, he has not been able to find out anything of the Godhead save what has been revealed in the Bible.

It is important that we have correct views concerning the Bible teaching on the Godhead. If we entertain false conceptions and wrong views of the Godhead, we will not be able to understand the nature of the Holy Spirit and our entire system of faith will be imperiled. Many have been the attempted explanations of the Trinity or Godhead. Some have taught that the Godhead is a threefold manifestation of one person. This theory makes the Godhead one God. There is a sense in which the three are one, but this unity does not destroy the three distinct personalities of the Godhead. Another false view is that there are three Gods; this theory ignores the unity of the Godhead. Both these views contradict the teachings of the Bible that God is three persons, yet one in essence and purpose. Jesus constantly referred to God as his Father and as a distinct person from himself. He also promised to send the Comforter from the Father. (John 15: 26.) Jesus could not send the Holy Spirit as a third divine person, if the Godhead were only one person showing himself in three different ways. The Godhead has evidently revealed himself to men in the Bible as three persons, and not as three aspects of one person. With this view of the Godhead, we are now ready to proceed with the unfolding of our sublime theme, the Holy Spirit. We should here resolve to consider prayerfully every statement that God has revealed to us of the Holy Spirit and get a clearer view of the Holy Spirit and his ministry in the redemption of our race.

The fact that the Holy Spirit is revealed in the Bible as a member of the Godhead makes this an important subject. Anything connected with the Godhead is important, and the more vitally connected with the Godhead the more important. Only in the Bible may we find the names which have been given to the Holy Spirit by divine authority. His name is "The Spirit," and Jesus says, "God is a Spirit" or "God is Spirit." (John 4: 24.) All the members of the Godhead are of the same nature; hence, they partake of the nature of the Holy Spirit, and the Holy Spirit partakes of the nature of the other members of the Godhead. If we can learn the nature of the Godhead, we will then have gained information as to the nature of the Holy Spirit.

HOLY SPIRIT A PERSON

INTRODUCTION.

Who is the Holy Spirit; must know to understand his nature and ministry; superstitions exposed.

I. A DIVINE PERSON.

1. Referred to with personal pronoun, masculine gender, singular number.
2. Same nature and essence as God.
3. Spoken of by Christ as a person.

II. HAS DIVINE ATTRIBUTES.

1. Has a mind. (Rom. 8: 27.)
2. Power of knowing. (1 Cor. 2: 10, 11.)
3. Power of volition. (1 Cor. 12: 11.)
4. Power to love. (Rom. 15: 30.)

III. THESE ATTRIBUTES ASCRIBABLE ONLY TO A PERSON.

1. Power of speaking. (1 Tim. 4: 1.)
2. Bears witness. (John 15: 26.)
3. Makes intercession. (Rom. 8: 26.)
4. Power of searching. (1 Cor. 2: 10.)
5. Power to forbid. (Acts 16: 6.)

IV. HAS FELLOWSHIP WITH GOD.

1. Associated with God.
2. Associated with Christ.
3. God a tri-unity, or one God and three persons.
4. "God" revealed himself as three persons.
5. Holy Spirit knows mind of God. (1 Cor. 2: 11.)

V. NAMES OF HOLY SPIRIT.

1. Different names for members of Godhead.
2. Many names for God.
3. More names for Christ.
4. Fewer names for Holy Spirit.
5. He is called "Holy Spirit," "Spirit," "Spirit of God," "Spirit of the Lord," "Spirit of Truth," "My Spirit," "Comforter."

HOLY SPIRIT A PERSON

"Howbeit when he, the Spirit of truth, is come, he shall guide you into all the truth: for he shall not speak from himself; but what things soever he shall hear, these shall he speak: and he shall declare unto you the things that are to come. He shall glorify me: for he shall take of mine, and shall declare it unto you." (John 16: 13, 14.)

We should know who the Holy Spirit is, his nature, his essence, his ministry, his relation to God, to Christ, and to man; in fact, we should study everything that the Bible reveals concerning the Holy Spirit. As far as it is possible for us, we should clear away all superstitions and traditions and let the Holy Spirit stand out as definitely and prominently in our minds as he does on the pages of inspiration. We are to see that the Holy Spirit is a divine person; "the Spirit of God" is God the Spirit. It is a grievous sin against the Holy Spirit to refuse or deny what the Bible teaches about the personality of the Holy Spirit. To deny what the New Testament teaches on his personality is to deny the testimony of Christ.

There is much confusion and superstition about the Holy Spirit in the minds of people. A clear understanding of the nature and work of the Holy Spirit will help to dispel and dissipate much of the confusion that exists about this subject. The Bible is not responsible for the vague mysticism which some. ascribe to the Holy Spirit; the ignorance of the personality of the Holy Spirit belongs to religious teachers; they have not sought to present in a clear and definite way what God teaches on this subject. Surely no one can charge God with the foolishness and ignorance that many hold with respect to the Holy Spirit. It is freely and frankly admitted that there is a profound mystery that belongs to the Holy Spirit; God and Christ have their mysterious side. However, there is a simple side to the Holy Spirit and his work; this we should seek to understand.

I. A DIVINE PERSON

The Holy Spirit is not a glorified "it." It is a grievous blunder growing out of dense ignorance to pray to God to send "it," or to ask that when "it" comes "it" will bring blessings to God's people. Neither is the Holy Spirit merely "an influence." He is not an impersonal and vague force released, in response to human need, to direct or influence the mind, disposition, or action of persons, whether sinners or saints. The Holy Spirit is far more than the mind, temper, or disposition of God or Christ; the Holy Spirit is not the Bible, New Testament, or Word of God. He is more than the vital element in Christ and his truth. The Holy Spirit vitalizes truth and makes it "sharper than any two-edged sword."

There is no such thing as an impersonal God. This would be a contradiction in terms; if there be a God, he must be personal. Personality involves the possession of personal qualities and attributes. There can be no such qualities unless there be commerce between persons. There can be no love without someone to love, or trust without someone to trust; there can be no honor without someone to treat with honor, or sympathy without someone with whom to sympathize; there can be no reverence without something or someone to reverence. This is not only true in the realm of human relations, but it is true with divine relations. The very being of God, as truly and fully personal, necessitates the possession of personal qualities that can thrive only in eternal communion between divine persons. The personality of the Holy Spirit necessitates personal attributes. The personality of a solitary deity would have no associates with whom to communicate and exercise attributes.

Christ while on earth frequently spoke of the other two members of the Godhead; he spoke of God as his Father, and frequently prayed to him. He also spoke of the Holy Spirit and his relation to the Holy Spirit. He said to his disciples, "But the Comforter, even the Holy Spirit, whom the Father will send in my name, he shall teach you all things, and bring to your remembrance all that I said unto you." (John 14: 26.) Again he said of the Holy Spirit that he would come from the Father, and "he shall bear witness of men." (John 15: 26.) And still again, he said, "Howbeit when he, the Spirit of truth, is come, he shall guide you into all the truth: for he shall not speak from himself; but what things soever he shall hear, these shall he speak: and he shall declare unto you the things that are to come. He shall glorify me: for he shall take of mine, and shall declare it unto you." (John 16: 13, 14.) In this quotation Jesus refers to the Holy Spirit or "the Spirit of truth" nine times; he uses the personal pronoun, masculine gender and singular number, nine times in referring to the Holy Spirit. These can properly be used only of a person.

A "person" has life, thought, volition, action, individuality, character, and influence. The Holy Spirit has all of these; he lives; he wills; he acts; he has a separate individuality, a particular character and possesses influence. The Holy Spirit has all of the marks of personality; he is one, and is always spoken of, like God and Christ, in the singular number. The Holy Spirit has life; the Spirit gives life. (Gal. 6: 8.) "The Spirit of God moved upon the face of the waters." (Gen. 1: 2.) In this the Holy Spirit is set forth as having a part in the creation of the material universe. The Spirit thinks and acts; these are attributes of a divine person. Since the Holy Spirit jointly with God and Christ formed the Godhead, he must be of the same nature and essence as God and Christ; since they are divine personages, the Holy Spirit must be so considered.

II. HAS DIVINE ATTRIBUTES

The New Testament speaks of the Holy Spirit as having attributes that belong to the other members of the Godhead. The Holy Spirit has a mind. "He that searcheth the hearts knoweth what is the mind of the Spirit." (Rom. 8: 27.) He empowered Peter on the day of Pentecost to preach the first gospel sermon. (Acts 2: 1-18.) At different times he inspired Peter, James, John, and Paul to write various books of the New Testament. All these actions indicate thought and a mind. The fact that the Holy Spirit has the attribute of volition is emphasized in the independent choice that the Holy Spirit makes. (Acts 16: 7.) Paul was confident that the Holy Spirit was choosing for him the perfect way of God. (Acts 21: 11-14.) The Holy Spirit had the power of knowing; the fact that he had a mind is evidence of the power of thinking and knowing. "But unto us God revealed them through the Spirit: for the Spirit searcheth all things, yea, the deep things of God. For who among men knoweth the things of a man, save the spirit of the man, which is in him? even so the things of God none knoweth, save the Spirit of God." (1 Cor. 2: 10, 11.) The Spirit possesses individuality. This is another characteristic of personality. The word individuality includes personality of a particular kind. (John 16: 7-11.) Individuality is not divided; it is indivisible; he does not think one thing and do another; he does not say one thing and mean another.

Not only does individuality imply personality, but it affirms character. The Holy Spirit possesses character. (John 16: 13-15.) Whatever is predicted of the Father and Son is also ascribed to the Holy Spirit. The Father and the Son are life; so is the Spirit. (Job 33: 4; John 3: 5, 6.) God and Christ are light; so is the Spirit. (1 Cor. 2: 9-12.) God and the Son are love; so is the Spirit. (Rom. 5: 3-5.) There is no divine attribute which belongs to the Father and Son that may not likewise be ascribed to the Spirit. The unity of the Godhead implies this, and the manifestations of the Spirit prove it. Hence, if we may speak of the character of God and Christ we may also speak of the character of the Holy Spirit. Every person has some influence; the Holy Spirit has influence. (Luke 24: 46-49.) The Holy Spirit has influenced people to do things. In no instance in all the Bible do we find where the Holy Spirit ever controlled men and did evil through them; he always worked that which was good. (Acts 6: 3; 2 Cor. 13: 14.) Hence, the influence of the Holy Spirit as a person is for good. The Holy Spirit has power to love. "Now I beseech you, brethren, by our Lord Jesus Christ, and by the love of the Spirit, that ye strive together with me in your prayers to God for me." (Rom. 15: 30.) Here the three members of the Godhead are mentioned. Throughout the Scriptures from their beginning (Gen. 1: 2) to their ending (Rev. 22: 17) we see God, the Word, and the Holy Spirit as divine beings living, speaking, acting, influencing, .blessing, reconciling, transforming, loving, and glorifying; the Holy Spirit is thus seen as not "a thing" or "it," but a glorious person, the Holy Spirit.

III. These Attributes Ascribable Only to a Person

The Holy Spirit as a divine person has the power of communicating thought to man; he has the power of speaking. "But the Spirit saith expressly, that in later times some shall fall away from the faith." (1 Tim. 4: 1.) The Holy Spirit speaks intelligently to intelligent creatures. This attribute belongs only to personality; again we conclude that the Holy Spirit is a person. One of the functions of the Holy Spirit was to bear witness of Christ. "The Spirit of truth, which proceedeth from the Father, he shall bear witness of me." (John 15: 26.) This can be ascribed only to a person. The Holy Spirit has power to make intercessions. "And in like manner the Spirit also helpeth our infirmity: for we know not how to pray as we ought; but the Spirit himself maketh intercession for us with groanings which cannot be uttered." (Rom. 8: 26.) It is also declared that the Spirit has the power of searching even "the deep things of God." (1 Cor. 2: 10.) These attributes can be ascribed only to an intelligent personality. The Holy Spirit has the power of restraining, of forbidding. (Acts 16: 6.) This and other things said of the Spirit can be ascribed only to a person; hence, all the attributes that we find revealed of the Holy Spirit belong to personality.

IV. Has Fellowship with God

The Holy Spirit as a member of the Godhead is associated in all divine acts with God and the Word. Such association and relationship necessarily imply a likeness in nature and a similarity in attributes. The Holy Spirit associates with God and Christ as a divine being. We cannot think of a mere force or inanimate thing as being companionable with God. Man had sweet communion and fellowship with God before he sinned. (Gen. 3: 8.) Man then was a suitable companion of God. The Holy Spirit has always been in fellowship with God; he has co-operated with God in the creation of the material world and in the creation of the spiritual realm. God has revealed himself in nature and in revelation; the revelation of God through Christ is the fullest revelation that we have of God. This revelation was made through Christ by the Holy Spirit. Without the Bible we cannot know anything of the person of Christ or the Holy Spirit. Both Christ, the living Word, and the Bible, the product of the Holy Spirit, clearly set forth the teaching that God is a "Tri-Unity," or one God in three persons. Each of these persons is set forth in the Bible as being possessed of the fullness of deity. Hence, "God" is revealed to us as three distinct persons. This is why the Holy Spirit knows the mind of God and the things of God. (1 Cor. 2: 11.) Here is one of the mysteries; we cannot explain how three divine persons make or compose one God. We accept the Bible teaching by faith on this question.

V. Names of Holy Spirit

Each member of the Godhead, being a distinct person, has different names and titles in the Bible. There are many names for God, such as Lord, Jehovah, Almighty, Father, Lord God, Jehovah God, Jehovah of Hosts, God of Israel, etc. All of these names describe some attribute or phase of character of God. There are more names in the Bible given to Christ than to God; there are approximately two hundred names and titles given to Christ in the Bible. However, there are fewer names given to the Holy Spirit than to any other member of the Godhead. These names are significant; they describe the nature, relation, function, and ministry of the Holy Spirit. We have such names as "Holy Spirit," "Spirit," "Spirit of God," "Spirit of the Lord," "Spirit of Truth," "My Spirit," and "Spirit of Jehovah." The conclusion is inescapable; the Holy Spirit has all the attributes and characteristics of a person; he is a person; he must be thought of and dealt with as a person. The Holy Spirit has just such names and titles as divine thought wished man to know. In the King James Version he is spoken of as "the Holy Ghost." "Ghost" is an archaic term that is never used in the modern translation to refer to the Holy Spirit. It helps to clear this member of the Godhead of confusion to speak of him in such appropriate names as are found in the Bible.

There are fewer aspects of the personality, nature, and work of the Holy Spirit revealed in the Bible than the other members of the Godhead; hence, there are fewer names given to the Holy Spirit in the Bible. It will assist in clarity of thought if we keep clearly in mind the distinctions between *person, personality,* and *nature.*

A person is a being conscious of self, subsisting in individuality and identity, and endowed with intuitive reason, rational sensibility, and a free will. A person may be said to signify the indivisible self of a rational nature, as distinguished from the natural attributes and functions which this self possesses and by means of which it is manifested. A *personality* may be defined as the sum of those qualities that make a *person* a *person* as distinguished from a member of some lower order of creation; it consists in the main of self-consciousness plus self-determination in view of moral ends. *Nature* may be described as that substratum or condition of being which determines the kind and attributes of the person, but which is clearly distinguished from *person* himself. A *person,* then, is the indivisible self which is and acts as a self-conscious being and free moral agent; his personality is that which makes him a person rather than a brute or a thing; his nature is the sum total of the traits of mind and heart which the self possesses and expresses more or less perfectly, consciously and unconsciously. Personality in God is the sum total of the infinite attributes resident in the inmost depth of his one divine nature; the three persons in the Godhead are the three individualities, the three personal centers of consciousness, the three separate self-conscious and self-determining persons or selves.

HOLY SPIRIT IN MATERIAL CREATION

Introduction.

Holy Spirit had distinct part in creation; he has had a part in all God's works; many have never studied his work in material creation.

I. Godhead in Creation.

1. God originated, provided, and rules.
2. The "Word" the agent in all creation. (John 1: 1-3, 10; 1 Cor. 8: 6; Col. 1: 16; Heb. 1: 2.)
3. Holy Spirit organized, gave laws, and guides.

II. Holy Spirit Organized Material Universe.

1. Three Hebrew words:
   a. "Bara," "created." (Gen. 1: 1, 27.)
   b. "Asah," "to make." (Gen. 1: 26.)
   c. "Yarsar," "to form." (Gen. 2: 7.)
2. At first material chaotic mass ("earth was waste and void") (Gen. 1: 2.)
3. Six days' work of creation, days of organization.
4. God worked through Holy Spirit.
5. Holy Spirit organized matter, gave form to it, vital force, and pro-creative power.
6. Holy Spirit launched creation upon its mission in the universe.

III. Holy Spirit Gave Laws to Perpetuate.

1. All things began by *miracle,* continued by *law.*
2. Vegetable and animal life began by *miracle.*
3. Man began by *miracle.*
4. Holy Spirit garnished the heavens. (Job 26: 13.)
5. Holy Spirit renews vegetable kingdom. (Psalm 104: 30.)
6. Holy Spirit everywhere. (Psalm 139: 7-10.)
7. Holy Spirit present wherever laws of universe are.
8. Formative acts of God continue through Holy Spirit.
9. Holy Spirit now makes man. (Job 23: 4.)

HOLY SPIRIT IN MATERIAL CREATION

"Thou sendest forth thy Spirit, they are created." (Psalm 104: 30.)

The Holy Spirit has had a very definite and distinct part in the creation of the material universe; his work as a member of the Godhead in the creation has received very little attention. It is as important to understand his work in this sphere as it is in any other sphere; with a clear understanding of his work we may cooperate in a more intelligent way. The function of the Holy Spirit is as broad and far-reaching in the universe as is the work of God. The Godhead has created the cosmos as it now appears. The Holy Spirit has functioned with God, the Creator, in all of his work. It is to appear in this study that the work of the Holy Spirit in the material world is as great as in the spiritual realm. If we understand his work in this realm, we may the better understand it in the redemption of man.

When we descend into the bowels of the earth and discover the rich deposits of iron, coal, gas, metallic ores of silver, gold, and precious stones, we ought to know that the Holy Spirit has had something to do in placing these there for the welfare of man. When we view the surface of the earth and traverse the rolling prairies, or climb the mountain heights, or descend into the valleys, we should know that the Holy Spirit has coordinated with God in this arrangement. When we admire the beauty of the flowers in the vegetable kingdom and enjoy the food from this source, again, we should learn that the Holy Spirit has made the rich provisions for our happiness. There is nothing with which we have to do in the vegetable kingdom that the Holy Spirit has not helped to bring about. When we turn our faces heavenward on a clear night and look at the stars, we should know that the Holy Spirit has helped in the arrangement of them. Everything beneath the earth, on the earth, or above the earth should remind us of the work of the Holy Spirit. When we study the laws of nature, we are studying the laws of God; when we witness the laws of nature in action, we see the Holy Spirit in action.

I. Godhead in Creation

The first mention made of God in the Bible is that he is the Creator; God has always existed; he is eternal. Material things or matter is not eternal. God has always existed and he has brought the material universe into existence; he is the Originator, Creator, and Founder of this material universe; it came into being by his fiat. He has omniscience and omnipotence; hence, all the wisdom, power, and authority in the universe came into existence by his decree. He planned creation and invested his wisdom and power in it; he is the Author as well as the Creator of "the heavens and the earth." "He hath made the earth by his power, he hath established the world by his wisdom, and by his understanding hath he stretched out the heavens." (Jer. 51: 15.) Jehovah spoke and the world came into existence; "the voice of Jehovah is powerful." (Psalm 29: 4.) God is not only omnipotent and omniscient, he is also omnipresent; he has all power, possesses all wisdom, and is everywhere at the same time. "But will God in very deed dwell on the earth? behold, heaven and the heaven of heavens cannot contain thee." (1 Kings 8: 27.) "Can any hide himself in secret places so that I shall not see him? saith Jehovah. Do not I fill heaven and earth? saith Jehovah." (Jer. 23: 24.) All the wisdom, power, and energy in nature came from God; he invested all these in nature when he created the universe.

The agent through whom God created "the heavens and the earth" was the Word. The creation took place "in the beginning." This was the eternity before the first that we have mentioned in Genesis. There are eight periods of time mentioned in Gen. 1, and this period designated as "the beginning" is the first period. This period had no beginning; it is the stretch of eternity before our universe was called into existence. During this indefinite period of time the heavens and the earth were created. The Godhead was present. Christ was there as the Word. "In the beginning was the Word, and the Word was with God, and the Word was God. The same was in the beginning with God. All things were made through him; and without him was not anything made that hath been made." (John 1: 1-3.) The "Word" was the member of the Godhead through whom God created all things. We may not know fully the part that the Word or Christ had in creation, but we do know that he was present "in the beginning" when the heavens and the earth were created. Moreover, we know that they were created by and through Christ; he was the divine agent in the creation. "Yet to us there is one God, the Father, of whom are all things, and we unto him; and one Lord, Jesus Christ, through whom are all things, and we through him." (1 Cor. 8: 6.) Again, Paul, in speaking of Christ, said: "For in him were all things created, in the heavens and upon the earth, things visible and things invisible, whether thrones or dominions or principalities or powers; all things have been created through him, and unto him; and he is before all things, and in him all things consist." (Col. 1: 16, 17.) The New Testament is still more definite in emphasizing that Christ is the divine agent through whom all things were created. "Hath at the end of these days spoken unto us in his Son, whom he appointed heir of all things, through whom also he made the worlds." (Heb. 1: 2.) No statement in the Bible could be more positive and definite than this which declares that the worlds were created through Christ.

We come now to examine more closely the part that the Holy Spirit had in the creation of the material world. God is the Creator; Christ, the Word, is the agent through whom God created all things; the Holy Spirit gives life, enacts laws, and organizes the material universe. Creation was not finished until the third member of the Godhead functioned. After the "heavens and the earth" were created, "the earth was waste and void; and darkness was upon the face of the deep: and the Spirit of God moved upon the face of the waters." (Gen. 1: 2.) The material of "the heavens and the earth" was unorganized; it "was waste and void." "Waste" means that it was not yet fully organized with respect to land and water, mountain and plain; the material had not assumed its final condition and arrangement as gaseous, liquid, and solid, in due proportion. "Void" means that it was destitute of organized beings, and that man had not yet appeared on the earth as its chief occupant. "Darkness was upon the face of the deep" means that the shoreless and chaotic sea of mingled elements was in unbroken darkness. The light of sun, moon, and stars could not penetrate this darkness.

The first work of the Holy Spirit was to "brood" or "move" upon "the face of the waters" and bring light. The separation of the light from darkness was the result of the Holy Spirit in moving upon the material universe. The six days of creation were days or periods of *organization*. Hence, the completion of the work of creation was done by the Holy Spirit. The ministry of the Holy Spirit in creation was to organize the matter, and set in motion all of the functioning of the parts of the universe. The details further of the work of the Holy Spirit are not revealed; we must be satisfied with the simple fact that the Holy Spirit was present in creation, and began his ministry with creation.

II. Holy Spirit Organized Material Universe

Creation could not, according to the divine plan, be completed without the work of the Holy Spirit. To "organize" is to arrange or constitute in interdependent parts; it means to systematize disordered parts. God called into existence through Christ, the Word, the material, and the Holy Spirit guided the arrangement of the elements into a complete system that we now call the "universe," which means all created things as constituting one system. There was no "universe" until after the Holy Spirit had functioned. "Universe" comes from two Latin words, "unus" which means "one," and "vertere," "versum," which means "to turn"; that is, turned, or combined, into one; this brought all created things into one system, our "universe." Hence, the "universe" is the work of the Holy Spirit.

There are three words in the Hebrew which need attention here. These words should be understood in order to appreciate the work of the Holy Spirit. The first one is "bara," which means "created," or called into existence; it means to cause to exist where previously to this moment there was no being. It is used in Gen. 1: 1 and is there uniformly translated "created." It is also used in Gen. 1: 27 with respect to the creation of man, and is there translated "created." The second word in the Hebrew here that needs attention is "asah," which means "to make"; it is used in Gen. 1: 26, where God said: "Let us make man in our image." Then follows the description of the material or fleshly part of man. There was made a creature from elements which already existed. The third word is "yarsar" and means "to form." It is used in Gen. 2: 7, where it is said that Jehovah "formed man of the dust of the ground." In a very distinct way man was "formed" from that which already existed. The Holy Spirit took material already in existence and fashioned it according to God's plan into the different creatures in the animal kingdom, and gave life unto them.

The work of the Holy Spirit in the creation of the material universe is thus clearly seen in the formation and making of the different creatures that inhabit the earth; it is further seen in the present order and arrangement of the system that we call the universe. All things are to continue as the Holy Spirit arranged them; the chaotic mass of material elements was arranged by the Holy Spirit during the six days' work of creation and is to continue in this order so long as the universe exists. In one sense it may be said that God did this; he worked through the Holy Spirit; the Holy Spirit under the supervision of the wisdom and power of God thus organized and launched creation upon its mission in the material universe.

III. HOLY SPIRIT GAVE LAWS TO PERPETUATE

The Holy Spirit organized the material universe and gave living force to matter, and arranged the stability of the organization. It is to continue as the Holy Spirit arranged it; this continuation is kept in order through the laws governing the existence and functioning of every material element. These laws, which we call natural laws, are destined to preserve and perpetuate the universe. There was placed in every vegetable the seed which should continue its existence. "And God said, Let the earth put forth grass, herbs yielding seed, and fruit-trees bearing fruit after their kind, wherein is the seed thereof, upon the earth: and it was so." (Gen. 1: 11.) This was the law for the stability and perpetuity of the vegetable kingdom; it should produce after its kind. This was the work of the Holy Spirit. In the creation of the animal kingdom we find that God said: "Let the earth bring forth living creatures after their kind, cattle, and creeping things, and beasts of the earth after their kind: and it was so."

(Gen. 1: 24.) This is the law given by the Holy Spirit, or given by God through the Holy Spirit, for the perpetuity of the animal kingdom; each one is to produce after its kind. This law has never been annulled or set aside; it will continue so long as the universe exists in its present order. This is sustained by the Holy Spirit. "By his Spirit the heavens are garnished." (Job 26: 13.) The "garnishing" of the heavens may mean the placing of each of the planetary bodies in space in its proper place, and sustaining it as it revolves in cycles of space so long as it exists. This work is done by the Holy Spirit and is continued by the Spirit. "Thou sendest forth thy Spirit, they are created; and thou renewest the face of the ground." (Psalm 104: 30.)

All things began by a special act of God that we call a "miracle." It was a miracle when God created "the heavens and the earth." It was a miracle when the vegetable kingdom was formed; it was a miracle when the animal kingdom was created; it was a miracle when man was first created. It matters not whether the seed or the plant existed first, it began with a miracle. It took a miracle to bring into existence the earth and everything that inhabits the earth. The Holy Spirit had his part in the working of all these miracles. The Holy Spirit gave the laws which perpetuate all of these things. As things began in miracles, they are continued through laws which the Holy Spirit has given. The Holy Spirit that formed the original seed or plant now procreates it by means of natural laws; every animal brought into existence by a miracle at first is procreated through the laws given by the Holy Spirit. Adam and Eve were created, but every other human being that has lived upon the earth has been born; this means that the human family is continued through the processes of the laws given by the Holy Spirit for their perpetuity. Since the laws of nature are universal, we look for the operation of the Holy Spirit to be universal. "Whither shall I go from thy Spirit? Or whither shall I flee from thy presence? If I ascend up into heaven, thou art there: if I make my bed in Sheol, behold, thou art there. If I take the wings of the morning, and dwell in the uttermost parts of the sea; even there shall thy hand lead me, and thy right hand shall hold me." (Psalm 139: 7-10.) This shows that wherever the laws of the material universe reach, there the Spirit of God goes and is ever present to guide and direct all the processes of the material world. Isaiah said: "Until the Spirit be poured upon us from on high, and the wilderness become a fruitful field, and the fruitful field be esteemed as a forest." (Isa. 32: 15.)   This may have direct reference to the revival of God's people, but it has its application to the product of the vegetable kingdom.   All the formative acts of God in the material universe are continued through the Holy Spirit.

God said, "Let us make man in our image, after our likeness." (Gen. 1: 26.)   The Holy Spirit was involved in the creation of man.   Man is a product of the Holy Spirit; the nature of the human soul comes from the nature of the Godhead.   "And Jehovah God formed man of the dust of the ground, and breathed into his nostrils the breath of life; and man became a living soul." (Gen. 2: 7.) Again we have the statement, "I have filled him with the Spirit of God, in wisdom, and in understanding, and in knowledge, and in all manner of workmanship." (Ex. 31: 3.)   And again we are informed that "there is a spirit in man, and the breath of the Almighty giveth them understanding." (Job 32: 8.)   Again we have the very valuable statement, "The Spirit of God hath made me, and the breath of the Almighty giveth me life." (Job 33: 4.)

HOLY SPIRIT IN SPIRITUAL CREATION

INTRODUCTION.

Two realms, material and spiritual; similarity in creation of both; they came from same source; man to live in both.

I. GODHEAD IN INCARNATION.

1. Only one member became flesh.
2. He was Immanuel. (Matt. 1: 23.)
3. Holy Spirit overshadowed Mary. (Luke 1: 35.)
4. Mary with child by Holy Spirit. (Matt. 1: 18, 20.)
5. Fullness of Godhead in him. (Col. 2: 9.)
6. God and Holy Spirit fully shared in incarnation.

II. FACTS ABOUT THE INCARNATION.

1. Jesus begotten of God. (John 1: 18; Acts 13: 33.)
2. This done through Holy Spirit.
3. God sent Christ to the world. (Rom. 8: 3.)
4. Jesus came of his free will. (Phil. 2: 6, 7.)
5. God came in Christ. (2 Cor. 5: 19.)

III. AN ANALOGY.

1. Same persons in material and spiritual realms.
2. Administration same in both.
   a. God originated and planned both.
   b. The Word, Christ, the agent in both.
   c. Holy Spirit organized and perfected both.
3. Holy Spirit worked with material in one, spirits in other.
4. Hence, a spiritual realm.

IV. HOLY SPIRIT GAVE LAWS FOR SPIRITUAL REALM.

1. Christ revealed Father's will. (John 4: 34.)
2. Holy Spirit spoke through apostles. (Matt. 10: 20; John 14: 26.)
3. Holy Spirit bears witness of Christ. (John 15: 26.)
4. Holy Spirit declares things of Christ. (John 16: 7-15.)
5. Holy Spirit repeated words of Christ.

HOLY SPIRIT IN SPIRITUAL CREATION

"Which things also we speak, not in words which man's wisdom teacheth, but which the Spirit teacheth; combining spiritual things with spiritual words." (1 Cor. 2: 13.)

In a treatment of the Holy Spirit in the creation of the spiritual realm, we are not interested in many of the theological theories. We had no deep concern about the age-long ontological arguments, or the science of reality; neither in the cosmological arguments, or the metaphysics which treats of the character of the universe as an orderly system; neither are we concerned about the teleological reasons, or evidences of design in nature. We are only interested in the simple reasons and statements given in the Bible. We are not attempting to prove the existence of the spiritual universe; we consider it, as we do God, that it exists and seek to know the part the Holy Spirit has had in its creation.

There are two realms—material and spiritual. There is a similarity in the creation of both; both originated from the same source. Man must live in both realms. He has a body and must live in the material realm so long as his spirit or soul remains in the physical body. He needs all of the physical elements that belong to life in that realm; if he is deprived of these, disease and death will result. Man is not wholly material; he has a spiritual nature, which is dependent upon spiritual elements for its temporal and eternal welfare. We are seeking to know the part that the Holy Spirit has had in the creation of this spiritual realm. It existed before Christ came to earth, but the coming of Christ modified the spiritual realm and set up a new order of things.

I. Godhead in Incarnation

"Incarnation" as here used means the uniting of the Word with humanity; it means the Word becoming "flesh, and" dwelling "among us." Only one member of the Godhead has ever dwelt in a body like ours. The mystery of divinity becoming humanity is simplified in the conception and birth of Jesus. He is called

"Immanuel" which means "God with us," or God in the flesh. (Matt. 1: 23.) Not all of the mystery is cleared from this great event. Only the simple side of this divine act is revealed to us. Mary was selected as the one who should cooperate with the Holy Spirit in uniting divinity and humanity. The angel said to her: "Thou shalt conceive in thy womb, and bring forth a son, and shalt call his name JESUS. He shall be great, and shall be called the Son of the Most High. . . . And Mary said unto the angel, How shall this be, seeing I know not a man? And the angel answered and said unto her, The Holy Spirit shall come upon thee, and the power of the Most High shall overshadow thee: wherefore also the holy thing which is begotten shall be called the Son of God." (Luke 1: 31-35.) This shows that the Holy Spirit had something to do with the miraculous conception of Jesus.

The incarnation is further emphasized by Matthew; he records: "Now the birth of Jesus Christ was on this wise: When his mother Mary had been betrothed to Joseph, before they came together she was found with child of the Holy Spirit." (Matt. 1: 18.) An angel said to Joseph: "Fear not to take unto thee Mary thy wife: for that which is conceived in her is of the Holy Spirit." (Matt. 1: 20.) These statements make it clear that the Holy Spirit was vitally connected with the incarnation. Hence, later it is stated that in Christ "dwelleth all the fulness of the Godhead bodily." (Col. 2: 9.) There were invested in Christ all of the attributes of deity. In his conception God and the Holy Spirit cooperated. All the members of the Godhead are functioning in the incarnation. It was such an important act that the three members of the Godhead act jointly in this great event.

II. FACTS ABOUT THE INCARNATION

The Scriptures clearly teach that both Christ and the Holy Spirit derived their deity from the Father as the fountainhead, and so they are subordinate to him; however, such derivation of deity and subordination do not by any means involve any quality of deity. The Father's fullness of deity is absolutely dependent upon the Son's deity and the deity of the Holy Spirit;

their dependence upon the Father for the derivation of their deity is no greater than the Father's dependence on their dependence. Hence, Christ is "the only begotten Son, who is in the bosom of the Father." (John 1: 18.) Again, "Thou art my Son, this day have I begotten thee." (Acts 13: 33.) So we see that God is the divine Father, Christ the divine Son; he was begotten by the Father through the Holy Spirit as the Holy Spirit overshadowed Mary when she conceived. These things are recited here that we may have clearly in mind the part that the Holy Spirit had in bringing the Word to earth, and his dwelling in a material body. Again, we have the union of divinity with humanity.

The incarnation is further emphasized in the fact that God sent Christ to the world. "For what the law could not do, in that it was weak through the flesh, God, sending his own Son in the likeness of sinful flesh and for sin, condemned sin in the flesh." (Rom. 8: 3.) "For God so loved the world, that he gave his only begotten Son, that whosoever believeth on him should not perish, but have eternal life." (John 3: 16.) Not only did God send his Son to die for the world, but the Son came of his own free will. "Have this mind in you, which was also in Christ Jesus: who, existing in the form of God, counted not the being on an equality with God a thing to be grasped, but emptied himself, taking the form of a servant, being made in the likeness of men; and being found in fashion as a man, he humbled himself, becoming obedient even unto death, yea, the death of the cross." (Phil. 2: 5-8.) So God sent Christ, and he voluntarily came to be a sin offering for the world. In a certain sense, God came *with* Christ since he is *in* Christ. "God was in Christ reconciling the world unto himself." (2 Cor. 5: 19.) Furthermore, we learn that the Holy Spirit was ever with Christ; he had the Spirit without measure. "For he whom God hath sent speaketh the words of God: for he giveth not the Spirit by measure." (John 3: 34.) Each member of the Godhead functioned in the incarnation; the three were united in the personal ministry of Christ.

III. An Analogy

There is a close analogy between the material realm and the spiritual. God is the Originator, Creator, and Supreme Ruler of the material universe; the Word is the agent through whom all things were made; the Holy Spirit is the organizer, the life imparter, lawgiver, and guide of the material realm. These members of the Godhead held a council at the creation of man; they are divine, one in substance, purpose, and design; yet they are three distinct persons and function in the work of creation. The same is true in the spiritual realm; God, the Father, originated and planned it; he brought about this new spiritual realm through the divine agent, Christ his Son. The Holy Spirit took the material that Christ had prepared and organized it into the kingdom of God on earth. On Pentecost the Holy Spirit came and through the apostles preached the gospel of the kingdom. The gospel as God's power to save the world was preached through the disciples of Christ.

When man sinned, he destroyed his spiritual relation to God; he broke the harmony of the world by sin; God permitted this condition to continue until the Christ came and his kingdom was established. In the creation of a new and higher spiritual realm, God made it possible for man to be redeemed from the ruin of the world and be rescued from the destruction which was pronounced upon the world. God planned the church; Christ came to earth and with his own blood made a sacrifice for the sins of the world; he called for disciples; some of them remained faithful to him; the Holy Spirit took these faithful ones and constituted this new spiritual realm, so frequently called by Christ the "kingdom of God," "the kingdom of heaven" his "church." "But now in Christ Jesus ye that once were far off are made nigh in the blood of Christ. For he is our peace, who made both one, and brake down the middle wall of partition, having abolished in his flesh the enmity, even the law of commandments contained in ordinances; that he might create in himself of the two one new man, so making peace; and might reconcile them both in one body unto God through the cross, having slain the enmity thereby: and he came and preached peace to you that were far off, and peace to them that were nigh: for through

him we both have our access in one Spirit unto the Father."
(Eph. 2: 13-18.) The "one new man" and the "one body" here
mean the church or the kingdom of God on earth. Each member
of the Godhead is mentioned in the creation of this new kingdom.

This analogy is further emphasized in the fact that God
originated and planned both the material and spiritual realms;
they would have some similarity because they have a common
origin. Both these realms were created through the Word, Christ,
the agent of creation; this gives another point of similarity between the two realms. Moreover, the Holy Spirit is the organizer
and perfecter of both realms. Hence, we conclude that since
the two realms have the same source, and were created by the
same agent, and organized and perfected by the same Holy Spirit,
there is a similitude between the two administrations. The
Holy Spirit gave the laws of the spiritual realm, as he had
given those of the material. The New Testament reveals to us
the laws that are to govern this spiritual creation. Not a single
word of instruction, law of action, or tenet of faith, but that came
through the Holy Spirit. After teaching his disciples the Father's
will, Jesus said: "The Holy Spirit, whom the Father will send
in my name, he shall teach you all things, and bring to your
remembrance all that I said unto you." (John 14: 26.) Again
Christ said: "Howbeit when he, the Spirit of truth, is come, he
shall guide you into all the truth: for he shall not speak from
himself; but what things soever he shall hear, these shall he
speak: and he shall declare unto you the things that are to come.
He shall glorify me: for he shall take of mine, and shall declare
it unto you." (John 16: 13, 14.) It is clear from these and
other Scriptures that the Holy Spirit gave the laws to govern
and rule the new spiritual creation. He took up his abode in
these laws and in and through them accomplished his work in
the church. The Holy Spirit worked with matter in the material realm, but he works with spirits in the spiritual realm.

IV. HOLY SPIRIT GAVE LAWS FOR SPIRITUAL REALM

As the Holy Spirit gave the laws for the government of all
matter in the material world, so he gave the laws which should
rule in the spiritual realm. The Holy Spirit took up his abode

in these laws, and gave to them the authority of Christ. The Bible is the guide given to man by the Holy Spirit. Christ came and revealed the Father's will. Jesus said: "My meat is to do the will of him that sent me, and to accomplish his work." (John 4: 34.) Again he said: "The Son can do nothing of himself, but what he seeth the Father doing: for what things soever he doeth, these the Son also doeth in like manner." (John 5: 19.) Christ had been with the Father; he knew his will; he revealed only the Father's will. He said: "I can of myself do nothing: as I hear, I judge: and my judgment is righteous; because I seek not mine own will, but the will of him that sent me." (John 5: 30.) Again he said: "When ye have lifted up the Son of man, then shall ye know that I am he, and that I do nothing of myself, but as the Father taught me, I speak these things." (John 8: 28.)

Here we have Jesus saying that he spake only the things that were taught him of the Father. To make it more emphatic, Jesus said: "For I spake not from myself; but the Father that sent me, he hath given me a commandment, what I should say, and what I should speak." (John 12: 49.) Now we have it clear that Christ spoke only the things which the Father had taught him.

Christ spoke these things to his apostles; the apostles, guided by the Holy Spirit, spoke these things to others. What the Spirit-guided apostles said was what Christ said. The Holy Spirit took the things of Christ and spoke them through the apostles to others. Christ said to his disciples: "For it is not ye that speak, but the Spirit of your Father that speaketh in you." (Matt. 10: 20.) When the apostles testified concerning Jesus, the Holy Spirit was bearing witness of Christ. The Holy Spirit was to take the things of Christ and declare them unto the world; this was done through the apostles. The Holy Spirit has used human instrumentality in speaking and writing God's will. Christ dwelt in the flesh as he ministered here upon earth; he used his material body in contacting the material realm; he used his body in suffering and in dying; Christ was clothed in the flesh. The Holy Spirit as a divine person has not had a human body, but he has used those who dwelt in the flesh to make known the will of God to the world. The Holy Spirit repeated the words of Christ, and has perfected the spiritual creation for man's redemption.

The prophet Isaiah had said, "Behold, my servant whom I have chosen; my beloved in whom my soul is well pleased: I will put my Spirit upon him, and he shall declare judgment to the Gentiles." (Matt. 12: 18.) This is spoken of Christ. The personal character and ministry of Christ harmonize with the work of the Holy Spirit. The personal conduct of Christ and his public ministry were conducted by the Holy Spirit. The Holy Spirit came upon Christ at his baptism, continued with him to the end, but in a more definite way did the Holy Spirit take up the words of Christ and guide his disciples in speaking. This was done that no mistake should be made; the apostles were to speak "as the Spirit gave them utterance." We do not have all of the words spoken by Christ on record. John said, "And there are also many other things which Jesus did, the which if they should be written every one, I suppose that even the world itself would not contain the books that should be written." (John 21: 25.) The Holy Spirit took up such words as in the wisdom of God were needed for the redemption of man and recorded them in the New Testament; hence, we have all that is necessary for us to know. "Every scripture inspired of God is also profitable for teaching, for reproof, for correction, for instruction which is in righteousness: that the man of God may be complete, furnished completely unto every good work." (2 Tim. 3: 16, 17.)

CHAPTER VI

HOLY SPIRIT IN OLD TESTAMENT

INTRODUCTION.

God the Creator, most prominent in Old Testament; Christ, in the New Testament; Holy Spirit, prominent in both.

I. DISPENSATIONS OF GODHEAD.

1. Gods dispensation by angels on earth.
2. Christ's dispensation on earth in the flesh.
3. Holy Spirit's dispensation on earth in the church.
4. One member on earth at a time.
5. Other two members in heaven at same time.

II. HOLY SPIRIT'S MANIFESTATIONS.

1. He appeared in creation. (Gen. 1: 2.)
2. He appeared in revelation. (Gen. 41: 16, 38.)
3. He gave prophetic vision. (Num. 24: 2.)
4. He revealed himself in workmanship. (Ex. 31: 3.)
5. He illustrated the incarnation. (Judges 6: 34.)
6. He gave power. (Ezek. 2: 1.)

III. PROPHETS SPOKE BY HOLY SPIRIT.

1. Holy Spirit preached through Noah. (1 Pet. 3: 20-22; 2 Pet. 2: 5.)
2. Holy Spirit spoke through Balaam. (Num. 24: 2.)
3. Holy Spirit on Saul. (1 Sam. 10: 10; 11: 6.)
4. David spoke by Holy Spirit. (Psalm 51: 11.)
5. Holy Spirit spoke through Isaiah. (Isa. 61: 1.)
6. Holy Spirit spoke through Ezekiel. (Ezek. 11: 5.)
7. Men of old spoke by Holy Spirit. (2 Pet. 1: 21.)

HOLY SPIRIT IN OLD TESTAMENT

"For no prophecy ever came by the will of man: but men spake from God, being moved by the Holy Spirit." (2 Pet. 1: 21.)

God as the Creator is most prominent in the Old Testament. He is mentioned in the first words of Genesis. "In the beginning God created the heavens and the earth." He frequently declares himself to be "God Almighty." (Gen. 17: 1; 35: 11.) He appeared in different ways and revealed himself in symbols, covenants, various confessions, and teachings. The manifestations of Jehovah in the Old Testament are as prominent as the manifestations of Christ in the New Testament. The Holy Spirit is prominent in both. Law, history, prophecy, and poetry in the Old Testament furnished a clear background for one definite, outstanding person, the Christ of the New Testament. All these manifestations are emphasized by the Holy Spirit in his recording them in the different books of the Bible.

What we know of God in the Old Testament came through the Holy Spirit, so all that we know of Christ in the New Testament came through the Holy Spirit. "Wherefore I make known unto you, that no man speaking in the Spirit of God saith, Jesus is anathema; and no man can say, Jesus is Lord, but in the Holy Spirit." (1 Cor. 12: 3.) What we know of Christ, of truth, of eternal life, the Holy Spirit reveals to us. The Holy Spirit has completed the Old Testament as he has the New Testament. The entire Bible is a product of the Holy Spirit. However, in this chapter we are to study the Holy Spirit and his work as revealed in the Old Testament.

I. DISPENSATIONS OF GODHEAD

There are the three members of the Godhead—God, the Creator, the Word, Christ, and the Holy Spirit. Each member of the Godhead has had his dispensation with man on the earth. A "dispensation" as used here means an epoch of time well marked by certain events; it means a system of principles, promises, rules ordained and administered during a certain period of time.

We do not refer here to the Patriarchal Dispensation, Jewish Dispensation, and Christian Dispensation. These are "dispensations" based upon different things. It is meant here that each member of the Godhead has had his dispensation with man, which has been definitely marked off as a period of time by certain outstanding events.

God's dispensation means that time from the creation of man to the coming of Christ. During this time God, through angels and other agencies, spoke to man and instructed him. "God, having of old time spoken unto the fathers in the prophets by divers portions and in divers manners." (Heb. 1: 1.) Sometimes God spoke directly to one as he did to Adam, Noah, and Abraham. Again he sent an angel to speak to man and reveal his will. Sometimes God revealed himself and his will in visions and dreams; he impressed his will on the mind of man through these means. This was his dispensation, and he used such agencies as his wisdom directed in revealing himself and his will to man. He was prominent and dominant in all of the affairs of his people during this dispensation. At times he spoke through the Holy Spirit to his messengers; in fact, we may understand that the Holy Spirit was functioning in all of the divine acts and revelations of God during this dispensation.

When the Word was made flesh and dwelt among us, when the Christ began his personal ministry on earth, then Christ's dispensation began. We do not mean by this that God had *nothing* to do with Christ's dispensation; we simply mean that the work of Christ was conspicuous, eminent, salient; this continued until Christ made his ascension back to the Father. Christ walked and talked with men during his personal ministry; he taught man the Father's will and wherever he went, like the pictures of him now, there was a halo of glory that surrounded him. He was "Immanuel," God with us in the flesh. He never followed any beaten path marked out by man, performed no program arranged by man, nor even did his own will, but the will of the Father. In all of these works and teachings he made God the Father stand out so that all could understand that he came from God and would return to God. His personal ministry occupies such a place in divine revelation that we may speak of his sojourn on earth as his dispensation.

Following the dispensation of Christ's personal ministry, and beginning on the first Pentecost after the resurrection of Christ, the dispensation of the Holy Spirit began. We now live in the period of time that we may call the Holy Spirit's dispensation. We do not mean that the Holy Spirit had nothing to do during God's dispensation or the dispensation of Christ's personal ministry, but that he takes the lead during this age as a member of the Godhead. The Holy Spirit is salient and present in all of the work of God and Christ in the redemption of man today. The Holy Spirit is the executing power of the Godhead during the church age. The Holy Spirit took up the work where Christ left it and carries it on to completion and to its final consummation. The Spirit age, so far as revelation instructs us, is the last dispensation.

Each member of the Godhead has now had his dispensation with man; the three members have cooperated in each dispensation, but one member has been made dominant in each dispensation. One member has been on earth, in person or by his representative, during these dispensations; the other two members seem to have yielded to the prominence of the one who was represented on earth. God is in his heavens; Christ has ascended back to heaven and the Holy Spirit has descended to earth. "Nevertheless I tell you the truth: It is expedient for you that I go away; for if I go not away, the Comforter will not come unto you; but if I go, I will send him unto you." (John 16: 7.) It was necessary that Christ return to the Father before the Holy Spirit would come; Christ must finish his work on earth and yield his place as a person to the Holy Spirit. In this way there would be left a member of the Godhead, in person or with a representative, among men.

II. Holy Spirit's Manifestations

The same prominence is not given in the Old Testament to the Holy Spirit that is given in the New Testament; this is probably true because the New Testament deals with the Holy

Spirit's dispensation. There are about sixteen books of the thirty-nine of the Old Testament which do not refer directly to the Holy Spirit; however twenty-three books of the Old Testament give clear references to the Holy Spirit; some of them make the Holy Spirit more prominent than others. The Holy Spirit is mentioned in the Old Testament with different names or titles. Sometimes he is referred to as just the Spirit; then, as the Spirit of God, Spirit of Jehovah, Spirit of the Lord, and Holy Spirit. The work of the Holy Spirit in the Old Testament appears in every feature as identical with his work in the New Testament; this helps to appreciate the work of the Holy Spirit as revealed in the Old Testament, for his work in the New Testament is made more emphatic than it is in the Old Testament.

The manifestations of the Holy Spirit in the Old Testament begin with the dawn of creation; the Holy Spirit appeared in creation. (Gen. 1: 2.) His first work as revealed in the Old Testament is upon the chaotic material universe, and then upon the creation of society, and finally upon individual character. The steps of his work appear to advance from the general confusion and disorder of matter to the narrow or more restricted field of humanity, and finally to the still more narrow field of individual character. The Old Testament clearly and frequently emphasizes the fact that the Holy Spirit appeared in God's revelation to man. Joseph told Pharaoh that the interpretation of dreams belonged to God; this was done by the Spirit of God. (Gen. 41: 16, 38.) Daniel told Nebuchadnezzar that God was a revealer of secrets. (Dan. 2: 28.) This was done through the Holy Spirit. It never appears to be an incredible or unnatural thing for the Spirit of God to make supernatural revelation to men, or to inspire in them the writing of his word, or the loving and doing of his will.

God in the Old Testament is frequently revealed as making his will known to man through visions and dreams. He appears in prophetic utterances to speak through the Holy Spirit. This came to Balaam. (Num. 24: 2.) The Spirit of God came mightily upon Saul, and "he prophesied among them." (1 Sam. 10: 10.) Ezekiel was brought in a vision by the Spirit into Chaldea;

there he had a vision in which Jehovah showed him certain things concerning Israel. (Ezek. 11: 24, 25.) In like manner the Holy Spirit seems to have guided men in ability to work for Jehovah. Oholiab of the tribe of Dan and Bezalel of the tribe of Judah were filled "with the Spirit of God, in wisdom, and in understanding, and in knowledge, and in all manner of workmanship." (Ex. 31: 3.) These men superintended the construction of the tabernacle.

We seem to find that the incarnation was illustrated in the Old Testament by the Spirit of Jehovah which came upon Gideon. "But the Spirit of Jehovah came upon Gideon." (Judges 6: 34.) The marginal reading for "came" is "clothed itself with"; that is, the Holy Spirit overshadowed Gideon as he did Mary in the incarnation. The same thought is expressed when we have God dwelling in us. "What agreement hath a temple of God with idols? for we are a temple of the living God; even as God said, I will dwell in them, and walk in them; and I will be their God, and they shall be my people." (2 Cor. 6: 16.) In like manner the Holy Spirit imparted power; he gave power to certain ones to do service for God. (Ezek. 2: 1, 2.)

III. Prophets Spoke by Holy Spirit

The Holy Spirit as revealed in the Old Testament spoke through the prophets to the people. The prophets were an important group or class of people in Old Testament history. "Prophet" means one who speaks for God; the prophet was God's mouthpiece to the people; this was done by the Holy Spirit. The Holy Spirit preached through Noah to the antediluvians; Peter represents Christ in his pre-fleshly state as preaching by the Holy Spirit to these people while the ark was being prepared. (1 Pet. 3: 18-22; 2 Pet. 2: 5.) The Holy Spirit spoke through Balaam (Num. 24: 2), and he was forced against his own will to speak God's message to Balak and the Moabites; Balaam attempted to curse the children of Israel. He desired to use the Holy Spirit in cursing the people whom God had blessed. Balaam attempted to bring two members of the Godhead into contradiction with each other. God had blessed Israel, and now Balaam with the Holy Spirit attempts to curse them. (Num. 22: 1 to 24: 25.)

The Holy Spirit came upon Saul, the son of Kish, and Saul prophesied. "And the Spirit of God came mightily upon him, and he prophesied among them. . . . Then the people said one to another, What is this that is come unto the son of Kish? Is Saul also among the prophets?" (1 Sam. 10: 10, 11.) At another time "the Spirit of God came mightily upon Saul" and he took the lead and won the battle for Israel. (1 Sam. 11: 6.) David spoke by the Holy Spirit. He said: "Cast me not away from thy presence; and take not thy Holy Spirit from me." (Psalm 51: 11.) Again, David said: "The spirit of Jehovah spake by me, and his word was upon my tongue." (2 Sam. 23: 2.) David was moved by the Holy Spirit in writing the Psalms. David also prophesied by the Holy Spirit; he was enabled to prophesy concerning Christ by the Holy Spirit. (Acts 13: 33, 34.)

Many of the prophets confessed that they were speaking by the Holy Spirit. Isaiah said: "The Spirit of the Lord Jehovah is upon me." (Isa. 61: 1.) Jeremiah said: "Now the word of Jehovah came unto me." (Jer. 1: 4.) Ezekiel said: "The Spirit lifted me up, and brought me unto the east gate of Jehovah's house." (Ezek. 11: 1.) Again, he said: "The Spirit of Jehovah fell upon me, and he said unto me, Speak, Thus saith Jehovah." (Ezek. 11: 5.) Daniel claimed to speak by the Holy Spirit; all the major prophets claimed the Holy Spirit as authority for what they said. The minor prophets attributed their messages to the Holy Spirit.

The New Testament honors the Old Testament as being the words of the Holy Spirit. Every quotation from the Old Testament found in the New Testament has the force of the voice of the Holy Spirit. Peter said: "For no prophecy ever came by the will of man: but men spake from God, being moved by the Holy Spirit." (2 Pet. 1: 21.) There were false prophets back in Old Testament times, as there are false teachers today. Jeremiah condemned those who did not speak by the Spirit of God. "How long shall this be in the heart of the prophets that prophesy lies, even the prophets of the deceit of their own heart? . . . The prophet that hath a dream, let him tell a dream; and he that hath my word, let him speak my word faithfully." (Jer. 23: 26-28.) The Holy Spirit is clearly, definitely, and frequently set forth in the Old Testament as a distinct person and functioning in all of the works of God. He is mentioned as the "Holy Spirit" three times in the Old Testament. "Cast me not away from thy presence; and take not thy holy Spirit from me." (Psalm 51: 11.) "But they rebelled, and grieved his holy Spirit; . . . where is he that put his holy Spirit in the midst of them?" (Isa. 63: 10, 11.)

The Holy Spirit is frequently referred to in the Old Testament. He is mentioned in the creation of the world (Gen. 1: 2), in the creation of man (Gen. 1: 26), in striving with wicked man before the flood (Gen. 6: 3), in the construction of the temple (1 Chron. 28: 11, 12), in withdrawing from the wicked (Psalm 51: 11). The omnipresence of the Holy Spirit is clearly declared in the Old Testament. (Psalm 139: 7.) He is also declared in prophecy as to his influence on the mental and moral character of Christ as the promised Savior. (Isa. 11: 2-5.) The Holy Spirit had a part in the restoration of the Jews from their captivity. (Isa. 32: 15; Ezek. 36: 27; 37: 9; Zech. 12: 10; 13: 1.) The Holy Spirit guided and blessed faithful Jews in rebuilding the temple. (Zech. 4: 6, 7.)

CHAPTER VII

HOLY SPIRIT IN NEW TESTAMENT

INTRODUCTION.

New Testament history of Holy Spirit; his advent and work fills it, as does Christ.

I. HOLY SPIRIT IN THE GOSPELS.

1. Holy Spirit in Matthew.
2. Holy Spirit in Mark.
3. Holy Spirit in Luke.
4. Holy Spirit in John.

II. HOLY SPIRIT IN ACTS.

1. Pentecost—advent of Holy Spirit. (Acts 2.)
2. Holy Spirit bears witness of Christ.
3. Apostles guided by Holy Spirit.
4. Church organized and developed by Holy Spirit.

III. HOLY SPIRIT IN THE EPISTLES.

1. Writers guided by Holy Spirit.
2. Christians taught how to live.
3. The promise and hope of heaven.

IV. FIGURES AND SYMBOLS OF HOLY SPIRIT.

1. The dove. (Matt. 3: 16.)
2. Anointing oil. (1 John 2: 20, 21.)
3. Seal and earnest of Holy Spirit. (Eph. 1: 13, 14.)
4. Water. (John 4: 11.)
5. Living water. (John 7: 37-39.)

HOLY SPIRIT IN NEW TESTAMENT

"For he whom God hath sent speaketh the words of God: for he giveth not the Spirit by measure." (John 3: 34.)

The New Testament presents a wide range of activities of the Holy Spirit; his person, advent, and relation to Christ are all discussed in the New Testament. His activities cover the full history of the Spirit in his relation to the salvation of souls. There are about two hundred sixty-four references to the Holy Spirit in the New Testament; many times the reference is just to the Spirit, Spirit of God, and the Spirit of Christ. Sometimes the definite article "the" is placed before the name, sometimes the indefinite article "a" is used. The number of uses shows the wide range of activities covered by the history in the New Testament. The most casual setting forth of the manifestations and activities of the Holy Spirit will quicken the entire spiritual life of believers in Christ; they should stimulate a higher thought concerning Christ and a deeper appreciation of the Holy Spirit.

Christ fills the New Testament; every book contains Christ as its great theme. As Christ fills the New Testament so the Holy Spirit who is associated with Christ fills it. All through his earthly ministry Christ had the companionship of the Holy Spirit. "How much more shall the blood of Christ, who through the eternal Spirit offered himself without blemish unto God, cleanse your conscience from dead works to serve the living God?" (Heb. 9: 14.) The dispensation of the Spirit is clearly revealed in the New Testament; hence, the New Testament may be called "the book of the Holy Spirit." To understand the mission and ministry of Christ is to understand the work of the Holy Spirit; to appreciate fully the power of the blood of Christ is to appreciate the importance of the work of the Holy Spirit. The Holy Spirit thus reveals Christ in the New Testament. "Wherefore I make known unto you, that no man speaking in the Spirit of God saith, Jesus is anathema; and no man can say, Jesus is Lord, but in the Holy Spirit." (1 Cor. 12: 3.)

I. Holy Spirit in the Gospels

There are a dozen or more references in the book of Matthew to the Holy Spirit. The first mention is: "When his mother Mary had been betrothed to Joseph, before they came together she was found with child of the Holy Spirit." (Matt. 1: 18.) Again, when the angel of the Lord appeared to Joseph in a dream, he instructed him to take Mary as his wife, "for that which is conceived in her is of the Holy Spirit." (Matt. 1: 20.) Again, John the Baptist said of Jesus that "he shall baptize you in the Holy Spirit and in fire." (Matt. 3: 11.) In verse 16, in giving an account of the baptism of Jesus, Matthew says that when he was baptized "the heavens were opened unto him, and he saw the Spirit of God descending as a dove, and coming upon him." (Matt. 3: 16.) In chapter 4, verse 1, Matthew says: "Then was Jesus led up of the Spirit into the wilderness to be tempted of the devil." Here we have brought clearly the Holy Spirit as a companion with Jesus.

Jesus, in talking to his disciples and instructing them in the work that they should do, stated that the Holy Spirit would guide them in their work. He was sending them forth on their limited commission which was restricted only to the Jews. He said: "For it is not ye that speak, but the Spirit of your Father that speaketh in you." (Matt. 10: 20.) Again, he said in quoting from Isaiah: "Behold, my servant whom I have chosen; my beloved in whom my soul is well pleased: I will put my Spirit upon him, and he shall declare judgment to the Gentiles." (Matt. 12: 18.) Jesus was accused of casting out demons by Beelzebub; he had answered this accusation and then said: "But if I by the Spirit of God cast out demons, then is the kingdom of God come upon you." (Matt. 12: 28.) A little further on Jesus discussed the blasphemy against the Holy Spirit; he had said that every sin should be forgiven, "but the blasphemy against the Spirit shall not be forgiven." (Matt. 12: 31.) Then in verse 32 he says: "Whosoever shall speak a word against the Son of man, it shall be forgiven him; but whosoever shall speak against the Holy Spirit, it shall not be forgiven him, neither in this world, nor in that which is to come." The Pharisees were gathered together attempting to ensnare Jesus, and he turned on them with questions; he asked them who the Christ should be, and they replied, "The son of David." Jesus then asked them: "How then doth David in the Spirit call him Lord?" (Matt. 22: 43.) The last reference that Matthew makes to the Holy Spirit is in giving the Great Commission: "Go ye therefore, and make disciples of all the nations, baptizing them into the name of the Father and of the Son and of the Holy Spirit." (Matt. 28: 19.)

Mark is the shortest of the four writers of the gospel; he makes fewer references to the Holy Spirit than the other writers of the gospel. There are only six references in Mark to the Holy Spirit. However, Mark begins his narrative with the baptism of John the Baptist; hence, he would omit all the references of the Holy Spirit in connection with the incarnation. His first reference is to the baptism of Jesus. "I baptized you in water; but he shall baptize you in the Holy Spirit." (Mark 1: 8.) The second reference is made with respect to the baptism of Jesus when he came "up out of the water, he saw the heavens rent asunder, and the Spirit as a dove descending upon him." (Mark 1: 10.) The next reference is a brief statement with respect to the temptation of Jesus after his baptism when the "Spirit driveth him forth into the wilderness." (Mark 1: 12.) His next reference is to the discussion on the blasphemy against the Holy Spirit, when Jesus said: "Whosoever shall blaspheme against the Holy Spirit hath never forgiveness, but is guilty of an eternal sin." (Mark 3: 29.) The next reference that Mark makes is in answer to the question that Jesus had asked about who the Christ is; they had answered, "The son of David." Jesus then said: "David himself said in the Holy Spirit, The Lord said unto my Lord, sit thou on my right hand, till I make thine enemies the footstool of thy feet." (Mark 12: 36.) The last reference is to his disciples when they should be persecuted that they should not be "anxious beforehand what ye shall speak: but whatsoever shall be given you in that hour, that speak ye; for it is not ye that speak, but the Holy Spirit." (Mark 13: 11.)

Luke mentions the Holy Spirit by name seventeen times, and one time he makes reference to him as "the promise of my

Father" (Luke 24: 49), which would mean that he makes eighteen references to the Holy Spirit. These references are found as follows: Luke 1: 15, 35, 41, 67; 2: 25-27; 3: 16, 22; 4: 1 (twice in this verse), 14, 18; 10: 21; 11: 13; 12: 10, 12; 24: 49. Luke records the Holy Spirit with respect to the birth of John the Baptist and the incarnation that the others do not mention. He records the descent of the Holy Spirit at the baptism of Jesus and his temptation and blasphemy against the Spirit and the Holy Spirit should speak through the apostles just as Matthew and Mark do.

John makes about two dozen references to the Holy Spirit; some of these references do not use the word "Spirit," but the pronoun in the masculine gender as referring to the Holy Spirit. He makes more references to the Holy Spirit than any other writer of the gospel. These references are as follows: John 1: 32, 33; 3: 5, 6, 8; 6: 63; 7: 39 (two references in this verse as two in 1: 33); 14: 16, 17, 26; 15: 26; 16: 7, 8, 9, 10, 11, 13, 14, 15. John represents the Holy Spirit as a person of the Godhead; he brings out more emphatically the personality of the Holy Spirit than any other writer. He always places emphasis on the personality of the Holy Spirit.

John first introduces the Holy Spirit in connection with John the Baptist; it is John who speaks of the Holy Spirit as "the Comforter"; he promises to send the Holy Spirit from the Father after he returns to the Father. John records much that the Holy Spirit would do when he came. The ministry of the Comforter in relation to the disciples is, first, his conviction of the world of the sinfulness of its rejection of Christ as Savior and Lord; the second ministry is the further unfolding to the disciples the truth about Christ in order to complete their equipment as messengers of Christ, and to build up the church as his body.

II. HOLY SPIRIT IN ACTS

Jesus gave his commission to his disciples to go into all the world and preach the gospel. They were to wait in Jerusalem until the Holy Spirit came. He came a few days after Jesus left the apostles and ascended to heaven. On Pentecost the Holy Spirit came and filled the apostles and they began to speak as the Spirit gave them utterance. The book of Acts records some of the things which some of the apostles did as they obeyed the commission. It was not necessary for the Holy Spirit to record everything that each of the apostles said and did; this would have involved much repetition, as they all taught the same thing and did the same thing with respect to the salvation of souls. They were all guided by the same Spirit.

There are about fifty-seven references to the Holy Spirit in the Acts; these record the part that the Holy Spirit had in guiding the apostles in speaking and his influence on sinners in conversion. We find that the Holy Spirit enabled the apostles to speak with other tongues and to work miracles. Nearly every phase of work of the Holy Spirit is mentioned in the book of Acts. There are two great lessons taught in Christianity—one, how to become a Christian; the other, how to live the Christian life. In Acts we have the question asked and answered by the Holy Spirit what one must do to be saved, or what one must do to become a Christian. The Holy Spirit is crystal clear in answering this question. He did not want anyone to be in doubt as to what the terms of salvation are. The Holy Spirit was to bear witness of Christ. (John 15: 26.) When the apostles preached the gospel of Christ through the Holy Spirit, they were bearing witness of Christ. The church was organized on the Pentecost that the Holy Spirit made his advent. Throughout the book of Acts we see the development of the church under the apostles guided by the Holy Spirit.

III. Holy Spirit in the Epistles

There are about one hundred thirty-two references made to the Holy Spirit in the Epistles and Revelation. References are made in each Epistle to the Holy Spirit except in Philemon, Second and Third John; hence, all the books of the New Testament except three contain references to the Holy Spirit. Of the twenty-seven books in the New Testament, twenty-four make reference to the Spirit. There are eight writers of the New Testament: Matthew, Mark, Luke, Peter, Paul, James, John, and Jude. Each writer makes reference to the Holy Spirit. Paul wrote thirteen, probably fourteen, books of the New Testament; he made reference to the Holy Spirit in each one of his books except Philemon. More references are made in the books of Romans than any other of the Epistles; in this book we have twenty-one references; First Corinthians contains the next greatest number, seventeen. In these Epistles Christians are taught how to live the Christian life and have the promise and hope of heaven given unto them if they will be faithful unto death.

IV. Figures and Symbols of Holy Spirit

The New Testament employs a great variety of figures of speech; these include the simplest simile to the most extreme hyperbole; in this general scope the figurative use of symbols has a large place, and especially in Revelation. The nature and the work of the Holy Spirit are indicated by certain symbols, visible signs or figures. We have the Holy Spirit presented as a dove at the baptism of Jesus. Again, the Holy Spirit may be referred to in 1 John 2: 20 as an anointing oil. "Ye were sealed with the Holy Spirit of promise, which is an earnest of our inheritance, unto the redemption of God's own possession, unto the praise of his glory." (Eph. 1: 13, 14.) "An earnest" is a pledge of security; it is usually money given in advance to guarantee that a promise will be kept. In discussing with the Samaritan woman at the well Jesus referred to the Holy Spirit as "water." "The woman saith unto him, Sir, thou hast nothing to draw with, and the well is deep: whence then hast thou that living water?" (John 4: 10, 11.) Again, Jesus said: "If any man thirst, let him come unto me and drink. He that believeth on me, as the scripture hath said, from within him shall flow rivers of living water. But this spake he of the Spirit, which they that believed on him were to receive: for the Spirit was not yet given; because Jesus was not yet glorified." (John 7: 37-39.) It is clear here that Jesus had reference to the Holy Spirit.

The figures and symbols of the Holy Spirit show different aspects of his nature and work in the salvation of man. The testimony of the four writers of the gospel—Matthew, Mark, Luke, and John—shows the work of the Holy Spirit and the conception of Christ, his presence at the baptism and temptation, and throughout the public life and ministry of Christ. The Holy Spirit was present in the miracles of Christ and was promised to his apostles in guiding them into all truth and in bringing to their remembrance all that Jesus had taught them. The Holy Spirit is very prominent in the Acts of the Apostles. Sometimes he is represented by figures and symbols, but most frequently by his personality. He was present in the establishment of the church on Pentecost and in the conversion of sinners; he was present in guiding the apostles in the early formation and organization of the church; he was present when Stephen was stoned; he had a part in bringing Philip and the eunuch together and the conversion of the eunuch. The Holy Spirit had a part in the conversion of Saul of Tarsus, and guided him in the extension of the gospel to the Gentiles. The Holy Spirit aided Barnabas in his ministry and guided Paul in establishing many churches. The Holy Spirit is mentioned frequently in simple terms and in figures in the Epistles. The Holy Spirit has a place in dwelling in the church and in abiding in the faithful disciples of Christ. During the miraculous age of the church the Holy Spirit was prominent in spiritual gifts and in other extraordinary manifestations. The Holy Spirit bears fruit in the lives of faithful Christians. The Spirit is the author of prophecy; in the book of Revelation the Holy Spirit is frequently represented in figures and symbols.

INSPIRATION OF THE BIBLE

INTRODUCTION.

Its importance; its truth strengthens faith; it is God's side of revelation.

I. TWO DISTINCT ELEMENTS.

1. The divine element.
   a. God gave a revelation.
   b. His thoughts, will, and wisdom.
2. Human element.
   a. Man chosen to record it.
   b. Human language used.

II. MEANING OF INSPIRATION.

1. God cooperating with man.
2. Supernatural influence of Holy Spirit on writers.
3. Divine illumination and guidance enabling men to select and correctly express God's will in human language.
4. Inspiration does not create fact-material.
5. No inspiration in paper, ink, or type.

III. INSPIRATION IN REVELATION.

1. "Revelation" is "unveiling."
   a. Divine revelation God's unveiling of truth about himself.
   b. Word of God expressed in human language.
2. Three epochs of divine revelation.
   a. Primitive revelation.
   b. Covenant revelation to Israel.
   c. Revelation through Christ.
3. A record of this revelation.
   a. Made *to* man.
   b. Made *for* man.
   c. Made *through* man.
4. Hence, the Bible.

INSPIRATION OF THE BIBLE

"Every scripture inspired of God is also profitable for teaching, for re-proof, for correction, for instruction which is in righteousness: that the man of God may be complete, furnished completely unto every good work." (2 Tim. 3: 16, 17.)

Much depends upon the truthfulness of the inspiration of the Bible; if it is not inspired, it falls to the low level of human production; even to the lowest and basest of human productions, for it claims to be inspired   If this claim is not true, the Bible cannot make one wise unto salvation. It is claimed for the Bible that it came from God and reveals the mind of God to man; if this claim is not true, the Bible does not reveal to man the love and power and wisdom of God. Furthermore, if the Bible is not inspired, man has no piece of literature that can claim inspiration; if there be no inspired will of God, man is left in sin without a ray of light to guide him home to glory. If it be proved that the Bible is inspired, then our faith can be strengthened in it. We want to know whether it is inspired.

By the Bible we mean the thirty-nine books of the Old Testament and the twenty-seven books of the New Testament. These are the books which are regarded by all Christians as of divine authority. We are not raising here the question as to what books are canonical; this belongs to another study, which does not come within the present scope of our investigation; neither are we raising the question as to whether there are other books that should be included in the Bible. We leave out of the present discussion all apocryphal books of the Old Testament as well as the New Testament. We are concerned only with the question as to whether the Bible as Christians now have it is a book from God. If it is inspired, it came from God; if it is not inspired, it is a fraud. The inspiration of the Bible belongs to God's side of revelation.

I. TWO DISTINCT ELEMENTS

The Bible is a composite book; it is not only composed of sixty-six books, with about forty different writers, over a stretch of more than fifteen hundred years, but it has the **divine element** and the human element in it. God's side of the Bible and the part that he had in producing it may be spoken of as the divine element of the Bible. The revelation that we have as the Bible came from God; he gave it; it contains his thoughts, mind, will, way, and wisdom. Inasmuch as it came from God, it should be regarded as the highest order of truth. The divine element lifts the Bible to supernatural plane and places it in a class to itself as a literary production. We have God's work in the natural realm and his work in the spiritual realm—God revealed in nature and God revealed in revelation. The inspiration of the Bible belongs to the divine side, or the divine element of the Bible.

The human element may be as pronounced as the divine element. God chose man to record his thoughts; he did not select angels to write the Bible. It was the wisdom of God to select men to write or make a record of his revelation to man. He chose to reveal his will to man in human language, not the dialect of angels. "If I speak with the tongues of men and of angels," but have not the divine aid, I could not express the will of God. God has ever worked through agencies; he has sought to use means in accomplishing his will. When man has been involved, God has always worked through men. This is true in the natural realm. He could produce a bountiful harvest in a moment of time and with one word, but that is not his way to produce harvest; his method has been to produce it through seed. There is needed the seed, soil, sunshine, moisture, and air for the production of any vegetable. So, when it comes to the spiritual nature of man, God has used man in developing characters that are pleasing to him. The divine element and human element have worked together in producing the Bible.

II. Meaning of Inspiration

It is necessary to understand the meaning of "inspiration." The word has a very interesting history; it literally means to "breathe in," or to be influenced by another. In the development of a theological nomenclature, it came to mean that the books of the Bible were written by men who were influenced by the Holy Spirit. The writers of the Bible are called inspired as breathed into by the Holy Spirit so that the product of their activities transcends human powers and becomes divinely authoritative.

Inspiration is usually defined as a supernatural influence exerted on the sacred writers by the Holy Spirit, by virtue of which their writings are given divine authority. In inspiration God, through the Holy Spirit, cooperates with man.

"Inspiration" may be used in a restricted sense and in a general sense; usually it is used to denote a divine and miraculous illumination and guidance of the human mind. It is that which enabled the writers of the Bible to select from their knowledge the proper material and correctly express that in human language. If the Bible was given by inspiration, then it is the word of God, and can make man wise unto salvation. Since the Bible has the divine and the human elements in its production, inspiration belongs to the divine element. It does not come within the scope of the present study to determine the exact ratio of the divine element to the human element; we have no exact measure of the divine influence, and no statement that will help us to determine the degree of certitude which belongs to any part of the Bible. It appears that sometimes the divine element was a chief factor; then, sometimes the human element was more dominant; and sometimes the two elements appear to be equal.

It is not the part of inspiration to create fact-material. The Holy Spirit did not create the fact-material. Inspiration never made a *fact* any more a *factor;* inspiration never made a *truth* any truer; inspiration never made a principle any more real. Inspiration only guided the speaker in speaking the truth on the subject; it enabled the writer to select and collect such fact-material as was needed; it guided the speaker or writer in expressing only principles. Even the Holy Spirit did not make a *principle, truth,* or *fact.* There is no inspiration in the scroll or parchment used by the writer; there was no inspiration in paper, ink, or type; these were used only by the one who was influenced by the Holy Spirit. Inspiration in using human agencies never violated a principle or law pertaining to human nature. The Holy Spirit guided the mind of the one inspired in operating according to the laws governing the activities of the mind.

We know that all written communications were made through

human instrumentality; Christ left no written documents upon the earth. We have a record of his writing only one time, and this was upon the ground and soon was erased. (John 8: 6.) God wrote upon the tables of stone the Ten Commandments. (Ex. 24: 12; 32: 15, 16.)   However, Moses threw these two tables of stone down and broke them. (Ex. 32: 19.)   God then called for Moses to return up into the mountain, and it seems that Jehovah told Moses what to write and that Moses engraved the Ten Commandments on the tables of stone the next time. (Ex. 34: 1-4, 28.)   No angel ever wrote anything that was preserved in the Bible. The human element runs throughout the Bible as does the divine element. We should not overlook the fact that the divine element is the inspiration of the Bible.

III. Inspiration in Revelation

"Revelation" simply means "unveiling" that which is "revealed." A divine revelation is God's unveiling the truth regarding himself in some manner and degree to the intelligence and heart of man.   Man can know God only as he thus reveals or unveils himself to man.   "But unto us God revealed them through the Spirit: for the Spirit searcheth all things, yea, the deep things of God.   For who among men knoweth the things of a man, save the spirit of the man, which is in him? even so the things of God none knoweth, save the Spirit of God.   But we received, not the spirit of the world, but the spirit which is from God; that we might know the things that were freely given to us of God.   Which things also we speak, not in words which man's wisdom teacheth, but which the Spirit teacheth; combining spiritual things with spiritual words." (1 Cor. 2: 10-13.)   In one of the prayers recorded that Jesus uttered, he said: "O Father, Lord of heaven and earth, that thou didst hide these things from the wise and understanding, and didst reveal them unto babes. . . . No one knoweth the Son, save the Father; neither doth any know the Father, save the Son, and he to whomsoever the Son willeth to reveal him." (Matt. 11: 25-27.)

Revelation is the word of God expressed in human language; revelation is the result of inspiration. God through the Holy Spirit illuminates the mind of man with his thoughts and enables man to express those thoughts, and when expressed they become revelation. The Bible is thus the product of inspiration; it is the final product expressed in the language of man—God's will to man. The Bible presents three epochs of divine relevation; these are clearly and definitely marked off from each other. They have been called "dispensations." The first has been called the "Primitive Revelation." This corresponds to the patriarchal dispensation. This was the period when God revealed himself to Adam in the Garden of Eden. During this time God was gradually unfolding his nature and personality to the patriarchs. He is revealed there as God the Creator of all things; later he is revealed as Lord God, which means, not only the Creator, but the Ruler of all things. Then he is revealed to Noah as the God who punishes wickedness. He is revealed to Abraham in different ways; he is God Almighty; he is his shield and great reward. He revealed himself to Isaac as the God who keeps his promises; to Jacob as the one who protects; and to Joseph as the one who is interested in human affairs.

The second epoch is the covenant revelation of God to Israel. This is synonymous with the Jewish dispensation; it is the period of time when the law of Moses was enforced. God revealed to Moses and through Moses to the children of Israel. The different statutes and ordinances were given to Moses and recorded in a book. The constitution of the law was written in the Ten Commandments. God's covenant with Israel, made at Sinai, contained all of the laws, statutes, ordinances, and promises to Israel. This covenant included their land inheritance in Palestine as promised to Abraham. The Holy Spirit spoke through Moses and guided him in his giving a record of all of these laws. During this epoch nearly all of the prophecies were given through the Holy Spirit and recorded as we now have them.

The third epoch of God's revelation was made through Christ. "God, having of old time spoken unto the fathers in the prophets by divers portions and in divers manners, hath at the end of these days spoken unto us in his Son, whom he appointed heir of all things, through whom also he made the worlds." (Heb. 1:

1, 2.) In Christ we have God revealed, not as the Creator and as the Lord, but as a Father. The fullness of the revelation of God is made through Christ. We have a fuller revelation of the love, mercy, justice, and wisdom of God made through Christ. We have his mind and will made known to us in Christ. The richest and fullest revelation of God is seen in Christ. Not only do we have the fullest revelation of God in Christ, but his revelation in Christ is complete. We need not expect any other revelation. This corresponds to the Christian dispensation.

God has spoken or revealed himself through Christ *to* man. No revelation of God is given to angels or to the lower creation; it is given directly to man. Man is the object to whom God has addressed his message. His revelation during the primitive age was *to* man; the law of Moses was given *to* man. Not only was the revelation made *to* man, but it was made *for* man. God gave his revelation for the benefit of man; he wanted man to know his mind; he wanted man to know his will, way, and wisdom; this was all done for man. Furthermore, his revelation was made *through* man. The Christ came and spoke to man and revealed God's will, but this was expressed later by the Holy Spirit *through* man. Every message that came through an angel, prophet, or Christ was later written by inspiration; that is, some man was inspired to write or record for permanent use these messages. Hence, a permanent and complete record of God's revelation *to* man and *for* man was made *through* man; this permanent record for future generations is called the Bible.

The Bible is the work of the Holy Spirit. The Old Testament was written by inspiration; Moses, who is the author of the first five books, was inspired, as was David and the prophets. Hence, we may ascribe the Old Testament to the special work of the Holy Spirit. Inspiration is at once recognized to proceed immediately from the Holy Spirit. The two quotations from the book of Job confirm these remarks. "But there is a spirit in man, and the breath of the Almighty giveth them understanding." (Job 32: 8.) "The Spirit of God hath made me, and the breath of the Almighty giveth me life." (Job 33: 4.) "The breath of the Almighty" as used here means "inspiration." These four questions need to be considered: (1) What are we to understand by the inspiration of the Holy Spirit? (2) What is inspired? (3) What are the evidences of the inspiration of the Old Testament? (4) What are the ends to be served by this work of the Holy Spirit?

In answering the first question we may say that "inspiration" properly means "God-inspired." The idea of breathing upon or breathing into the soul is that which the word naturally conveys, thus God breathed into the nostrils of Adam the breath of life. The writers of the Old Testament were simply his instruments in producing the Old Testament. In answering the second question we may say that the writings of those who were inspired have been preserved by the Jews; they are reckoned as the canonical books of the Old Testament. God has preserved his own book; it can be ascribed only to him that it has not been perverted nor destroyed. The answer to the third question may take all of the evidences as to the authenticity and canonicity of the Old Testament. Each book of the Old Testament carries with it its own proof. A self-evidencing light attends all the books of the Bible. We look out on the works of God, and we feel they proclaim their own author; so also do the books of the Bible. Men could not have written them, they could as well have made the sun, or moon, or stars, or earth. The human mind could not have conceived the Ten Commandments, or the life of Jesus Christ. The answer to the fourth question is simple enough. The Scriptures were written to make men wise unto salvation. They are profitable "for teaching," "for reproof," "for correction," and "for instruction in righteousness." (2 Tim. 3: 16, 17.) The grand and glorious end is that "the man of God may be complete, furnished completely unto every good work."

Christ endorsed the Old Testament with its threefold division—law, prophets, and Psalms—when he said, "All things must needs be fulfilled, which are written in the law of Moses, and the prophets, and the psalms, concerning me." (Luke 24: 44.) Again, Christ said that "David in the Spirit" called him Lord. (Matt. 22: 43.) Again Christ called the Old Testament "the word of God." (John 10: 35.) Christ came to fulfill the law and the prophets. (Matt. 5: 17.) Moreover Jesus commanded the Jews to search the Old Testament Scriptures, for they testified of him. (John 5: 39.) Hence, the testimony of Jesus is the spirit of prophecy. (Rev. 19: 10.)

HOLY SPIRIT IN INSPIRATION

INTRODUCTION.

Three divine-human persons or things—divine-human man, Christ; divine-human institution, the church; divine-human book, the Bible.

I. DIFFICULT POSITIONS.

1. If *none* of the Bible is inspired, it sinks to the level of human productions, as it claims to be inspired.
2. If *only a part* is inspired, *what part?* Who is able to say?
3. Either the *entire Bible* is inspired, *or only a part,* or *none.*

II. THEORIES OF INSPIRATION.

1. Some scholars have put them under five heads.
2. Others under fewer heads.
3. Most common theories.
   a. The verbal and plenary theory.
   b. The natural theory.
   c. The noematical or thought theory.

III. HOW TO TEST A THEORY.

1. If a proposed theory serves to explain all the facts and phenomena involved in the case, it should be accepted as true and valid.
2. If it does not do this, it should be rejected.

IV. THE THEORIES TESTED.

1. Verbal theory fails to account for the human element.
2. The natural theory fails to account for the divine element.
3. The thought theory contradicts revealed truth. (Matt. 10: 19, 20.)

V. THE TRUTH OF INSPIRATION.

1. All false theories rejected, we may understand the truth.
2. Holy Spirit exercised a special providential and miraculous influence over both the words and thoughts of the writers.

HOLY SPIRIT IN INSPIRATION

"Be not anxious how or what ye shall speak: for it shall be given you in that hour what ye shall speak. For it is not ye that speak, but the Spirit of your Father that speaketh in you." (Matt. 10: 19, 20.)

There are three things or persons which should be considered in the study of the inspiration of the Bible. One is a divine-human person, Christ; the divine element and the human element compose Jesus as we know him in the flesh. He was as divine as his Father, God, and as human as his mother, Mary. We see clearly the blending of divinity and humanity in the divine personage of the Christ. Again, the church is a divine-human institution; it is divine in that God designed it, established it, and Christ reigns over it. It is human in that it is composed, not of angels, nor spirits, but of human beings; every member of the body of Christ, the church, is a human being. The third divine-human thing in the world is the Bible. The inspiration of the Bible represents the divine element of it, and the men by whom and through whom it was given and has been preserved constitute the human element.

The Bible is truly the history of the self-manifestation of God; all of its annals, captivities, exiles, conquests, wars, changing dynasties, priesthoods, altars are subordinate to the thought of God. During the period of about fifteen or sixteen hundred years about thirty-six or forty writers, belonging to a peculiarly religious people, gave to the world sixty-six books which, because of a most remarkable unity, are called one book, the book, the Bible. Claim is made for these books the phenomena of inspiration. The men who wrote these books were inspired; they were holy men. There must be holy men if there be a holy book. The Bible, as a book of the revelation of God, unfolds the idea of God together with his will, way, and wisdom; it is furthermore the story of the development of these holy men, the penmen of the Holy Spirit.

I. Difficult Positions

Different attitudes are sustained toward the inspiration of the Bible; different positions are held even by those who claim to believe the Bible. Of course, atheists, agnostics, and infidels deny the inspiration of the Bible; they deny that it was given by the Holy Spirit. If the Bible is not inspired, it sinks to the low level of human production; it is self-contradictory and mendacious, since it claims to be inspired and to guide men in the way of life everlasting; it makes promises of salvation and gives a hope of heaven. However, if it is not inspired, it holds out false hopes and deludes those who have put their faith in it. Since millions trust the Bible, as the word of God, it is the most mendacious book that ever has been given to man.

Another attitude or position with respect to inspiration is held; there are some who admit that a part of the Bible is inspired, while other parts of it are not inspired. Here the difficulty arises when one attempts to draw the line between the parts that are inspired and those which are not. Since the Bible itself does not tell us which part is not inspired, how can we know? If *only* a *part* is inspired, *what part?* Who is able to say? If the divine element of inspiration and the human element of the Bible are not so blended in every detail, how can we claim that it is a book from God? If the divine and human parts are so mingled, but not blended, what claim to inspiration may be made? Will it not require an inspired man to point out to us the part that is inspired, and that which is not inspired? These are difficulties which the one who affirms that only a part of the Bible is inspired must meet.

We are forced in the study of inspiration to accept one of three disjunctions. Either the *entire* Bible is inspired, or *only a part* of it is inspired, or *none* of it is inspired. We have here a simple trilemma, and must take one of the disjunctions. Which is the more tenable? We must hold to the position that *none* of the Bible is inspired, or adhere to the position that *only a part* of it is inspired, or that *all* of the Bible is inspired. The believer takes the position that the *entire* Bible is inspired; this is the only tenable position that a Christian can take. The Christian takes the responsibility of proving his position; his is a positive and affirmative position. The Christian is ready to shoulder the responsibility of his affirmation that the *entire* Bible is inspired.

II. THEORIES OF INSPIRATION

Before examining further the evidence of inspiration, it is necessary to dispose of the different views that have been held concerning inspiration. False theories have arisen; these must be disposed of before we can appreciate the study of inspiration. Some scholars have summed up these different views and collected them under five heads or theories. This seems to be too many for close logical reasoning. Still others include all the views under two or three heads. Those who group them under two theories have reduced them to the simplest classification to be made. A variety of views and positions with only shades of minor differences may be grouped under fewer heads.

The most common theories considered in our study of inspiration will be grouped under three heads. It is thought that all of the salient views may be examined under these three theories. First, we consider the verbal or plenary theory. The verbal theory is sometimes called the literalistic theory. The proponents of this theory hold that the Holy Spirit put the words into the mouth of the speaker or guided the pen even in writing the words of the original manuscript. This position would make the writers of the Bible mere passive instruments of the Holy Spirit; the writers did nothing more than act as the mere amanuenses of the Holy Spirit; they merely recorded the words of the Holy Spirit as one would record the words of another in giving a direct quotation.

The natural theory of inspiration admits of many different grades and shades of meaning. Some make it consist wholly in the natural influence of the subject on the powers of the human mind; still others admit that there may be some providential influence on the mind. The theory reduces itself to the simple position that the writers of the Bible were inspired only as writers today are inspired. They would claim no more inspiration for the writers of the Bible than they would claim for Milton, Shakespeare, Burns, or any other poet. The result of this theory would make the books of the Bible merely literary productions with all of the errors that belong to human productions; the thoughts of the Bible have no higher source than the intellects of men, according to this theory. The Bible, according to it, does not express the mind of God.

The third theory has been variously named. By some it has been called the "Noematical Theory of Inspiration." This term comes from two Greek words meaning "mind" and "thought." It means that the Holy Spirit merely gave the thought to man and left man free to express that thought in his own way. This theory denies that the words were given to man and affirms that only the thoughts came from God. The exponents of this theory concede that the thoughts were all suggested by the Holy Spirit, but that is all that came from the Holy Spirit. These different positions must be weighed; the truth that is in them must be sifted and retained and the errors discarded. It is our further study to proceed and glean, as far as possible, the clear, axiomatic, scriptural truth about inspiration.

III. How to Test a Theory

The student of the subject of inspiration is at once confronted with a serious task of learning how to test the different theories presented and learn the truth from them. When a theory is presented, one ought to be able to examine in detail that theory and determine whether to accept or reject it. The question is raised: How may we test a theory? Fortunately for us, there are some well-defined and simple rules to follow in testing a theory in any branch of science. These have been worked out and formulated in plain, understandable English; furthermore, they have been tested in so many cases that they are about ready to take the place of axioms. Any proposed theory may be tested by these standards and the truth of them determined. If a proposed theory serves to explain all of the facts, principles, and phenomena involved in the case, it should be accepted as true and valid. However, if this theory does not explain fully and clearly all of the facts, principles, and phenomena, then it should be rejected. This seems to be a clear and definite way of testing the theories of inspiration.

IV. THE THEORIES TESTED

It now becomes a simple matter to test these theories of inspiration by the rules that have been suggested. The verbal theory. If holy men of old who spoke by the Holy Spirit were mere penmen of the Holy Spirit, it seems that all the books of the Bible would have been written in the same style. Job, David, Isaiah, Matthew, Mark, Luke, John, Paul, and Peter would use the same style of writing, or the Holy Spirit would choose to use one style for Job, another for David, and still another for Paul. This does not account for the variety of styles used in writing the Bible. It is freely granted that the Holy Spirit has the power and wisdom to choose any style, and he could choose to use the style that the writers used in their ordinary speech or writings. But why should we conclude that the Holy Spirit would use the style of Isaiah and not permit Isaiah to use his own style? Why should the Holy Spirit choose to use the style of David, and not permit David to use his own style? This theory would not account for the human element in the Bible; it breaks down when we see that it does not account for the human elements that are in the Bible.

When the test is made, the natural theory breaks down because it fails to account for the supernatural element in the Bible. It fails utterly to account for those wonderful attributes of Jehovah which are revealed in the Bible. No man could know the processes of creation and the steps of development without divine aid. No one was present at the creation who kept any record of the stages of development, and yet Genesis gives an outline of creation. Geology or any other science cannot account for the divine element in the Bible. The Christ as a perfect character could not have been invented by finite mind. Wise men of the east came to his cradle and wise men of the west started from the cross; the greatest men of all history have been those who have believed in the Christ of the New Testament.

The noematical theory, or the thought theory, does not meet and satisfy all the requirements in the case. This theory claims that only the thought was given to the writer and that he was left free to use his individual style in expressing that thought for permanent record. Christ told his apostles that they should give no thought as to what they should speak, for it would be given them in the hour that they needed it; he then added: "For it is not ye that speak, but the Spirit of your Father that speaketh in you." (Matt. 10: 20.) Paul declared: "Which things also we speak, not in words which man's wisdom teacheth, but which the Spirit teacheth; combining spiritual things with spiritual words." (1 Cor. 2: 13.) Again Paul said: "When ye received from us the word of the message, even the word of God, ye accepted it not as the word of men, but, as it is in truth, the word of God, which also worketh in you that believe." (1 Thess. 2: 13.) When submitted to the rigid test, this theory, like the others, breaks down.

V. THE TRUTH OF INSPIRATION

There is some truth in all of the theories that have been advanced; however, there is so much error connected with them that they must be rejected. The false theories having been set aside, we may more clearly understand the truth about inspiration. The Holy Spirit seems to have exercised a special providential and miraculous influence over both the words and the thoughts of the writer. With this view we would conclude that in the original manuscripts there were no words or thoughts that were not in strict harmony with the will of God. This does not touch the question of whether or not the copyists and translators have been faithful in giving to us a true copy of the mind of God in the Bible. It is thought that our copy of the Bible is free enough from human errors that we can believe in the present copy of the Bible as inspired.

The Holy Spirit endorsed the inspiration of the Old Testament through the inspiration of the New Testament writers. The Old Testament is sometimes called the "sacred writings." (2 Tim. 3: 15.) Again the prophets and other writers of the Old Testament are endorsed as speaking by the Holy Spirit by the New Testament writers. "And when they agreed not among themselves, they departed after that Paul had spoken one word, Well spake the Holy Spirit through Isaiah the prophet unto your fathers." (Acts 28: 25.) The writer of the Hebrew letter in referring to the Old Testament Scriptures said, "And the Holy Spirit also beareth witness to us." (Heb. 10: 15.) After this statement, Jer. 31: 33 and following verses are quoted. Peter wrote, "For no prophecy ever came by the will of man: but men spake from God, being moved by the Holy Spirit." (2 Pet. 1: 21.) Paul in writing to the church at Rome speaks of the law as being "holy, and the commandment holy, and righteous, and good." (Rom. 7: 12.) Again, it is said that "God, having of old time spoken unto the fathers in the prophets by divers portions and in divers manners." (Heb. 1: 1.) So God spoke through the prophets by the Holy Spirit; the message that they bore was the message of God; it was the message of the Holy Spirit, as they spoke as the Holy Spirit moved them. The Holy Spirit thus inspired the writers to speak God's message to the people. If we can never understand the full meaning of inspiration, we can understand that the Holy Spirit guided the pen of the writers of the Bible. We cannot understand all of the qualities that belong to electricity, but we do know that it has light, heat, and power; so the Holy Spirit guided speakers and writers in delivering just God's message and nothing else but his message in writing the Bible.

DEGREES OF INSPIRATION

INTRODUCTION.

No errors in the original manuscripts; every theory rejected which does not recognize the Holy Spirit in *every word* as well as in *every thought.*

I. THREE ELEMENTS IN DIVINE ADMINISTRATION.

    1. The natural element.

        a. God acts through certain fixed laws.

        b. These are constant in physical, moral, and spiritual realms.

    2. Providential element.

        a. Power exercised through natural laws increased or diminished as God proposed.

        b. Joseph in Egypt an example.

    3. The miraculous element.

        a. If natural forces sufficient, God never uses providential.

        b. If natural and providential insufficient, miraculous used.

II. DIVINE ECONOMY.

    1. God never employs unnecessary means.

    2. He uses learning and talent of writers of Bible.

    3. An equal degree of inspiration not necessary.

    4. Paul better educated than other writers.

III. EXAMPLES OF DIFFERENT DEGREES.

    1. Christ had the highest. (John 3: 34.)

        a. Holy Spirit to abide with him. (John 1: 33.)

        b. He spoke with authority. (Matt. 7: 29.)

    2. Inspiration of apostles.

        a. Had baptism of Holy Spirit.

        b. Classed above prophets.

    3. Inspiration of Paul.

        a. He claimed inspiration. (1 Cor. 2: 13.)

        b. Had higher degree at one time than at another.

        c. Spoke by commandment of Lord. (1 Cor. 7: 10.)

        d. Spoke his own judgment. (1 Cor. 7: 12, 25, 40.)

DEGREES OF INSPIRATION

"The Spirit of Jehovah came mightily upon David from that day forward. . . . Now the Spirit of Jehovah departed from Saul, and an evil spirit from Jehovah troubled him." (1 Sam. 16: 13, 14.)

No matter what view of inspiration we accept, there were no errors in the original manuscripts of the Bible. It is not claimed that the translators were inspired so that no error was made in translation; it is only claimed that the Holy Spirit guided the writers so that the complete will of God was expressed by the writers. It is believed that the overruling providence of God has preserved a copy of the original manuscripts so that today the Bible expresses the will of God and is able to make men wise unto salvation. This copy we call the Bible.

Every theory which does not recognize the Holy Spirit in *every word* as well as in *every thought* is to be rejected. The Bible is a product of the Holy Spirit. We must recognize it as such. The only guide that we have is the Bible; if it is not a book from God, then God our Creator has placed us in this world without speaking a word to us or giving us any instruction as to our origin and destiny. Man is left without any token of divine blessings in a spiritual way, if the Bible did not come from God. If it came from God, it is inspired; if it did not come from God, it is not inspired. Since God through the Holy Spirit has given us the Bible, we may trust him that he will preserve it so that man may know God's will and be guided by his wisdom.

I. THREE ELEMENTS IN DIVINE ADMINISTRATION

As we study God in his universe, we recognize that there are three elements in his administration of affairs; we mean by this that God's power is exercised in three ways. We must know these in order to appreciate the work of the Holy Spirit in inspiration. The first element that we recognize is the natural element; this is the simplest and most common method that we recognize in the universe. These methods or laws are frequently called the laws of nature. God works through nature; the Holy

Spirit gave the laws by which the natural realm or material world is governed; he exercises through the Holy Spirit his power and sustains the world in its present order. These laws of nature are constant in the physical, moral, and spiritual realms; they have never been changed since the material world was created; they will never be changed so long as its present order remains. All the power and energy exercised and manifested through these laws come from God. He reigns through the Holy Spirit over all nature.

Another element in the administration of the universe is the providential element. Some have ignored or even denied God's exercising any providential care over his universe; they even deny any providential care over man. The power or extraordinary energy that is exercised above the power exerted through natural laws is called providential; the providential power is exercised through natural laws; this power may be increased or diminished according to the will or purpose of God. The providential element is the plus element above the power exerted through the natural laws. The natural laws give direction to the extra care and power that God exercises. This is done through the Holy Spirit. A clear example of the exercise of the providential element is seen clearly in the case of Joseph in Egypt. God cared for him; the story as recorded in Genesis clearly reveals the fact that there is a power that is guiding and using Joseph in Egypt and caring for his brethren that is not seen in others. As we view God's care over Joseph, we see that only natural laws are revealed. No new law or principle is brought into the affairs; the hand of God guides in a special way the affairs through natural laws.

The third element in the divine administration of affairs is the miraculous element. The supernatural element is seen in some of the administrations of God's power; this we call the miraculous element. When God's purpose cannot be accomplished through the ordinary means, he has used other means. If the forces through natural laws are sufficient to accomplish God's will in the administration of affairs, he never uses the providential element. If his purpose can be carried out through the natural laws by the extra providential element, no other divine energy is expended. However, if the purpose of God cannot be carried out through the ordinary channels of the natural laws, supplemented with the energy of the providential element, then the miraculous element is employed. The miraculous element is only used when the natural and providential elements are insufficient. Sometimes the miraculous element is exercised independent of all laws and forces of nature. The miraculous element may be through the laws of nature or above them. God's will must be done; he is the sovereign ruler of the universe; he is omnipotent. We do not expect the miraculous power of God to be used today; he has established his laws that pertain to the redemption of man, and there is no need for the miraculous element to be used.

A close examination of the miraculous manifestations of divine administration shows that the natural and providential elements are united with the miraculous element in many instances. When this is the case, the miraculous element is a supplement to the other two elements. When the flood was brought upon the earth, the forces of nature were evidently employed to bring the flood of waters upon the earth; however, this was a miracle; the miraculous element in this instance worked through the natural laws. When the waters of the Red Sea were divided, or when the river Jordan was divided for the children of Israel to cross, it seems that the miraculous element was contrary to the natural element. The natural element was suspended and the miraculous power exercised. When the sun and moon stood still at the command of Joshua, the miraculous element was manifested above the natural element. When the shadow on the dial of Ahaz (Isa. 38: 8) was turned back ten steps, the miraculous element seems to run counter to the natural element. God has power to manifest himself contrary to the laws of nature; he is limited in the exercise of his power only by his own will.

II. Divine Economy

There is what we call the "Law of Parsimony"; this law forbids the use of anything, energy, or person that is not necessary to accomplish the end that God has in purpose. It also bids us provide the fewest agencies which solve a problem or explain a phenomenon. If the natural element is sufficient, God never uses the providential or miraculous; he observes his own law of parsimony. He never employs unnecessary means in his work; he never wastes any energy; he never gives too much instruction; he never has been extravagant with his commands or promises; all that he has said and done were necessary. He used all the learning and talents of the several writers of the Bible so far as these natural means were available. He has followed this law of parsimony in inspiration of the Bible. An equal degree of inspiration was not necessary in all of the writers of the Bible. There were some facts, events, principles, truths, and experiences that the writers did not know; these had to be supplied by the Holy Spirit. Then there were some of these things which the writers knew; these they needed the Holy Spirit to guide them in just speaking or writing only the truth about these things.

These were some of the events in the experience of Moses, with which he was perfectly familiar; he needed the Holy Spirit to guide him in writing just those things that God wanted to be preserved for future generations. Again, there were events connected with creation, Adam, and the deluge which Moses needed the Holy Spirit to inform him about these things. Some of the prophets had an accurate knowledge of the condition of affairs in Israel; they did not need the Holy Spirit to *inform* them of these things, but they did need the Holy Spirit to guide them in selecting just such things as were best to be included in the divine record. Paul was better educated than some of the other writers of the New Testament; these attainments helped him to be better informed on some of the affairs than other writers. The Holy Spirit used the talents and attainments that Paul had and guided him in writing the major portion of the New Testament. Paul knew the events connected with his own conversion, yet he needed the Holy Spirit to guide him in relating only such things as were necessary for others to know.

III. Examples of Different Degrees

It may seem strange to some to speak of different degrees of inspiration. However, it will appear clear as we go on in this study to each one. Christ had the highest degree of inspiration.

He was a member of the Godhead and knew the mind of God and the Holy Spirit. "For he whom God hath sent speaketh the words of God: for he giveth not the Spirit by measure." (John 3: 34.) Here we have it declared that Christ had the Holy Spirit without measure; this implies that others had a different degree of the Holy Spirit, if we may so speak of his influence. The Holy Spirit was to remain with Christ; this implies that he did not remain with others all the time as he did with Christ. At the baptism of Jesus, we have the testimony of John who said: "I knew him not: but he that sent me to baptize in water, he said unto me, Upon whomsoever thou shalt see the Spirit descending, and abiding upon him, the same is he that baptizeth in the Holy Spirit." (John 1: 33.) The Holy Spirit came upon him and abided with him; hence, Christ spoke with authority, and not as scribes. (Matt. 7: 29.)

The apostles had the next degree of the Holy Spirit or inspiration. They were baptized in the Holy Spirit; they received the fullest measure of the Spirit with the exception of Christ, who had the Spirit without measure. The apostles were classed with the prophets; they were frequently "filled with the Holy Spirit." (Acts 2: 4; 4: 8; 9: 17; 13: 9.) They had power to perform miracles and confirm the word which they spoke by the Holy Spirit. No one can read the record as given in Acts without being convinced that the apostles had the highest degree of the Holy Spirit in the early church. Christ had promised the Comforter, or the Holy Spirit, to them; he came upon them at Pentecost; he guided them; they testified for Christ and preached the gospel to the unsaved by the Holy Spirit.

Paul was inspired; he spoke by inspiration; he wrote by inspiration. The thirteen or fourteen books of the New Testament written by Paul constitute a large portion of the New Testament. He seems to have had a higher degree at one time than at another. He claimed inspiration. "Which things also we speak, not in words which man's wisdom teacheth, but which the Spirit teacheth; combining spiritual things with spiritual words." (1 Cor. 2: 13.) Again he said: "For I make known to you, brethren, as touching the gospel which was preached by me, that it is not after man. For neither did I receive it from man, nor was I

taught it, but it came to me through revelation of Jesus Christ
. . . to reveal his Son in me, that I might preach him among the
Gentiles; straightway I conferred not with flesh and blood: neither
went I up to Jerusalem to them that were apostles before me: but
I went away into Arabia; and again I returned unto Damascus."
(Gal. 1: 11-17.)

Sometimes Paul wrote by the commandment of God; that is,
he wrote the commandment of God. He said: "But unto the
married I give charge, yea not I, but the Lord." (1 Cor. 7: 10.)
Here he expresses the will of God, the commandment of God.
He had the Holy Spirit and thus spoke by the Holy Spirit in expressing the commandment of God. At another time, though
guided by the Holy Spirit, he said: "But to the rest say I, not
the Lord." (1 Cor. 7: 12.) Here Paul wrote his own inspired
judgment in the matter without having a direct commandment
from God. Again he said: "If any man thinketh himself to be a
prophet, or spiritual, let him take knowledge of the things which
I write unto you, that they are the commandment of the Lord."
(1 Cor. 14: 37.) So it appears that Paul wrote his own judgment on some things. (1 Cor. 7: 12, 25, 40.) It is clear furthermore that the Holy Spirit exercised a very special providential
and miraculous influence over both the words and the thoughts
of the writers of the Bible. When they needed the degree of inspiration to *inform* them, this was given; when they needed only
the degree to *guide* them in selecting the material which they had
in hand, they were given only this power. Luke had material on
hand and needed only the Holy Spirit that he might trace "the
course of all things accurately from the first." (Luke 1: 1-3.)

The Bible begins, as we should expect, with God (Gen. 1: 1),
and it ends with man, who was the last of God's creation. "The
grace of the Lord Jesus be with the saints. Amen." (Rev. 22:
21.) "The saints" are mentioned in the last verse of the Bible
as "God" is mentioned in the first verse of it. No one has ever
claimed that the Bible was actually written by the hand of God; it
is claimed that God *through man* wrote the Bible. It is not claimed
that God arranged the books in the order that we know them or
have them in our Bible; inspiration did not arrange the books
of the Old Testament as we have them in our Bible; neither did

the Holy Spirit arrange the books of the New Testament in their present order. The Holy Spirit did not divide the Bible into chapters and verses; these divisions were made by man long years after the Holy Spirit had guided the writers in giving to us the original manuscripts of the Bible. There have been many translations of the Bible, and these translations were made from copies of the original manuscripts. The Holy Spirit did not make these translations, but the overruling providence of God is thought to have protected the Bible and we now have it as a revelation of God's will to man. There is a progressive development of thought from the first of Genesis to the last of Revelation. This continuity may be seen in reading the Bible through; one book is a sequence of another. As we read through Genesis, we close that book with the feeling that there is something else to follow. There is implied at the close of each book of the Bible the word "continued" until we come to Revelation; there is nothing to be added to the "Amen" of Revelation.

INSPIRATION OF THE OLD TESTAMENT

INTRODUCTION.

Much proof of inspiration; thirty-nine books of the Old Testament; these given by the Holy Spirit.

I. OLD TESTAMENT WRITERS CLAIMED HOLY SPIRIT.

   1. The writers of the law.
      a. Moses and the Pentateuch. (Deut. 18: 15; 31: 9, 34.)
      b. Law through Moses. (Ex. 19: 7-10; John 1: 17.)
      c. Joshua had Holy Spirit. (Josh. 1: 5, 8.)
   2. The writers of the Psalms.
      a. David spoke by Holy Spirit. (2 Sam. 23: 1, 2.)
      b. Solomon guided by Holy Spirit. (1 Kings 6: 11.)
   3. The prophets claimed inspiration.
      a. Each of the major prophets had Holy Spirit. (Isa. 1: 1, 2; Jer. 2: 1; Ezek. 2: 2; Dan. 9: 20. 22.)
      b. Each of the minor prophets made this claim.

II. OLD TESTAMENT ENDORSED BY CHRIST.

   1. Threefold division. (Luke 22: 43.)
   2. Christ endorsed David. (Matt. 22: 43; Mark 12: 46.)
   3. Christ called Old Testament "word of God." (John 10: 35.)
   4. He came to fulfill law and prophets. (Matt. 5: 17.)
   5. Testimony of Jesus' spirit of prophecy. (Rev. 19: 10.)

III. HOLY SPIRIT ENDORSED OLD TESTAMENT.

   1. Holy Spirit endorsed Old Testament through New Testament writers.
   2. "Scriptures" in New Testament refer to Old Testament.
   3. "Every scripture inspired of God." (2 Tim. 3: 16.)
   4. God spoke in the prophets. (Heb. 1: 1.)
   5. Men of Old Testament moved by Holy Spirit. (2 Pet. 1: 21.)
   6. Old Testament called "sacred writings." (2 Tim. 3: 15.)

INSPIRATION OF THE OLD TESTAMENT

"I will put my Spirit within you, and cause you to walk in my statutes, and ye shall keep mine ordinances, and do them." (Ezek. 36: 27.)

It has been said that the Old Testament is the New Testament concealed, and that the New Testament is the Old Testament revealed. There is much truth in this statement. We see in the Old Testament the gradual unfolding of the idea of God, his plan, and the redemption of man. The Old Testament is the background of the New Testament; it is in the Old Testament that the deep roots of the New Testament find nourishment. Everywhere throughout the history of man from Adam to the close of Malachi we recognize the invisible presence and the constant operation of the Holy Spirit. It is claimed that the Old Testament is inspired. and, therefore, reveals the will of God to man. The reader is impressed, as he turns the pages of the Old Testament with the inspiration of the Holy Spirit; there is a deep undercurrent that outcrops here and there of the work of the Holy Spirit in the Old Testament.

There is abundant proof of the inspiration of the Old Testament, both internally and externally; the canonicity of the thirty-nine books of the Old Testament is based upon the proof of the inspiration of these books. The external evidence increases from year to year; archaeology is discovering new evidence from time to time. There is now so much external evidence discovered that it is spoken of as "the testimony of the spade." The discoveries which have been made in recent years in Bible lands are cumulative evidence of the inspiration of the Bible. However, we are more interested in this discussion in the internal evidence of the inspiration of the Bible. We will present internal evidences in this study.

I. OLD TESTAMENT WRITERS CLAIMED HOLY SPIRIT

Even a casual reading of the Old Testament impresses one with the work of the Holy Spirit. There are so many clear and emphatic claims made by the writers that it is tedious to repeat

them.   The Old Testament abounds in numerous claims of
inspiration.   The inspiration of the Old Testament is so clear,
so accurate, and so absolute that no one can justify himself before
God or intelligent men without accepting without doubt the
evidence of inspiration.   Moses wrote the Pentateuch.   As we
read these five books, we are impressed with the fact that Moses
had the Spirit of God.   No one could have written Genesis
without the aid of the Holy Spirit.   Exodus contains forty chapters; in this book we find "God spake these words" one hundred
sixty-one times; that is an average of a little more than four
times to each of the forty chapters of this statement.   Truly
we do not find that "God suggested or inspired these *thoughts*,"
but on each occasion it is recorded "God spake these *words*."

Moses was the great lawgiver; he was called up on Mount Sinai
and there God gave the law to him, and he in turn gave it to the
people.   (Ex. 19: 7-10; Deut. 18: 15; 31: 9, 34; John 1: 17.)
Joshua succeeded Moses in the leadership of Israel; Joshua was
"full of the spirit of wisdom; for Moses had laid his hands upon
him: and the children of Israel hearkened unto him, and did as
Jehovah commanded Moses."   (Deut. 34: 9.)   Again, Joshua
made a copy of the book of the law and kept it for his guidance.   (Josh. 1: 1, 5, 8.)   "Jehovah thy God is with thee whither-
soever thou goest."   Jehovah was with Joshua as he was with
Moses in leading the children of Israel and fighting their battles
for them.   So the Pentateuch and the book of Joshua were given
by inspiration.

The writers of the Psalms were inspired.   David wrote many
of the Psalms and the internal evidence shows that he wrote by
inspiration.   "Now these are the last words of David.   David the
son of Jesse saith, And the man who was raised on high saith,
The anointed of the God of Jacob, and the sweet psalmist of Israel:
the Spirit of Jehovah spake by me, and his word was upon my
tongue."   (2 Sam. 23: 1, 2.)   Jesus said: "How then doth David
in the Spirit call him Lord?"   (Matt. 22: 43.)   The Psalms
breathe the Spirit of God in devotion to God.   In the Psalms we
have the devotional worship expressed.   There is praise to God
for his goodness and mercy to the people; through the Psalms the
children of Israel praised God.   Solomon, David's wise son, wrote

the Proverbs, Ecclesiastes, and the Song of Solomon, while David wrote or compiled many of the Psalms. Job was probably written by Moses, but it shows that the Holy Spirit guided in its composition. Hence, the devotional part of the Old Testament was given by inspiration.

The prophets all claimed to speak by inspiration; from Samuel to Malachi the Holy Spirit guided the prophets. We have them divided into two classes—the major prophets and the minor prophets. The major prophets are Isaiah, Jeremiah, Ezekiel, and Daniel; all major prophets claimed to speak the word of God by the Holy Spirit. (Isa. 1: 1, 2; Jer. 2: 1; Ezek. 2: 2; Dan. 9: 20, 22.) There are sixty-six chapters in Isaiah, fifty-two in Jeremiah, forty-eight in Ezekiel, and twelve in Daniel, one hundred seventy-eight chapters in all of the major prophets. This is a large portion of prophecy in the Old Testament. There are twelve minor prophets, and each of these claimed to speak the word of God; they spoke by the Holy Spirit. (Hos. 1: 1; Joel 1: 1; Amos 1: 3; Obad. 1: 1; Jonah 1: 1; Mic. 1: 1; Zeph. 1: 1; Hag. 1: 2; Zech. 1: 3; Mal. 1: 1.) These prophets were all burdened with the word of God; the Holy Spirit spoke through them to the people.

II. Old Testament Endorsed by Christ

The history of the earthly ministry of Christ testifies that he endorsed the Old Testament Scriptures. He even endorsed the threefold division of the Old Testament—the law, the prophets, and the Psalms. "These are my words which I spake unto you, while I was yet with you, that all things must needs be fulfilled, which are written in the law of Moses, and the prophets, and the psalms, concerning me." (Luke 24: 44.) Hence, Christ endorsed the Pentateuch and the history of the Old Testament; he gave full endorsement to the prophets; he frequently said concerning the prophecies that they "must needs be fulfilled." This could not be truthfully said if the Old Testament was written by uninspired men. Christ fulfilled the prophecies concerning himself; he was the antitype of the types of him in the Old Testament. Frequently Matthew refers to the birth of Jesus and says that this was done that "it might be fulfilled which was spoken by the Lord through the prophet." (Matt. 1: 22.)

Christ endorsed David and said that he spoke by the Holy Spirit. "And Jesus answered and said, as he taught in the temple, How say the scribes that the Christ is the son of David? David himself said in the Holy Spirit, The Lord said unto my Lord, Sit thou on my right hand, till I make thine enemies the footstool of thy feet." (Mark 12: 35, 36.) Christ then endorsed the Psalms and that which David prophesied. A further endorsement of the Old Testament is observed in that Christ spoke of it as "the word of God." (John 10: 35.) "If he called them gods, unto whom the word of God came (and the scripture cannot be broken)." Christ could not call the Old Testament Scriptures the word of God if they were not inspired. Again, the fact that he came to fulfill the law and the prophets shows that he regarded "the law and the prophets" as inspired. "Think not that I came to destroy the law or the prophets: I came not to destroy, but to fulfil." (Matt. 5: 17.) Again, we have John bearing testimony and saying: "The testimony of Jesus is the spirit of prophecy." (Rev. 19: 10.) Again, Jesus said: "Ye search the scriptures, because ye think that in them ye have eternal life; and these are they which bear witness of me." (John 5: 39.) The evidence that Jesus endorsed the Old Testament is cumulative; however, we need no further proof of the testimony of Jesus to the inspiration of the Old Testament.

Dr. Harry Rimmer has calculated the number of quotations that Christ used from the Old Testament. Matthew contains 1,181 verses; 603 verses are the words of Jesus; this is fifty-one per cent of all of the verses. Eighty-three of these verses are Old Testament quotations, or fourteen per cent of the verses used by Jesus are from the Old Testament. Mark contains 609 verses; 275 of these are quotations of Jesus; thus forty-five per cent of the verses in Mark are the words of Jesus; thirty-four of these verses, or thirteen per cent, are from the Old Testament. Luke contains 1,251 verses, of which 570 are the words of Jesus; this is forty-five per cent of the verses; forty-two of these verses, or seven per cent of his quotations, are from the Old Testament. John contains 879 verses; 417 of these, or forty-nine per cent, are quotations from Jesus; 417 of these quotations of Jesus, or forty-nine per cent, are from the Old Testament. The four gospels contain 3,920 verses, and 1,865 of these are the words of Jesus; this is forty-eight per cent of all the verses; of his quoted conversation, 179 verses are literally Old Testament words. *Ten per cent of the daily conversation of Jesus was Old Testament verses literally quoted.* Truly Jesus endorsed the Old Testament as inspired.

III. Holy Spirit Endorsed Old Testament

The Holy Spirit spoke through the apostles; they were to speak by the Holy Spirit. "For it is not ye that speak, but the Spirit of your Father that speaketh in you." (Matt. 10: 20.) As inspired men spoke we have the Holy Spirit speaking. Hence Paul said: "But the Spirit saith expressly, that in later times some shall fall away from the faith." (1 Tim. 4: 1.) Hence, the Holy Spirit spoke through the writers of the New Testament. Every writer of the New Testament endorsed the Old Testament. We find more than two hundred eighty-four quotations from the Old Testament in seventeen books of the New Testament. These two hundred eighty-four quotations from the Old Testament are quoted from twenty-five of the Old Testament books. Each time that a quotation is made emphasis is given to the inspiration of the Old Testament. The writers of the New Testament were inspired, and when they quoted from the Old Testament they gave the force of inspiration to the books from which they quoted, or at least they gave the force of inspiration to the quotations which they made.

"Scriptures," when used in the New Testament, refer to the Old Testament. It is used a number of times by the writers of the New Testament, and must always refer to the Old Testament. It may be used occasionally to include New Testament Scripture, but its primary use is to refer to the Old Testament. "Every scripture inspired of God is also profitable for teaching, for reproof, for correction, for instruction which is in righteousness: that the man of God may be complete, furnished completely unto every good work." (2 Tim. 3: 16, 17.) This is a general statement and may refer both to the Old Testament and the New Testament. Since "every scripture" is inspired of God, then the New Testament Scriptures would be inspired of God. In this way "scripture" as used here would include the New Testament as well as the Old Testament. Furthermore, the Holy Spirit in writing Hebrews endorsed the prophets. "God, having of old time spoken unto the fathers in the prophets by divers portions and in divers manners, hath at the end of these days spoken unto us in his Son, whom he appointed heir of all things, through whom also he made the worlds." (Heb. 1: 1, 2.) God spoke through the prophets; he did this by the Holy Spirit. This would enforce claim that the prophets were inspired.

The Holy Spirit further emphasized the inspiration of the Old Testament when he spoke through Peter and said: "For no prophecy ever came by the will of man: but men spake from God, being moved by the Holy Spirit." (2 Pet. 1: 21.) Again, this shows that the Old Testament writers, and especially the prophets, spoke by the Holy Spirit. When one speaks "from God," that one speaks by the Holy Spirit; hence, his words are the words of God and express the will of God. Moreover, the Old Testament is called "the sacred writings." "But abide thou in the things which thou hast learned and hast been assured of, knowing of whom thou hast learned them and that from a babe thou hast known the sacred writings which are able to make thee wise unto salvation through faith which is in Christ Jesus." (2 Tim. 3: 14, 15.) These "sacred writings" have reference to the Old Testament Scriptures as we now have them. Paul had access to the Septuagint Version, which contains all the thirty-nine books of the Old Testament. Hence, the thirty-nine books of the Old Testament are called by the Holy Spirit "sacred writings." This would give full and complete endorsement to the Old Testament Scriptures as inspired of God.

It is true that the Old Testament is frequently referred to as the "sacred writings," "scriptures," and "word of God." It pleased God to deliver his message to the world through man; thus man needed to be guided as to what should be written; he needed to know what to leave out of the Bible as well as to know what should be put into it. This could not be left to the mere judgment of man; some higher power must guide in this work; some superior wisdom to that of man must be used in writing the Bible. The prophets in the Old Testament and the writers of the New Testament were able to peer into the future and see coming events; this is proof that the Holy Spirit guided them. The writers of the Old Testament and the New Testament refer to and quote each other, which shows that their writings were true and given by the Holy Spirit.

The Old Testament contains many prophecies that have been fulfilled. The prophecies were written before the events occurred; inspired men have pointed out that certain prophecies have been fulfilled. (Matt. 1: 33; 2: 6, 18; 3: 3, etc.) Christ himself pointed out that certain prophecies were fulfilled in his life. He said, "Today hath this scripture been fulfilled in your ears." (Luke 4: 21.) He came and fulfilled every prophecy pertaining to his earthly ministry; he answered every type in the Old Testament that pertained to him and his kingdom on earth. The shadows of the Old Testament point unerringly to the reality of the substance. The Old Testament would contain many types, shadows, and prophecies without any meaning, if Christ and his kingdom had not fulfilled them. Truly, "the Old Testament is the New Testament concealed and the New Testament is the Old Testament revealed."

Chapter XII

ALLEGED DISCREPANCIES OF OLD TESTAMENT

INTRODUCTION.

No contradiction in Old Testament; some apparent ones. These should be noted in this discussion.

I. ALLEGED DISCREPANCIES ABOUT GOD.

1. His omniscience. (Psalm 139: 2-4; Gen. 22: 12; Deut. 8: 2.)
2. His forgetfulness. (Gen. 8: 1; Isa. 49: 15.)
3. His omnipresence. (Psalm 139: 7-10; Isa. 66: 1; Lev. 3: 8; 4: 16.)
4. Eternity of God. (Psalm 90: 2; Hab. 3: 3.)
5. Invisibility of God. (Gen. 32: 30; Ex. 33: 20.)

II. ALLEGED DISCREPANCIES ABOUT MAN.

1. Covering sins. (Psalm 32: 1; Prov. 28: 13.)
2. David's conduct. (Psalm 119: 176; Psalm 119: 110.)
3. Israel's transgression. (Jer. 2: 22; 4: 14.)
4. Judging of David. (Psalm 7: 8; 113: 2.)

III. ALLEGED HISTORICAL DISCREPANCIES.

1. Meaning of Jacob's name. (Gen. 25: 26; 27: 36.)
2. Abraham's inheritance. (Gen. 13: 15; 15: 18; Acts 7: 5.)
3. Abraham's only son. (Gen. 12: 2; 25: 6.)
4. Joseph's name. (Gen. 30: 23; 30: 24.)
5. Passover slaying at home. (Ex. 12: 7; Deut. 16: 1-7.)
6. Abraham's age. (Gen. 12: 4; 11: 26, 32; Acts 7: 4.)
7. Place of the ark. (Num. 2: 17; 10: 21, 33.)
8. Place of Aaron's death. (Num. 20: 27, 28; 33: 38; Deut. 10: 6.)
9. Ahaziah's age. (2 Kings 8: 28; 2 Chron. 22: 2.)

ALLEGED DISCREPANCIES OF OLD TESTAMENT

"For this cause God sendeth them a working of error, that they should believe a lie: that they all might be judged who believed not the truth, but had pleasure in unrighteousness."   (2 Thess. 2: 11, 12.)

It seems in order to discuss some of the "alleged discrepancies" in the Old Testament in connection with the inspiration of it. If our conclusion is true that the Old Testament is inspired, or was given by inspiration, then there should be no errors in it. The Holy Spirit never makes an error; there were no discrepancies or contradictions in the original manuscripts of the writers of the Old Testament.   If there be any errors, they have been made by uninspired men in translating and copying the Old Testament. Even if there should be found a discrepancy now, it cannot be charged against the Holy Spirit.   All errors, if there be any, in the Old Testament arise since the Holy Spirit had anything to do with the composition of the books of the Old Testament.

It is freely granted that there are some apparent contradictions, but these are not *real* contradictions; there are many *alleged* discrepancies, but no *real* ones.   There are many passages in the Old Testament which are difficult to understand.   Oftentimes the *seeming* discrepancies disappear when a clear understanding of them is had.   Many of the alleged discrepancies are the product of the imagination of critics, who are influenced in a great degree by dogmatic prejudice.   They will disappear when viewed in the light of their context.   No doctrine or faith is impaired by any alleged discrepancy; no promise is obscured by them; no command is confused by them.   They do not hinder anyone in understanding the complete text of the Old Testament Scriptures.   We are now to look at some of the difficulties and alleged discrepancies in the Old Testament, that our faith may be strengthened in the proof of the inspiration of the Old Testament.

I. ALLEGED DISCREPANCIES ABOUT GOD

Since God is made so prominent in the Old Testament, and since there is a gradual unfolding of the nature and characteristics of God, it is in order to begin with the alleged discrepancies about him. It is claimed by some that there is a discrepancy in the record of God's omnipotence. In Jer. 32: 27 the question is asked if there is anything too hard for Jehovah; this is asked with an affirmative answer, which teaches that God has all power. Then in Judges 1: 19, the statement is made that Jehovah was with Judah and that he drove out the inhabitants of the hill country. but that he could not drive out the inhabitants of the valley. This would make it appear that Jehovah was not able to drive out those in the valley; hence, God does not have all power. It is clear from the context that God is able to do all things that are consistent with his will. In Judges the pronoun "he" refers to Judah and not to God. The American Standard Version makes this clear.

The omniscience of God is also challenged by some. It is claimed that there are discrepancies in the Old Testament about what God knows. In Psalm 139: 2-4, it is stated that God knows all about one; that he can search and know even the very thoughts. While in Gen. 22: 12, the statement is made that has been interpreted that God did not know that Abraham feared him until after he had offered Isaac as a sacrifice; that he just found this out by Abraham's obedience. There is no discrepancy here as Jehovah tested Abraham. God knew what Abraham would do, and tested him to strengthen Abraham's faith. God established by actual experiment that which he previously knew. The same is true with respect to Israel; he tested Israel and let them know what had lain hidden in the divine mind; it was now revealed and verified to Israel. (Deut. 8: 2.)

Again, it is claimed that there is a discrepancy in the statements made about the forgetfulness of God. In Isa. 49: 15, it is stated that God would not forget, yet in Gen. 8: 1 it is stated that "God remembered Noah," as though he had forgotten him. There is no discrepancy here, for the writer of Genesis is speaking "after the manner of men." God left Noah in the ark for many long months as if he had forgotten him, although he had not done so.

The omnipresence of God is also brought to view in the light of a discrepancy. In Psalm 139: 7-10 it is claimed that God was everywhere at the same time, and yet in Gen. 3: 8 we have the statement that Adam and Eve "hid themselves from the presence of Jehovah God amongst the trees of the garden." This is given to show that God was not omnipresent; that Adam and Eve and others could hide themselves from God. The "presence of Jehovah God," from which Adam hid himself, and Cain and Jonah (Gen. 4: 9-15; Jonah 1: 3) fled, was the visible and special manifestation of God to them at that time; it does not have any reference to the characteristic of God's omnipresence.

In like manner the eternity of God is challenged. Critics have said that there is a discrepancy between Psalm 90: 2 and Hab. 3: 3. In Psalm 90: 2 it is taught that God is from everlasting; that he is eternal; but in Hab. 3: 3 some have interpreted it to mean that God really came from Teman and from Mount Paran. It is strange that one would attempt to teach that God originated in time at a certain place. The Scripture simply refers to the wonderful display of divine power and glory which the Israelites witnessed in connection with the giving of the law. Teman and Paran were regions south of Palestine. Really these is no discrepancy here.

The invisibility of God as set forth in the Old Testament is also made the occasion of claims for alleged discrepancies. In Gen. 32: 30 it is stated that Jacob saw God "face to face," but in Ex. 33: 20 it is stated that no one could see God and live. There is no discrepancy here, as Jacob saw only the manifestation of the representative of God. God is a Spirit. (John 4: 24.) No one can see a spirit; spirits are invisible; hence, God is invisible. However, he has sent angels to represent him and other representatives which may be manifested to the physical eye. There are many other alleged discrepancies about God, but these can all be made clear by prayerful study.

II. ALLEGED DISCREPANCIES ABOUT MAN

There are many alleged discrepancies in the Old Testament about man; these may disappear as the light of truth and reason is turned upon them. In Psalm 32: 1 a blessing is pronounced upon the one whose "sin is covered," but in Prov. 28: 13 a condemnation is placed upon the one that covereth his sins. This is

claimed to be one of the discrepancies about man. In the first
the covering of sin means its remission or atonement, while in
Proverbs, as the context evinces, it refers to its unjustifiable con-
cealment; in Psalms there is an allusion to God's gracious act in
forgiving sin, while in Proverbs reference is made to man's wicked
act in conniving at sin and hiding it. No one is justified in making
a discrepancy here.

David's conduct is frequently mentioned as a case of discrepancy.
In Psalm 119: 176 the writer confesses that he had gone astray
like a lost sheep, but in Psalm 119: 110 he claims that he had
not erred from God's precepts. In the first reference David does
not charge himself with any moral obliquity, but sets forth his
desolate and perilous condition. Troubles and misfortunes which
David experienced in this world caused him to state that he was
like a lost sheep in his fleeing from the presence of Saul, while
Saul was attempting to kill him. There is no discrepancy here
when the text is understood; there is nothing to keep one from
accepting the inspiration of the Old Testament.

In Jer. 2: 22 and 4: 14 another discrepancy is claimed. In the
first reference Israel is represented as being unable to cleanse
itself from sin, yet in Jer. 4: 14 it is claimed that Israel could
wash itself and be cleansed from all sin. In the first place no one
could cleanse themselves from sin; only God could do that.
One must repent of sin before forgiveness may be enjoyed. Israel
had to repent and comply with God's conditions of forgiveness;
when Israel did this, then it was forgiven. There is no contradiction here. In like manner it is claimed that Jerusalem was a
delight to God in Psalm 87: 2, 3 and Psalm 132: 13, but in
Jer. 32: 31 a statement is made that Jerusalem had provoked
the anger of God and should be removed from before his face.
In the passages from Psalms there is no reference to Jerusalem
according to her earthly aspects with her streets and walls and
palaces. In Jeremiah there is reference made to literal Jerusalem; it should be destroyed because it was unfaithful to God.

Another discrepancy is alleged between Psalm 7: 8 and Psalm
113: 2. Here we have in the first passage David desiring to be
judged of the Lord, while in the second passage he desires not
to be judged by Jehovah. The first text has reference to one

particular case, the controversy between David and Kish, a Benjamite; many think that this has reference to Saul; some think that reference is made to Shimei. David knew himself to be innocent of the crimes alleged against him by his enemy. Yet, David knew that he was not perfect; he knew that he was guilty of sin, but not the sins of which he was charged. There is no discrepancy here.

III. ALLEGED HISTORICAL DISCREPANCIES

There are many alleged historical discrepancies; critics have seached for every possible discrepancy or contradiction. Some have attempted to show that Bible history and profane history do not agree; others claim that there are discrepancies between historical statements in the Old Testament. They mention the meaning of the name Jacob. In Gen. 25: 26 his name is given to mean "to seize the heel" or "heel-grasper," while in Gen. 27: 36 it is given to mean "supplanter." A close study will show that these meanings are different shades of meaning of the same name. The "heel-grasper" could also be "the supplanter." Again, Abraham's inheritance as mentioned in Gen. 13: 15 and 15: 18 is interpreted to contradict what Stephen said in Acts 7: 5. In Genesis the inheritance is promised to the seed of Abraham, not to Abraham personally, but in Acts 7: 5 we have the statement that Abraham had no inheritance "to set his foot on." This is true and harmonizes with the statements in Genesis.

Another discrepancy is charged between Gen. 22: 2, Heb. 11: 17, and Gen. 25: 6. In the first reference Isaac is spoken of as the only son of Abraham, while in Gen. 25: 6 we learn that Abraham had several other sons. Isaac was Abraham's "only son" by Sarah, as well as the only one in the line of promise, the theocratic line. There is no contradiction here. In like manner, the name of Joseph has been cited as an alleged discrepancy. In Gen. 30: 23 Joseph's name appears to mean "taken away my reproach," while in verse 24 it is given to mean "Jehovah add to me another son." There is no contradiction here. The apparent incongruity is dissipated by the fact that Joseph's birth was a proof that God had *removed* from Rachel the reproach of barrenness, while at the same time it also excited the wish that

he would add another son.   There is no discrepancy and very
slight basis of an alleged one.

Again, some have sought to make a discrepancy between Ex.
12: 7 and Deut. 16: 1-7.   In Exodus the children of Israel are
commanded to slay the passover at home, while in Deuteronomy
they are forbidden to slay the passover lamb in their homes, but
are commanded to bring it to the common altar.   In the first
passage the Israelites were in Egypt and had no common altar,
but in the second passage they were given instruction in anticipation of the common altar at the place that God designated.

Again, a discrepancy is charged with respect to the age of Abraham.   In Gen. 12:4 his age at migration is seventy-five years,
but in Gen. 11: 26, 32; Acts 7: 4 his age is apparently one
hundred thirty-five years.   In Gen. 11: 26 Abraham may be mentioned first simply on account of his importance in the history;
Moses is usually named before Aaron, yet Aaron was older than
Moses.   So Abraham may have been the youngest son, born
when Terah was one hundred thirty years old; it would then
follow that Abraham left Haran at the age of seventy-five, his
father having died at the age of two hundred five; this removes
the difficulty.   In like manner the apparent discrepancies in the
place of the ark, as recorded in Num. 2: 17; 10: 21, 33, and
the place of Aaron's death as mentioned in Num. 20: 27, 28;
33: 38, and Deut. 10: 6, and the age of Ahaziah, 2 Kings 8:
28 and 2 Chron. 22: 2, all may be cleared with but little effort
when the context is understood.   There are no discrepancies which
would prevent one's believing in the inspiration of the Old Testament.

There are other alleged discrepancies in the Old Testament.
For instance it is said that "the word of Jehovah came unto Jonah"
(Jonah 1: 1), and that God is everywhere; then how could Jonah
flee from the presence of the Lord? (Jonah 1: 3.)   There is no
trouble in understanding this.   In a certain sense Jehovah is omnipresent, and in another sense Jonah could flee the presence of
Jehovah.   When Jonah fled from the presence of duty as commanded by Jehovah, he was fleeing from the presence of Jehovah.
Anyone who attempts to get away from obedience to God's command is attempting to get away from the presence of God. Another

charge brought against the Bible is in the "imprecatory psalms." It is charged that in these psalms we may "detect traces of human prejudice and passion." It should be understood that the language may often be interpreted to mean that which the Holy Spirit did not intend it to mean. David wrote many of the psalms; he makes his enemies the enemies of God. When David was faithful to God, his enemies, because of his faithfulness to Jehovah, were enemies of Jehovah. Hence, the imprecation that David expresses is the condemnation of Jehovah on his enemies. Again, Noah's imprecation is cited by critics of the Bible as being unworthy of Jehovah. This is found in the curse that was pronounced upon Canaan, the grandson of Noah. Shem and Japheth were blessed, and the son of Ham was cursed. (Gen. 9: 25-27.) This is more a prophecy concerning Ham than a condemnation; the history of the descendants of Ham reveals the fact that it was a prophecy which was fulfilled. Another similar case is Sarah's attitude to Hagar and Ishmael. (Gen. 21: 10.) In this case Jehovah signified that the affairs here were to be typical of that which should take place in the Christian age. See Gal. 4.

CHAPTER XIII

INSPIRATION OF NEW TESTAMENT

INTRODUCTION.

New Testament claims inspiration; if not inspired, no complete record of Christ, or origin of Christianity; no one without Holy Spirit could have written it.

I. RELATION OF NEW TESTAMENT TO OLD TESTAMENT.

   1. Inspiration of Old Testament proof of inspiration of New Testament.
   2. Old Testament incomplete without the New.
   3. Old Testament and New Testament present one great system.
   4. Holy Spirit the author of both.
   5. Complete harmony between the two testaments.

II. PROMISES OF CHRIST.

   1. Holy Spirit promised to apostles.
   2. He would bring words to their remembrance. (John 14: 26.)
   3. Holy Spirit should guide them. (John 16: 12-15.)
   4. This promise repeated after resurrection. (Acts 1: 5, 8.)
   5. This promise fulfilled. (Acts 2: 1-4.)
   6. Miraculous power manifested. (Acts 8: 5-8; 1 Cor. 12: 7-11.)

III. TESTIMONY OF NEW TESTAMENT WRITERS.

   1. Paul's testimony. (Rom. 9: 1-3; 1 Cor. 2: 4-16.)
   2. Peter's testimony. (1 Pet. 1: 10-12.)
   3. John's testimony. (1 John 5: 6-9; Rev. 1: 1, 10, 11.)
   4. Testimony of other writers—Matthew, Mark, Luke, James, Jude.

INSPIRATION OF NEW TESTAMENT

"We received, not the spirit of the world, but the spirit which is from God; that we might know the things that were freely given to us of God." (1 Cor. 2: 12.)

From the beginning of Genesis, and all through the Old Testament, God partially revealed himself in one way and another; far back in prehistoric times he spoke to different ones, and then, as the centuries rolled on, he clearly and more fully revealed himself to his chosen people, Israel. He raised up for himself a chosen people through whom he might make his will and his ways known to the world at large. Old Testament history, cumbered as it is with the wreckage of human sins and failures, is the story of how God made himself known to the Hebrew people through their outstanding leaders and prophets. However, it was not possible for God to reveal himself in the fullness of his moral and spiritual perfections through imperfect human instruments of revelation. No mere man could by any possibility be great enough or holy enough to serve as a channel for the full disclosure of deity.

It is a cardinal tenet of Christianity that in Christ Jesus we have the supreme revelation of God to man; through Christ God has made known his nature, his will, his love, his wisdom. "In him dwelleth all the fulness of the Godhead bodily." (Col. 2: 9.) Such a profound and far-reaching revelation of God must be preserved for future generations. The New Testament gives us a record of this revelation of God through Christ to man. The New Testament is with us; it has been with us nearly two thousand years; from whence did it come? Did the writers of the New Testament foist it upon the world as a creation of their own imagination? The historicity of Jesus is too firmly established in the minds and hearts of so many millions of believers that it can never be undermined. No atheist or infidel can ever remove Christ to the icy altitudes of an incomprehensible and unapproachable creature of imagination. In the very nature of things man is constitutionally incapable of discovering and comprehending a perfect character; man cannot escape the trammels of his finite limitations of mind and heart. He is wholly dependent on the God who made him to reveal to him an absolutely perfect character.

If the New Testament is not inspired, we have no complete record of Christ as the revelation of God to man. If it is not inspired, we have no history of the origin of Christianity. No one without the Holy Spirit could have invented the perfect character of Jesus and the books of the New Testament. The writers of the twenty-seven books of the New Testament claim inspiration. The New Testament contains in full the one and only account of the origin of Christianity. There may be fragments of this account found in the writings of the early Christians and even in profane history, but nowhere is there to be found a different New Testament. No one can prove that the true account was lost, and that we now have a spurious account. Neither is it probable that a false account, so elaborate, so perfect, and so cunningly devised, has been put in the place of the true account. No one *would* have forged the books of the New Testament if he could, for they are opposed to deceivers and liars; no one would write such condemnation of such sins and appeal to history and risk fatal exposure. Moreover, none *could* have forged such books if they *would;* they could not so wisely have drawn the line between the Old Testament and the New; they could not have invented the many undesigned coincidences between the historic portions of the New Testament and the Epistles; they could not have invented the perfect character and life of Christ; neither could they have formulated so profound a system of morals and religion. Furthermore, even if any could or would have forged them, it would have been impossible to secure for them the acceptance and circulation among the churches. It should not be forgotten that the church existed nearly a quarter of a century before even the first book of the New Testament was written. How could the books of the New Testament have been forged and passed off as genuine? The only rational conclusion is that they were given by the Holy Spirit as the internal evidence shows.

I. Relation of New Testament to Old Testament

There is such a relation between the Old Testament and the New that the inspiration of the Old Testament serves as incontestable proof of the inspiration of the New; the two books are not two separate volumes independent of each other. It has been proved that the Old Testament is inspired; hence, the force of the evidence of the Old Testament is tantamount to the inspiration of the New Testament. The Old Testament and the New are so related that they must stand or fall together; the proof of the inspiration of the one may be considered as proof of the inspiration of the other. The inspiration of the Old Testament is as clear as a demonstration can be made; hence, the New Testament is inspired even with greater clarity of evidence.

Anyone who reads the Old Testament from Genesis to Malachi will see that the Old Testament is incomplete; there are promises in it made by God that must be kept. There are types which look forward to antitypes; there are prophecies which must be fulfilled; there are shadows of things to come, which point to the substance in the future. The priesthood under the law prefigured the priesthood under Christ; the bloody sacrifices of animals under the law looked to the future for their deep significance. In many ways the Old Testament is incomplete without the New. If the Old Testament was given by the Holy Spirit, the New Testament was predicted by the Holy Spirit at the same time.

It is as clear as a mathematical demonstration that the Old Testament and the New present one grand and glorious system; every part of the Old Testament coordinates completely with every part of the New Testament. In the New Testament we have the fulfillment of the prophecies, the antitypes of the types, the substance of the shadows, and the realization of the promises. Neither human sagacity, nor mathematical calculation, nor fortunate guessing, nor chance, nor an ingenious interpretation can account for the many antitypes, fulfillment of prophecy, and realization of promises that are clearly set forth in the New Testament; this can be done only by the fact that the New Testament was written by the Holy Spirit. Since the Holy Spirit is the

author of both, we have complete harmony between the two
Testaments. The two Testaments may be compared to two
hemispheres—it takes the two to complete the sphere; they are
component parts of one great whole; they are the products of the
one Holy Spirit. The existence of the one was a pledge for
the existence of the other.

II. PROMISES OF CHRIST

Among the many blessings of Christ and his abundant teachings,
we find that he promised the Holy Spirit to his apostles. "Behold, I send you forth as sheep in the midst of wolves: be ye
therefore wise as serpents, and harmless as doves. But beware
of men: for they will deliver you up to councils, and in their
synagogues they will scourge you; yea and before governors
and kings shall ye be brought for my sake, for a testimony to
them and to the Gentiles. But when they deliver you up, be not
anxious how or what ye shall speak: for it shall be given you in
that hour what ye shall speak. For it is not ye that speak, but
the Spirit of your Father that speaketh in you." (Matt. 10:
16-20.) Again, he promised his apostles: "And when they lead
you to judgment, and deliver you up, be not anxious beforehand
what ye shall speak: but whatsoever shall be given you in that
hour, that speak ye; for it is not ye that speak, but the Holy
Spirit." (Mark 13: 11.) Again, Jesus told his apostles that
when they were brought before "kings and governors" for his
sake, that it should turn out as a testimony for him. Hence, he
said: "Settle it therefore in your hearts, not to meditate beforehand
how to answer: for I will give you a mouth and wisdom, which
all your adversaries shall not be able to withstand or to gain-
say." (Luke 21: 14, 15.) Moreover, Jesus made a definite
promise to his apostles that he would send the Holy Spirit to
them after he returned to the Father. While he was here on
earth he kept his apostles with him for many months, and taught
them many things that they should teach others. He was not
willing to trust the frail memory of even his apostles. He had
repeated much of his teachings frequently to them, yet their
memories might fail them in reproducing his teachings later to
others. He informed them that he would be taken from them;

hence, he promised, "but the Comforter, even the Holy Spirit, whom the Father will send in my name, he shall teach you all things, and bring to your remembrance all that I said unto you." (John 14: 26.)

Not only did Christ promise his apostles that the Holy Spirit should bring to their remembrance all that he had taught them, but he made the specific promise that the Holy Spirit would guide them into all truth. This assurance was given with the highest degree of positiveness. He said: "Howbeit when he, the Spirit of truth, is come, he shall guide you into all the truth: for he shall not speak from himself; but what things soever he shall hear, these shall he speak: and he shall declare unto you the things that are to come." (John 16: 13.) Hence, according to the promise that Jesus made to his apostles, they spoke as the Holy Spirit brought to their remembrance the words of Jesus. This promise was not only made before Jesus left his apostles, but after his resurrection, and before his ascension to the Father, he repeated the promise that they should receive the Holy Spirit. He said: "But ye shall be baptized in the Holy Spirit not many days hence. . . . But ye shall receive power, when the Holy Spirit is come upon you." (Acts 1: 5-8.) This promise was fulfilled; a record of its fulfillment is found in Acts 2: 1-4. With the Holy Spirit came the power to work miracles. The record found in Acts bears witness that the apostles frequently manifested this power by working miracles. (Acts 8: 5-8, 14-17; 10: 44-46; 1 Cor. 12: 7-11.) Miraculous gifts of the Holy Spirit were bestowed upon Timothy (2 Tim. 1: 6), Barnabas (Acts 13: 1), Philip (Acts 8: 6), and others; these received spiritual gifts in order to confirm the word which they preached. The apostles had the power to bestow such gifts.

III. Testimony of New Testament Writers

There are eight writers of the New Testament and twenty-seven books. The apostles were generally known to the churches and did not need to make the claim that they were inspired. The miracles which they had performed bore witness to the fact that they had the Holy Spirit, and that they wrote under his influence. However, there are incidental remarks made by them that their writings were inspired. Paul wrote probably fourteen books of the twenty-seven. He said: "I say the truth in Christ, I lie not, my conscience bearing witness with me in the Holy Spirit, that I have great sorrow and unceasing pain in my heart." (Rom. 9: 1, 2.) Again, Paul said: "But to each one is given the manifestation of the Spirit to profit withal. For to one is given through the Spirit the word of wisdom; and to another the word of knowledge, according to the same Spirit: to another faith, in the same Spirit; and to another gifts of healings, in the one Spirit; and to another workings of miracles; and to another prophecy; and to another discernings of spirits: to another divers kinds of tongues; and to another the interpretation of tongues: but all these worketh the one and the same Spirit, dividing to each one severally even as he will." (1 Cor. 12: 7-11.)

Peter, another one of the apostles, wrote two books of the New Testament, the two letters that bear his name. He said: "Concerning which salvation the prophets sought and searched diligently, . . . searching what time or what manner of time the Spirit of Christ which was in them did point unto, . . . to whom it was revealed, that not unto themselves, but unto you, did they minister these things, which now have been announced unto you through them that preached the gospel unto you by the Holy Spirit sent forth from heaven; which things angels desire to look into." (1 Pet. 1: 10-12.) The testimony of John to the inspiration of his writings is as emphatic as that of other writers. (1 John 5: 6-9; Rev. 1: 1, 10, 11.) The testimony of Matthew, Mark, Luke, James, and Jude, the other writers of the New Testament, bears marks of the Holy Spirit. Hence, we conclude again that the New Testament was given by the Holy Spirit.

Christ promised the Holy Spirit to guide his apostles in their work. (John 16: 13.) The Holy Spirit was to refresh their memory and give them the words that they were to use. (John 14: 26.) He was to bear witness of Christ (John 15: 26), and would speak through the apostles on the occasion that should arise. Jesus said to them, "For it is not ye that speak, but the Spirit of your Father that speaketh in you." (Matt. 10: 20.) On the day of Pentecost the apostles "were all filled with the Holy Spirit, and began to speak with other tongues, as the Spirit gave them utterance." (Acts 2: 4.) Peter, on this occasion, was guided by the Holy Spirit in all that he said. The Holy Spirit spoke through Peter to the multitudes that assembled on that occasion. Paul said, "How that our gospel came not unto you in word only, but also in power, and in the Holy Spirit, and in much assurance; even as ye know what manner of men we showed ourselves toward you for your sake." (1 Thess. 1: 5.) Hence, God revealed through the Spirit his gospel to Paul and others. Paul said to the church at Corinth that "God revealed them through the Spirit: for the Spirit searcheth all things, yea, the deep things of God. For who among men knoweth the things of a man, save the spirit of the man, which is in him? even so the things of God none knoweth, save the Spirit of God." (1 Cor. 2: 10, 11.)

The claim to inspiration is made in the New Testament. Ananias said to Saul that Jesus had appeared to him "that thou mayest receive thy sight, and be filled with the Holy Spirit." (Acts 9: 17.) In writing to the church at Rome Paul says that he was "called to be an apostle, separated unto the gospel of God" (Rom. 1: 1), and that he was an apostle by the will of God. Paul did not receive his message from man but from God. This was done through the Holy Spirit. (Gal. 1: 11-17.)

ALLEGED DISCREPANCIES OF NEW TESTAMENT

Introduction.

Alleged discrepancies urged inspiration of New Testament; no discrepancies in the "Autograph Manuscripts"; all errors, if any, made since.

I. Possible Occasion for Discrepancies.

    1. Do not have original mansucripts.

    2. Many ancient manuscripts.

    3. Various translations.

II. No Material Changes.

    1. Two possible classes of changes:

        a. Intentional.

        b. Unintentional.

    2. No material fact or doctrine changed.

    3. Genuineness and integrity involved here.

    4. The changes, if any, are not proof against inspiration.

III. Some Alleged Discrepancies.

    1. Genealogies of Jesus.

    2. Different accounts of four writers of gospel.

    3. Two accounts of Sermon on Mount.

    4. The inscription on the cross.

    5. Paul's mistake. (Num. 25: 9; 1 Cor. 10: 8.)

    6. Differences in quotations.

    7. Only one mediator. (1 Tim. 2: 5; Rom. 8: 26.)

ALLEGED DISCREPANCIES OF NEW TESTAMENT

"Paul also, according to the wisdom given to him, wrote unto you; . . . wherein are some things hard to be understood, which the ignorant and unstedfast wrest, as they do also the other scriptures, unto their own destruction." (2 Pet. 3: 15, 16.)

It is thought wise at this time to discuss the "alleged discrepancies" here of the New Testament because of its bearing on the subject of inspiration. It is claimed by all believers in the New Testament that it is inspired; that it is the product of the Holy Spirit. However, the charge is made against the New Testament that there are errors and discrepancies and contradictions; if this be true, then the books of the New Testament were not given by the Holy Spirit; or if given by the Holy Spirit, then the Holy Spirit made errors, and is not to be relied upon. In order to clear our subject of inspiration, attention is given here to some of the discrepancies which are charged against the New Testament.

No discrepancies were made in the "Autograph Manuscripts" or original manuscripts of the New Testament. Our conception of the work of God is that he made no mistakes; Christ made no mistakes; the Holy Spirit made no mistakes; our conception of each member of the Godhead is that the work of each is perfect. The work of God partakes of his nature, so the work of Christ and the Holy Spirit partake of their nature; their work must have the characteristic of perfection. Hence, the original manuscripts of the New Testament were free from error; we believe in the inerrancy of the "Autograph Manuscripts" of the New Testament. All errors, if any, that may *now* be found in the New Testament have been made by uninspired men. We are to see in this study whether any errors have been made since the original copies of the books of the New Testament were made and signed by the respective writers.

I. Possible Occasion for Discrepancies

How do we know that the New Testament, as we have it today, is genuine and authentic? How can we demonstrate that the

books of the New Testament were written by the Holy Spirit,
and that we have them now as they were then written? Can
believers in the New Testament admit that there are errors in
it? What influence will such an admission have on the faith
of Christians? If any errors, what force have they today? Can
the original manuscripts be produced? It is not known that a
single one of the original manuscripts is in existence. No one
can go and put his hand upon a document and claim truthfully
that it is one of the original documents of a book of the New
Testament. We do not mean to say that these original manuscripts are not in existence now; we simply mean to say that no
one knows that they exist today; they may still be in existence,
and may be found sometime in the future. We are not committed to the idea that they are still in existence; we simply do
not know. They are not necessary, and again, men might worship them if they were in existence now. If the original manuscripts are not obtainable, how then can we prove that the books
of the New Testament as we have them today express the will
of God as given us by the Holy Spirit?

There are many ancient manuscripts of the New Testament
in existence now; none of these is claimed to be the "Autograph
Manuscripts," or those used by the writers of the New Testament.
Some of these manuscripts are very ancient, reaching back to
the fourth century of our era. The history of the extant manuscripts of the New Testament covers a period extending from the
fourth century to the invention of printing by John Gutenberg
in A.D. 1440. There are three great manuscripts of the New
Testament which have come down to us from the fourth and
fifth centuries; they are the Codex Vaticanus, Codex Sinaiticus,
and the Codex Alexandrinus. The Codex Vaticanus is called
the "Vatican Manuscript"; it is claimed to be the oldest of all
existing documents known to man of the New Testament. It is
kept in Rome and belongs to the Catholic Church. It should be
noted that the Roman emperor, Constantine, ordered in A.D. 330
fifty large copies of the Scriptures to be made; printing was
invented in 1440, or about the middle of the fifteenth century.
The Bible was among the first documents to be printed.

At the time that the Bible was first printed, there were in possession of certain scholars more than two thousand manuscripts of the

Bible; most of these manuscripts were written between A.D. 1000 and 1500. Some of these date as far back as the eighth and ninth century. There were many fragments of manuscripts in existence; these could all be put together and a complete copy of the New Testament had. Since the middle of the fourteenth century, there are in existence so many copies that comparisons may be made and all differences checked. We have the writings of such men as Origen, Clement, Tertullian, Irenaeus, and Eusebius; these give quotations from books of the New Testament. Their quotations bear strong evidence of the existence of the New Testament.

Since the start of printing, there have been many copies of the New Testament printed in the various languages of the time. A translation is a change from one language to another; all translations, at the best, are the work of uninspired men, who, though holy and faithful, are yet unable to give an inerrant copy of the sacred oracles; however, they can check their work by the ancient manuscripts and keep them fairly accurate. Our translation today of the New Testament does not have to contain all of the cumulative errors that may have been made in other translations. It is a translation "out of the original tongues, being the version set forth A.D. 1611, compared with the most ancient authorities and revised A.D. 1881-1885." This we call "the American Revised Version."

II. No Material Changes

It is claimed that our version of the New Testament set forth clearly and accurately the mind of God as given by the Holy Spirit through the writers of the New Testament. All the errors, if there be any, must arise during the period of time from the original manuscripts to the present time. The original manuscripts contained no errors. Has the New Testament been changed by passing through the different translations? Have any changes in the original text been made by copyists? We can know that there are no changes since the fourth century, as we have an ancient manuscript written during the fourth century. We can compare our New Testament with that ancient document and see that we have an exact copy of it. All errors and changes can be corrected by going back to the ancient manuscripts. Hence, the only material changes that are possible, if there be any, are those which were made between the original manuscripts up to the fourth century. Some of the books of the New Testament were not written until very near the close of the first century; hence, the possible time for errors to be made is very short; about two hundred years would cover the time for those possible errors and changes. There were not so many times during this period when copies would be made. No printing was done; all writing was done by hand, and this was a slow and tedious task. Not many scribes would thus copy the entire New Testament in a generation at that time. We must take into account the overruling providence of God in protecting the New Testament from errors.

There are only two possible classes of changes to be expected; these are the *intentional* changes and the *unintentional* changes. No one has ever been able to show that any intentional change has been made; the one who so affirms shoulders the responsibility of proving that an intentional change was made in that short period of time between the original manuscripts and the ancient manuscripts that we now have. No one knows how many copies were made nor what scribes made them; hence, it is utterly impossible for anyone to prove that any changes have been made. The "intentional" changes could be divided into two classes— those *honestly* made and those *dishonestly* made. The honestly made changes would be in a change of words as a synonym for a word. A dishonest change would be one that would modify the facts which are recorded or change the doctrine that is taught. The "unintentional changes" would arise from one who is copying and failed to see correctly the original, or one who is acting as an amanuensis and failed to hear distinctly, or his memory not accurate; hence, he would err in his work.

However, these errors or changes would not materially change the original thought as expressed by the Holy Spirit. Since it cannot be proved that any changes of either kind have been made, no one should doubt our present text of the New Testament. We have an example in literature which illustrates the present case. Scholars today are willing to give credibility, genuineness, and authenticity to Virgil, one of our classics today; yet, no one has the original writings of Virgil, and the copy that we have now, the oldest copy of Virgil, dates from the fourth century, and was written more than three hundred years after the death of Virgil. Virgil lived at about the time of Christ on earth. All the changes, if any, are no proof against the inspiration of the New Testament. Inspiration belongs to the original copy of the books of the New Testament.

III. Some Alleged Discrepancies

It is in order to notice some alleged discrepancies charged against the New Testament. It is charged that the genealogies of Jesus recorded in Matthew and Luke are different and conflict. There may be difficulties in these genealogies, but certainly there are no contradictions between them. Matthew carefully traces the genealogy of Joseph from Abraham down to Jesus; he emphasizes the kingly line of descent. Luke traces the genealogy from Joseph back to Adam; he stresses the fact that Jesus is the "Son of Man"; Luke gives Mary's side of the genealogy through Heli, who was the father, or father-in-law of Joseph. Two different purposes are expressed in the genealogies and hence, necessarily, they are different. The same charge is made against the different accounts of the four writers of the gospel. It is claimed that since all four of them wrote by the same Holy Spirit they should be identical. The critic fails to recognize the fact that the Holy Spirit could and did emphasize the same points through four different writers. It would have been useless to have written four copies of the gospel with them all identical. Matthew sets forth Christ as a King; Mark presents him as the Divine Servant; Luke presents him as the Son of Man; John emphasizes his divine nature. Hence, the writers would have to relate different things.

Another charge is made against the inspiration of the New Testament that there are two accounts of the Sermon on the Mount, and that these accounts differ. It is true that Matthew records some things, many things, in his account of the sermon that Luke does not mention, also Luke records some things that Matthew does not mention. However, nothing that Matthew records contradicts anything that Luke records. There are not two accounts of the same sermon, but two separate and faithful records of *two different sermons*. Jesus frequently repeated some things. Another case in point is the inscription that was placed on the cross. All four of the writers of the gospel give a record of this inscription, but their records vary. The charge is made that if the Holy Spirit guided the writers there would be no difference in the records. It should be remembered that the inscription placed over the head of Jesus on his cross was written in three languages—in Hebrew, Greek, and Latin. One writer could give the translation of one language and others give the translation of another language. It seems clear that there should be a difference in the quotations; however, they all mean the same thing, and there is no contradiction between them.

Another alleged discrepancy is made in charging that the quotations from the Old Testament are not exact; that, if the Holy Spirit wrote the Old Testament, and the Holy Spirit wrote the New Testament, why should not the Holy Spirit give the exact quotation? The explanation is that the writers did not attempt in all instances to give exact quotations. It should be remembered that the Holy Spirit knew the exact and full meaning of his own words as recorded in the Old Testament, and only he can infallibly reproduce his message in other words. Again, it is charged that the New Testament declares Christ to be the only mediator between God and man. The Holy Spirit said: "For there is one God, one mediator also between God and men, himself man, Christ Jesus." (1 Tim. 2: 5.) Then, in Rom. 8: 26, we have: "And in like manner the Spirit also helpeth our infirmity: for we know not how to pray as we ought; but the Spirit himself maketh intercession for us with groanings which cannot be uttered." There is an apparent contradiction here, but no real one. Paul simply means that the Holy Spirit aids the Christian in praying.

PART TWO

PART TWO

Chapter I

HOLY SPIRIT AND CHRIST

Introduction.

Difficult to separate Holy Spirit and Christ; mystery shrouds much of the relationship between them, yet some facts revealed.

I. Holy Spirit in Incarnation.

1. Mary overshadowed by Holy Sprit. (Luke 1: 35.)
2. Christ begotten by Holy Spirit. (Matt. 1: 20.)
3. Also begotten of God. (John 1: 14, 3: 16.)

II. Jesus Full of Holy Spirit.

1. Holy Spirit came at his baptism. (Matt. 3: 16; Luke 3: 22.)
2. Led of Holy Spirit. (Matt. 4: 1.)
3. Had Holy Spirit without measure. (John 3: 34.)
4. Jesus full of Holy Spirit. (Luke 4: 1, 14.)
5. Holy Spirit giveth life. (John 6: 63.)
6. In Christ is life. (John 1: 3.)

III. Holy Spirit Aided Christ in His Work.

1. Holy Spirit promised to Jesus. (Matt. 12: 18.)
2. Cast out demons by Holy Spirit. (Matt. 12: 28.)
3. Christ spoke by Holy Spirit. (Luke 4: 18, 21.)
4. Holy Spirit with him in all things. (Acts 1: 2.)
5. God with him in all things.
6. Christ rejoiced in Holy Spirit. (Luke 10: 21.)

IV. Holy Spirit with Christ in Life and Death.

1. Holy Spirit with him at birth.
2. Filled with Holy Spirit through life.
3. Holy Spirit with him in death.
4. Raised from dead by Holy Spirit. (Rom. 8: 11.)

HOLY SPIRIT AND CHRIST

"The Spirit of the Lord is upon me, because he anointed me to preach good tidings to the poor." (Luke 4: 18.)

It is difficult to separate Christ and the Holy Spirit during his personal ministry; in fact, it is difficult to separate in mind the members of the Godhead in any of the work of redemption. The complete cooperation of the Holy Spirit with Christ is clearly set forth not only in the prophecies, but in the New Testament teachings. As the Holy Spirit was one in the counsels of the Godhead in the eternal past, as he now and ever will be in the progress of God's kingdom, so was he one with Christ during his earthly ministry. Mystery shrouds much of the relationship existing between Christ and the Holy Spirit, but that does not set aside the revealed facts. We can accept the declarations of the Scriptures with unfaltering faith, whatever may be the theories of man.

There are some very important facts revealed about the relation of the Holy Spirit and Christ; these we need to study. They come within the scope of the present treatise on the Holy Spirit. The Holy Spirit predicted through the prophets the major facts in the life and death of the Christ before he ever came to earth; hence, the Holy Spirit had a part in arranging the program for the earthly ministry of Christ. After he came the Holy Spirit was associated with him in all of the details of his earthly life. The time of the coming of Christ was clearly and frequently foretold; he was to come "in the latter days," or at the end of the Mosaic dispensation. (Isa. 2: 2.) Again, it was foretold that he would come during the existence of the second temple; that is, while the second temple was standing. (Mal. 3: 1.) He was to be born in Bethlehem of Judea. (Mic. 5: 2.) He was to come through the tribe of Judea. (Gen. 12: 3; Heb. 2: 16; 7: 14.) He was to be in the line of David. (Isa. 11: 10.) The Holy Spirit foretold all of these and many other things concerning the Christ. We are now to see his close connection with Christ while he was on earth.

I. Holy Spirit in Incarnation

As the Holy Spirit had foretold through the prophets the coming of Christ, and had clearly and definitely prophesied of the nature of his work on earth, his betrayal, trial, and crucifixion, we may expect him to be present in the incarnation. By "incarnation" we mean the union of a member of the Godhead with humanity; the assuming of a body of human flesh by a divine being is called "incarnation." There is a difference between incarnation and transmigration; in transmigration we have the soul or spirit of a human being entering into a body of flesh, while in incarnation we have a divine being entering into a fleshly body. We cannot remove or uncover the mystery that belongs to incarnation; we are not attempting to go "beyond" what is written; we simply want to study "what is written."

The angel Gabriel was sent to Mary as she lived in Nazareth, and informed her that she was "highly favored" of the Lord; he bid her not to be afraid, "for thou hast found favor with God," the angel said. Further instruction was given her that she should "bring forth a son, and shalt call his name JESUS." Mary was confused as to what was meant, and asked the angel: "How shall this be, seeing I know not a man?" The angel Gabriel answered her and said: "The Holy Spirit shall come upon thee, and the power of the Most High shall overshadow thee: wherefore also the holy thing which is begotten shall be called the Son of God." (Luke 1: 35.) This was a fulfillment of the prophecy that "a virgin shall conceive, and bear a son, and shall call his name Immanuel." (Isa. 7: 14.) It was also a fulfillment of the promise which was made to Eve in the Garden of Eden before Adam and Eve were separated from the garden. "I will put enmity between thee and the woman, and between thy seed and her seed: he shall bruise thy head, and thou shalt bruise his heel." (Gen. 3: 15.) The Christ was to be the seed of the woman; in a peculiar and extraordinary, or supernatural way, the Christ was to be of the seed of the woman. Mary knew not a man until after the Christ was born. (Matt. 1: 25.)

Emphasis is further placed upon this fact by the statement of the angel to Joseph in a dream when he said: "Joseph, thou son of David, fear not to take unto thee Mary thy wife: for that which is conceived in her is of the Holy Spirit." (Matt. 1:20.) Hence, we have clearly the divinity of Christ set forth through the relation of the Holy Spirit to him in the incarnation. This is as far as we can go in the exegesis of the text of the Scriptures; man knows only what is revealed to him about the incarnation. He may not understand all that is said concerning it, but it is simple enough for us to understand that the Holy Spirit had to do with the incarnation.

Not only is it revealed that Christ was begotten of the Holy Spirit, but that he was begotten of God. "And the Word became flesh, and dwelt among us (and we beheld his glory, glory as of the only begotten from the Father), full of grace and truth." (John 1:14.) "For God so loved the world, that he gave his only begotten Son, that whosoever believeth on him should not perish, but have eternal life." (John 3:16.) Frequently Christ is spoken of in the New Testament as "the only begotten of the Father" and his "only begotten Son." We see now that Christ was begotten of the Father through the Holy Spirit. When God is prominent, he is spoken of as God's only begotten Son; when the Holy Spirit is prominent, he is spoken of as having been begotten by the Holy Spirit. These two members of the Godhead co-operated in the incarnation.

II. JESUS FULL OF HOLY SPIRIT

Not only was the Holy Spirit prominent in the incarnation, but he ever accompanied the Christ. At his baptism the Holy Spirit was present. "And Jesus, when he was baptized, went up straightway from the water: and lo, the heavens were opened unto him, and he saw the Spirit of God descending as a dove, and coming upon him." (Matt. 3:16.) Mark records this event with these words: "And straightway coming up out of the water, he saw the heavens rent asunder, and the Spirit as a dove descending upon him." (Mark 1:10.) Luke records this event: "And the Holy Spirit descended in a bodily form, as a dove, upon him, and a voice came out of heaven." (Luke 3:22.) John the Baptist bears testimony that he did not know Christ until God who had sent him to baptize said: "Upon whomsoever thou shalt see the Spirit descending, and abiding upon him, the same is he that baptizeth in the Holy Spirit. And I have seen, and have borne witness that this is the Son of God." (John 1: 33, 34.) The physical manifestation of the power of the Holy Spirit came in the form of a dove, and remained with Christ. Soon after his baptism Christ was led of the Holy Spirit into the wilderness where he endured the temptations. "Then was Jesus led up of the Spirit into the wilderness to be tempted of the devil." (Matt. 4: 1.) Mark says: "And straightway the Spirit driveth him forth into the wilderness." (Mark 1: 12.)

So far the Holy Spirit has manifested his presence with Christ from his conception. His abundant presence has been designated with the terms without measure. "For he whom God hath sent speaketh the words of God: for he giveth not the Spirit by measure." (John 3: 34.) God gave the Holy Spirit in his fullness without measure to Christ as the Messiah; he gave the Spirit by "measure" to apostles, prophets, and others; that is, they had the Holy Spirit in modified degrees. Not only is the relation of the Holy Spirit to Jesus described as being without measure, but his relation to Jesus is described by Luke as being "full of the Holy Spirit." (Luke 4: 1, 14.) The truth now stands out clearly in the record. Christ's earthly life was under the complete control and influence of the Holy Spirit; the witness of the Spirit had been given him at his baptism and he was now "full of the Holy Spirit."

We have learned that the Holy Spirit gave life. Jesus said: "It is the spirit that giveth life; the flesh profiteth nothing; the words that I have spoken unto you are spirit, and are life." (John 6: 63.) The life-giving and origin of life is in the Christ, but he gives life through the Holy Spirit. "All things were made through him; and without him was not anything made that hath been made. In him was life; and the life was the light of men." (John 1: 3, 4.) All life originated with Christ; this life is sustained by the Holy Spirit. Two divine persons not only can be, but must be, one at the center of their being; oneness on the part of two divine beings requires a third person as the bond of union. Hence, we see in the Godhead, God as the Creator, Christ as the agent, and the Holy Spirit as the organizer and lawgiver of all created things, yea of the universe.

III. HOLY SPIRIT AIDED CHRIST IN HIS WORK

There are three great facts relative to the coming of Christ into the world, namely: God sent Christ (Rom. 8: 3), Christ came of his own free will (Phil. 2: 6, 7), and God came in Christ (2 Cor. 5: 19). All of these affirmations about the incarnation are true at one and the same time; they open to us a most fruitful field of thought. The incarnation, which the Holy Spirit had was important, opened the way for men to enter into fellowship with God, Christ, and the Holy Spirit; while only the Christ of the Godhead actually came in the flesh, the Father and the Holy Spirit fully shared in the incarnation through the power of infinite sympathy. The Holy Spirit continued his presence, influence, and cooperation with Christ during his personal ministry. "Behold, my servant whom I have chosen; my beloved in whom my soul is well pleased: I will put my Spirit upon him, and he shall declare judgment to the Gentiles." (Matt. 12: 18.) It was prophesied that the Holy Spirit would be with the Messiah and we find a fulfillment of this prophecy claimed by the Christ. He even cast out demons by the Holy Spirit; that is, the Holy Spirit gave him power to cast out demons. Jesus acknowledged this fact. "But if I by the Spirit of God cast out demons, then is the kingdom of God come upon you." (Matt. 12: 28.)

The Father was delighted to fill his Son with his Holy Spirit, and to remain with his Son through the Holy Spirit during his sojourn on earth. While Christ was here in the flesh, he went into the synagogue at Nazareth and there was delivered unto him the book of Isaiah and he found the place where it was written, "The Spirit of the Lord is upon me, because he anointed me to preach good tidings to the poor." He then closed the book and said: "Today hath this scripture been fulfilled in your ears." (Luke 4: 18, 21.) Here we have Christ stating that he was speaking by the Holy Spirit. Even after Jesus had been crucified, buried, and raised from the dead, and just before his ascension, he gave commandment "through the Holy Spirit unto the apostles whom he had chosen." (Acts 1: 2.) God was with Christ in all things through the Holy Spirit; "he rejoiced in the Holy Spirit" (Luke 10: 21), and taught by the Holy Spirit. Hence, the Holy Spirit aided him in all of his personal ministry.

IV. Holy Spirit with Christ in Life and Death

From the beginning of Christ's perfect life on the earth, from the incarnation, throughout his entire mission and ministry among men, the Holy Spirit fully cooperated with him. Whatever separation in person there may be, or in office, their cooperation was continued and complete. It seems that the Christ while on earth, as the Son of man, recognized his dependence upon the Holy Spirit. Yea, even more, the New Testament teaches that the only work done by the Holy Spirit during our Lord's earthly life was through his divine person, and only so many were moved upon by the Holy Spirit as came into personal contact with Christ or to whom he imparted personally his influence and power.

The Holy Spirit was with Christ at his birth; he was filled with his power and influence throughout his earthly life; the Holy Spirit was with him in working miracles, and was with him in his death. Christ shed his blood as an atonement for sin in his death. His blood through the Holy Spirit became the cleansing power of sin. "For if the blood of goats and bulls, and the ashes of a heifer sprinkling them that have been defiled, sanctify unto the cleanness of the flesh: how much more shall the blood of Christ, who through the eternal Spirit offered himself without blemish unto God, cleanse your conscience from dead works to serve the living God?" (Heb. 9: 13, 14.) Furthermore, Christ was raised from the dead by the Holy Spirit. "But if the Spirit of him that raised up Jesus from the dead dwelleth in you, he that raised up Christ Jesus from the dead shall give life also to your mortal bodies through his Spirit that dwelleth in you." (Rom. 8: 11.) So, we find that the Holy Spirit predicted the coming of Christ, was present in his incarnation, at his baptism, aiding him in speaking, with him in death, with him in the resurrection, with him in his ascension and coronation, and finally came to earth on Pentecost.

The crowning work of the Holy Spirit is to glorify Christ; he was with him in the incarnation, in his public ministry, in his life and in his death. The Spirit would lead men to glorify Christ by leading them to obey him and honor him in their worship. The Holy Spirit reveals to man that Christ is man's Mediator; this is wonderful; Christ is the only mediator between God and man.

"For there is one God, one mediator also between God and men, himself man, Christ Jesus." (1 Tim. 2: 5.) The mediatorial work is in harmony with the glorious person of Christ. The Spirit leads people into a constant fellowship with him as their Prophet, Priest, and King. The Holy Spirit glorifies Christ by making him the head of the church. (Eph. 5: 23.) He is the head of every man (1 Cor. 11: 3), and every faithful Christian has sanctified Christ in their hearts as Lord (1 Pet. 3: 15).

Furthermore, the Holy Spirit glorifies Christ by giving him the supremacy which belong to the Son of God. He is not only supreme over every heart, but he is supreme over his own church. His supremacy extends to all things. The Holy Spirit glorifies Christ in every true act of worship. All the worship that we give to God goes through Christ as our Mediator. He is our High Priest and all of our sacrifices are made to God through him. We praise God in worship through Christ. Our prayers are all made "in the name of Christ." The songs of his redeemed people are given to him and reflect his praise. "And I saw, and I heard a voice of many angels round about the throne and the living creatures and the elders; and the number of them was ten thousand times ten thousand, and thousands of thousands; saying with a great voice, Worthy is the Lamb that hath been slain to receive the power, and riches, and wisdom, and might, and honor, and glory, and blessings." (Rev. 5: 11, 12.)

CHRIST'S TEACHING ABOUT HOLY SPIRIT

INTRODUCTION.

Christ had much to say about Holy Spirit; he revealed God to man
he also revealed Holy Spirit to man; his teachings should be studied

I. PERSONALITY OF HOLY SPIRIT REVEALED.

1. Revealed personality of God.

2. Revealed personality of Holy Spirit.

3. Holy Spirit's relation to God and Christ requires personality.

II. DISPENSATION OF HOLY SPIRIT.

1. Each member of the Godhead has his dispensation.

2. Holy Spirit supreme in this age.

3. No appeal from the words of Holy Spirit.

4. New Testament given during this dispensation.

III. CHRIST PROMISED ADVENT OF HOLY SPIRIT.

1. Prophets foretold his coming.

2. John the Baptist promised this to his disciples.

3. Christ promised Holy Spirit to his disciples.

4. Apostles to wait for him.

5. Reasons for his coming.

IV. THE MISSION OF HOLY SPIRIT.

1. Work through apostles.

2. Work through others.

3. To further work of Christ.

4. Relation of Holy Spirit to world.

CHRIST'S TEACHING ABOUT HOLY SPIRIT

"For if I go not away, the Comforter will not come unto you; but if I go, I will send him unto you." (John 16: 7.)

Various names are applied to the Holy Spirit in the gospels; sometimes just Spirit is used, at other times Spirit of the Lord, and Spirit of God, and Comforter. In the gospels reference is made to the Holy Spirit nearly fifty times; Comforter is used four times by John; the other writers do not refer to the Holy Spirit as the "Comforter." Christ revealed God to man; he was the image of God and those who saw him saw God. He revealed the Father's will, his way, his wisdom. His express mission to earth was to do the will of God, and thus by example and precept has he revealed God to man. In the Old Testament we have glimpses of God; we have angels representing him; we have prophets speaking his message to the people; but in Christ we have the full and complete revelation of God to man.

Christ also revealed the Holy Spirit to man. He has spoken more often about the Holy Spirit than any other; we have a fuller revelation of the Holy Spirit in the teachings of Christ than anywhere else in the Bible. The personality of the Holy Spirit is clearly set forth by Christ and his work is definitely outlined by Christ. Christ as clearly and fully reveals the nature and work of the Holy Spirit as he does the character of God. We are to study the Holy Spirit as he appears in the teachings of Christ. This is an important study. Christ has not said a single word about the Holy Spirit, or anything else, that is not important and needed as instruction to man. He makes the Holy Spirit stand out prominently in his every reference to him.

I. Personality of Holy Spirit Revealed

Every phase of the nature of the Holy Spirit and his work has been revealed by Christ; that is, all the phases of which we have any knowledge. John has recorded more about the personality of the Holy Spirit in the teachings of Jesus than any other writer. Chapters thirteen to seventeen of the Gospel According to John

record more of the teaching on the personality of the Holy Spirit
than other portions of his writings. These chapters explicitly
assert Christ's teaching on this great theme. The "Spirit" is
mentioned eight times by name; once he is called the Holy Spirit
(John 14: 26); three times the Spirit of truth (John 14: 17;
15: 26; 16: 13); and four times he is called the Comforter
(John 14: 16, 26; 15: 26; 16: 7). This enumeration of references does not exhaust the total number of references made to the
Holy Spirit. Jesus is about to complete his earthly ministry, a
life which has been rendered in service to God and man, and is
now ready to be offered in sacrifice for the sins of the world.
The teachings of Jesus upon the great theme or the personality
of the Holy Spirit is not philosophical, but practical; not ab-
stract, but concrete; not general, but specific; not systematic, but
occasional; his teachings were given in answer to questions and
as his disciples needed the instruction.

Christ revealed the personality of God; he revealed all the
traits of character of which we have a record. We do not know
whether God has any other trait of character which Christ did
not reveal; we do know that all the traits of character that we
see in Christ are in God. Christ fully and completely revealed
God to man; in doing this he revealed the will, way, wisdom,
power, love, mercy, justice, and long-suffering of God to man.
He has clearly revealed the personality of the Holy Spirit as he
did the personality of God. Christ never attempted to give a
formal definition of God; neither does he attempt to give a definition of the Holy Spirit. Christ never used any high-sounding
titles, but usually spoke of God by the simple and familiar name
of "Father." He revealed the relation of the Holy Spirit to
the Father, and the relation of the Holy Spirit to himself. He
also taught the relation that the Holy Spirit would bear to his
disciples, and then his relation to the world.

Since the Holy Spirit is a member of the Godhead, he must
bear such relationship to the other two members as will comport
with the nature of the other two. Personality is required to be so
closely associated with God and Christ. God and Christ are
spiritual beings; they are divine personalities; hence, for the
Holy Spirit to be one with them, he must be a personality. It

is very shallow reasoning for one to think of the Holy Spirit as being something other than a personality. The personality of the Holy Spirit was not so clearly set forth in the Old Testament; he is not there regarded as a separate person, but has always been such. The use that Christ makes of the personal pronoun and masculine gender in speaking of the Holy Spirit helps to set him forth as a divine person.

II. DISPENSATION OF HOLY SPIRIT

In a former chapter discussion is had of the three dispensations of the Godhead. God's dispensation is that period of time before the incarnation of Christ; it began with the creation of man and continued through the epochs of the patriarchal age and to the latter days of the Mosaic age to the coming of Christ. The period of time during the personal ministry of Christ may be called the dispensation of Christ. So the period of time when the Holy Spirit is supreme is called the dispensation of the Holy Spirit. The Holy Spirit is supreme during this age. The subordination of the Word and the Holy Spirit to God during his dispensation is clearly revealed in the Old Testament, so the subordination of God and the Holy Spirit is clearly seen in the teachings of Christ in the New Testament; also the subordination of God and Christ is made prominent in the dispensation of the Holy Spirit.

There is no appeal from the Holy Spirit; his words are final for us. People could reject Christ during his dispensation, and later accept the Holy Spirit in his teaching through the apostles; however, no one can reject the teachings of the Holy Spirit and expect another dispensation; we are now living in the last dispensation. However, God in Christ is omnipresent through the Holy Spirit in all of the affairs that pertain to the redemption of man. It is a glorious privilege to live under the administration of the Holy Spirit. It was great to live during the days of the fleshly ministry of Christ; it was great to hear him preach and see him work miracles. It is just as great to live under the Spirit's dispensation and see the wondrous work the Holy Spirit does through the truth of God.

The New Testament was written by the Holy Spirit during his dispensation. For sometime after the church was established, oral instruction was given by the Holy Spirit. The early Christians had the Old Testament Scriptures, but not the New; hence, they were dependent upon oral instruction for guidance in living the Christian life; but when the New Testament was written, Christians could be instructed by the written word. The New Testament is a textbook for Christians during this dispensation; it was given by the Holy Spirit. All the duties of the Christian life are to be found in the New Testament. The guidance of Christians by the New Testament is the guidance of the Holy Spirit. The New Testament is a product of the dispensation of the Holy Spirit. Christ predicted this when he told his disciples that the Holy Spirit would guide them in all truth.

III. CHRIST PROMISED ADVENT OF HOLY SPIRIT

The Holy Spirit in the teachings of Jesus is said to be sent or given by the Father. "I will pray the Father, and he shall give you another Comforter, that he may be with you for ever, even the Spirit of truth." (John 14: 16, 17.) Again, Jesus said: "But the Comforter, even the Holy Spirit, whom the Father will send in my name, he shall teach you all things, and bring to your remembrance all that I said unto you." (John 14: 26.) Christ also teaches and affirms that the Holy Spirit would be sent in answer to his prayer; he said that the Holy Spirit would be sent "in my name." Again, Jesus taught that he would send the Holy Spirit. He said to his disciples: "It is expedient for you that I go away; for if I go not away, the Comforter will not come unto you; but if I go, I will send him unto you." (John 16: 7.) Again, Christ said that the Holy Spirit would not "speak from himself; but what things soever he shall hear, these shall he speak: and he shall declare unto you the things that are to come. He shall glorify me: for he shall take of mine, and shall declare it unto you." (John 16: 13, 14.) Hence, the Holy Spirit is sent by the Father in the name of Christ; he is sent by the Father and the Son. We see here the primacy of God the Father is recognized by Christ in the sending of the Holy Spirit.

The Holy Spirit is sent by the Father and by the Son; twice Jesus promised that the Father would send the Holy Spirit, and twice he declares that I will send the "Spirit." "But when the

Comforter is come, whom I will send unto you from the Father, even the Spirit of truth, which proceedeth from the Father, he shall bear witness of me." (John 15: 26.) No loftier promise could be made than for God and Christ to cooperate in sending the Holy Spirit to complete the work of Christ on earth. Hence, the Holy Spirit has the sanction of God and Christ in his work. The prophets had foretold the advent of the Holy Spirit. (Joel 2: 28-32; Acts 2: 16-21.) John the Baptist was filled with the Holy Spirit (Luke 1: 15); his father Zacharias was filled with the Holy Spirit (Luke 1: 67). John prophesied that Christ would baptize in the Holy Spirit. (Matt. 3: 10-12; Mark 1: 7, 8; Luke 3: 9, 16, 17; John 1: 33.)

We have seen that Christ promised the Holy Spirit to his disciples (John 14: 16, 26; 15: 26; 16: 7), and that he was to guide the apostles into all truth and bring to their remembrance the things which Christ had taught them. However, the Holy Spirit was not to come to them until after Christ ascended to the Father. The apostles were to wait in Jerusalem until the Holy Spirit should come. "And behold, I send forth the promise of my Father upon you: but tarry ye in the city, until ye be clothed with power from on high." (Luke 24: 49.) The apostles waited in Jerusalem until this promise was fulfilled. "The former treatise I made, O Theophilus, concerning all that Jesus began both to do and to teach, until the day in which he was received up, after that he had given commandment through the Holy Spirit unto the apostles whom he had chosen: to whom he also showed himself alive after his passion by many proofs, appearing unto them by the space of forty days, and speaking the things concerning the kingdom of God: and, being assembled together with them, he charged them not to depart from Jerusalem, but to wait for the promise of the Father, which, said he, ye heard from me: for John indeed baptized with water; but ye shall be baptized in the Holy Spirit not many days hence." (Acts 1: 1-5.)

IV. The Mission of Holy Spirit

The mission of Christ to earth was frequently announced by the prophets before the advent of Christ; many of the details of his life, his teaching, his church, his death, burial, resurrection, and ascension were mentioned by the prophets. Some misunderstood his mission, but this was their fault, and not the fault of the prophets, neither of John the Baptist, nor Christ. These all stated his mission. In like manner, the prophets and Christ designated the mission of the Holy Spirit. The mission of the Holy Spirit was succinctly declared by Christ to be that of taking of his things and declaring them unto others. Christ had revealed the Father's will to the disciples; they are to proclaim his teachings to the world for all ages; Christ is not willing to trust their frail memory; hence, the Holy Spirit is to guide them in expressing that which they have been taught to others. His mission is to take the work of redemption where Christ left it and further it on to the final consummation. The apostles were to go into all the world with the gospel of Christ; the Holy Spirit was to guide them in their speaking and writing.

Christ made his contacts with man through his fleshly body; that is, while he dwelt in his body of flesh. The divine being of the second member of the Godhead formed no contacts with man apart from his fleshly body. He held conversations with his disciples after his resurrection, but he was still manifested to them through his fleshly body. So the Holy Spirit forms his contacts with man *through* man. The Holy Spirit makes no contact with the world, save through the apostles and others. The Holy Spirit proceeded *from* the Father *through* the Son rather than simply from the Father, so the Holy Spirit reaches the hearts of people through his message to them. We find his message in the New Testament. The Holy Spirit was to dwell in the disciples and to teach them the things of Christ and guide them in doing what Christ had commanded. He is to testify to the world the gospel of Christ and bring conviction of sin to the lost. "Nevertheless I tell you the truth: it is expedient for you that I go away; for if I go not away, the Comforter will not come unto you; but if I go, I will send him unto you. And he. when he is come, will convict the world in respect to sin, and of righteousness, and of judgment: of sin, because they believe not on me; of righteousness, because I go to the Father, and ye behold me no more; of judgment, because the prince of this world hath been judged." (John 16: 7-11.) Here we have a terse outline given by Christ of some of the work of the Holy Spirit.

All of the persons of the Godhead were concerned in the creation; the work of creation, at least various phases of it, is in the Scripture referred indifferently to God without any distinction as to the persons of the Godhead. "In the beginning God created the heavens and the earth." (Gen. 1: 1.) Again, it is said that all things were created through Christ. (John 1: 3, 10; Eph. 3: 9; Col. 1: 16; Heb. 1: 1, 2.) Again, creation is applied to the Holy Spirit. (Gen. 1: 2; Job 26: 13; 33: 4; Psalm 33: 6; 104: 30.) The great work of the Holy Spirit in the world, if we are permitted to distinguish one part of his work from another, is to perfect men in the sight of God; in other words, the salvation of man is his highest work. The Holy Spirit's work must relate to the creation of all things, both material and spiritual. In every work effected by the Father, Son, and the Holy Spirit in common, the power to bring forth proceeds from the Father, the power to arrange from the Son, the power to perfect from the Holy Spirit.

Chapter III

HOLY SPIRIT AND PENTECOST

INTRODUCTION.

Pentecost a significant day; no day before or after like it; the prophets, John the Baptist, and Christ pointed to it.

I. PENTECOST IN THE OLD TESTAMENT.

1. An annual feast of the Jews.
2. Its names in Old Testament.
3. Came on first day of week. (Lev. 23: 11, 16.)
4. Commemorate bondage in Egypt. (Deut. 16: 12.)
5. Mentioned three times in New Testament. (Acts 2: 1; 20: 16; 1 Cor. 16: 8.)

II. COMING OF HOLY SPIRIT.

1. His physical manifestations.
2. The assembling of the multitude.
3. The speaking with tongues.
4. The fulfillment of prophecy.

III. PENTECOST A NOTABLE DAY.

1. Illumination of minds of apostles.
2. Power to express and impress.
3. A full gospel preached.
4. Christ the center.
5. Beginning of salvation through Christ.
6. The birthday of the church.

HOLY SPIRIT AND PENTECOST

"I will pour forth of my Spirit upon all flesh: . . . before the day of the Lord come, that great and notable day." (Acts 2: 17-20.)

The thought has frequently been presented that the history of God's dealing with man includes three dispensations or periods of divine self-manifestation. First is that of the Father, from the creation to the incarnation; the second is that of the Son, during the life of Christ upon earth; the third is that of the Holy Spirit, extending from Pentecost till the second coming of Christ. Pentecost is a significant day in the redemption of man. The birth of Christ was a great event, but we are not told so very much about its significance; it has its place in the divine calendar. The crucifixion of Christ marks another great event in the scheme of man's redemption, then Pentecost is the next day of significant events. Few have understood fully the far-reaching events that occurred on Pentecost; they have not realized its importance in the history of man's redemption.

When Jesus led his eleven apostles out to the slopes of the Mount of Olives, and from that point ascended to his Father, they returned from the Mount of Olives and went into the upper chamber where they were abiding (Acts 1: 13), waiting for "the promise" of the Holy Spirit. They did not know how long they would remain there in suspense; all must have had a feeling that something extraordinary was about to occur. A larger body is next mentioned as "these all with one accord continued stedfastly in prayer, with the women, and Mary the mother of Jesus, and with his brethren." (Acts 1: 14.) Then, in verse 15, we read of a still larger company of about one hundred twenty. Peter, during this period of waiting, arose in the midst of the company and reminded them that "it was needful that the scripture should be fulfilled, which the Holy Spirit spake before by the mouth of David concerning Judas, who was guide to them that took Jesus." (Acts 1: 16.) Matthias was selected to take the place of Judas, "and he was numbered with the eleven apostles." (Acts 1: 26.) This company had a right to expect some notable event to occur as some of the prophets and John the Baptist and Christ had all foretold some events that should take place on this great and notable day.

I. Pentecost in the Old Testament

There were many feast days connected with the law; these feast days were great occasions for worship and celebration. Perhaps the Jews did not always look to the deep significance of these feast days in their calendar. The first great feast in the Jewish year was the Passover; it came at the evening of the fourteenth day of the first month, which was called Abib, or Nisan (Ex. 12: 2; 13: 4), and corresponded to the last of March and the first of April of our calendar. The second great feast designated by the law was Pentecost; this feast came in the third month, or Sivan (Esther 8: 9), of the sacred year of the Jews. Pentecost lasted only one day; it was determined by counting fifty days from the sixteenth of Nisan, seven weeks, and the next or fiftieth day was the day of Pentecost; it fell on the sixth day of Sivan. The feast of unleavened bread followed the Passover; it continued seven days and came to be reckoned with the Passover. The third great feast was the feast of tabernacles or of ingathering; it began on the fifteenth day of the seventh month, Tisri, and continued till the twenty-second day of that month.

"Pentecost" is not found in the Old Testament. This feast has three names in the Old Testament; they are "feast of weeks" (Ex. 34: 22; Deut. 16: 10), "feast of harvest" (Ex. 23: 16), and "day of first-fruits" (Num. 28: 26). The fourth name for this feast is "Pentecost" and is found only in the New Testament. It always came on the first day of the week. (Lev. 23: 11, 16.) Some have thought that it had connection with the giving of the law; however, this is not clear. It came at the end of the reaping season, when all the wheat and barley had been cut and gathered. It was held at the central sanctuary. (Deut. 16: 11.) The people were expected to assemble at the place of the altar and hold their celebration. As the altar was at the temple, and the temple was located in Jerusalem, so Pentecost was celebrated at Jerusalem. It is thought that a commemoration of the bondage in Egypt was held at this time; however, it seems that the agricultural phase of the feast received greatest emphasis. This feast is mentioned by name three times in the New Testament. (Acts 2: 1; 20: 16; 1 Cor. 16: 8.) Pentecost was a festival of good cheer; it was a day of joy. Freewill offerings were to be made to the Lord (Deut. 16: 10) and it was to be marked by a liberal spirit toward the Levite, the stranger, and orphans and widows. (Deut. 16: 11, 14.) This day was chosen by the Christ to be the day upon which the Holy Spirit should come.

II. COMING OF HOLY SPIRIT

There was no mention of any great event connected with the celebration of Pentecost in Old Testament times. This is the only great feast among the Jews which is not mentioned as the memorial of some event in the history of the Jews. Some Jews claimed that it commemorated the giving of the law from Mount Sinai, as the law was given on the fiftieth day after the deliverance from Egypt; however, there is no mention of this fact in the Old Testament, nor by Josephus or Philo; there is no proof that the law was given fifty days after the departure from Egypt. Whether any great event in the history of Israel was celebrated or commemorated at Pentecost or not, we do know that Pentecost has been made a memorable day by the coming of the Holy Spirit. The apostles had spent about ten days in prayer, waiting patiently and prayerfully for the fulfillment of the promise of the Christ. Not only had he promised them the power which they needed, but the presence of the Holy Spirit. Jesus had never deceived his disciples, but had always gone beyond their hopes. They had desired a temporal kingdom; they expected an earthly kingdom but they were to receive a spiritual kingdom. They had desired to crown him King of the Jews but they were to help prepare the world for the grander coronation of Lord of lords and King of kings; they did not know these things while he was with them.

There were physical manifestations of the descent of the Holy Spirit. Christ had taught his disciples and associated with them in his fleshly body; they are now to learn what Christ will do and teach through the Holy Spirit in his new, his spiritual body, the church. In that new spiritual body of Christ the Holy

Spirit is the vital life element. The first physical manifestation on that Pentecost was the "sound as of the rushing of a mighty wind"; this "sound" broke the silence and calmness that had settled upon the apostles after the ascension of the Christ and the brief interview with the two angels. The second physical manifestation was lambent jets or flames of fire which appeared to flicker in the air, and distribution of gifts to each of the apostles were made emphatic. "There appeared unto them tongues parting asunder, like as of fire; and it sat upon each one of them." (Acts 2: 3.) These flickering manifestations of light were "like as of fire"; they were not really flames of fire, but "like as of fire"; that which is like fire is not fire. Wind and fire were mentioned in the Old Testament as symbols of the presence of God. (See Jon. 1: 4 and Jer. 5: 14.) The sound as a physical manifestation appealed to the ear, and the tongues "like as of fire" appealed to the sight; hence, these two avenues were appealed to with the physical manifestations of the presence of the Holy Spirit. "And they were all filled with the Holy Spirit, and began to speak with other tongues, as the Spirit gave them utterance." (Acts 2: 4.) Here was another physical manifestation of the presence of the Holy Spirit; the apostles "began to speak with other tongues." This appealed to their intelligence; they were able to speak with tongues, or in a language that they had not learned. Whatever may be the physical phenomena that accompanied the presence of the Holy Spirit, the important fact is that the apostles "were all filled with the Holy Spirit."

There is no doubt that this wonderful manifestation was the beginning that morning of the fulfillment of promise that Christ had made to his apostles. It was soon noised abroad that something extraordinary was taking place. We do not know at what time the apostles left the room where they were abiding; we do know that all Jerusalem was filled with Jews and proselytes who had come to Jerusalem to keep the Feast of Pentecost. When this was noised abroad, the multitude came together; it was about nine o'clock that morning when the multitude assembled. Sometime earlier than that the Holy Spirit had come upon them. The physical manifestations helped to bring together the multitude; it should be remembered that the multitude did not receive the Holy Spirit, for many of them did not know what was taking place; Peter had to explain the phenomena to them. The Holy Spirit wrought a veritable revolution or change in the apostles; they were now ready to face the multitude with a clear explanation of what had just taken place and preach the gospel to the multitude.

The physical manifestations of the "sound," tongues "like as of fire" and speaking "with other tongues," are incidental; they are simple corollaries to the presence of the Holy Spirit. As Christ is the Son of God, so the Holy Spirit is the gift of God; the Holy Spirit is the Father's gift on behalf of his Son. It is only natural that extraordinary manifestations accompany the Holy Spirit on this transcendent event, so the Holy Spirit takes out a claim to all the territory of the lives of the apostles and gives to them the power of speaking with other tongues. The gift of tongues is a manifestation to the unbelieving Jews, bearing witness to the presence of the Holy Spirit with the apostles.

III. Pentecost a Notable Day

Pentecost is a notable day because on it at this time the minds of the apostles were illuminated and set right. Much of the teachings of Christ had been dark and unintelligible to the apostles; they now have a clearer conception of the Messiahship of Christ, and acceptance of his death, not as an overthrow, but as ordered by Jehovah for a great end; the view of his resurrection now becomes illuminated to them. Peter, later speaking of this event, says that they were begotten "again unto a living hope by the resurrection of Jesus Christ from the dead." (1 Pet. 1: 3.) The apostles now were filled with rapture at the dawning perception of the inconceivable spiritual glory which was yet to come. The apostles now have power to express themselves, or to proclaim the new truth as the message of the gospel; they proved that at least sufficient assimilation of truth had taken place to enable them to utter it freely, courageously, and powerfully. They had power to impress others with their message. The Holy Spirit was now speaking in them; hence, the wonderful immediate impression made by the apostles.

The apostles are now ready with the aid of the Holy Spirit to preach a full and complete gospel as God's power to save through Christ. They could not preach this before because they did not understand it. They probably did not understand all that was said on this day by themselves. The fundamental facts of the gospel—the death, burial, and resurrection of Christ—could now be preached by them with forceful significance. (1 Cor. 15: 1-4.) Christ is made the center of the gospel; Christ had told his apostles that when the Holy Spirit should come "he shall glorify me: for he shall take of mine, and shall declare it unto you." (John 16: 14.) The Holy Spirit is to make as his subject in preaching through the apostles the Christ as the central theme of every sermon.

Furthermore, Pentecost is a notable day because it is a day of beginnings. On this day we have the beginning of the preaching of the gospel in its fullness; the facts of the gospel could not have been preached until after they had occurred; hence, this was the first time that the gospel was preached in fact. This day is the beginning of salvation through Christ; for the first time in the history of the race of man is the question asked: "What shall we do?" "What must I do to be saved?" The answer was quickly, accurately, and fully given by the Holy Spirit. This was the beginning of the gospel plan of salvation.

Pentecost was further made notable because it became the birthday of the church. The church had existed in the eternal purpose of God. (Eph. 3: 10, 11.) The church of Christ did not exist under the old covenant, but it existed in prophecy. (Isa. 2: 2-4; 9: 6; Dan. 2: 44.) Then the church existed in preparation. John the Baptist had made ready material for the coming of Christ (Matt. 3: 2, 13-17); Jesus, during his personal ministry, had further prepared the way for the establishment of his church. The Holy Spirit now comes and takes the prepared material and organizes it into the church. As the Holy Spirit took the chaotic matter of the material realm and organized it into a complete system, so he now takes the disorganized material prepared by John the Baptist and Christ and organizes it into the church. So Pentecost is the natal day of the church.

The Holy Spirit spoke through the apostles, or they spoke "as the Spirit gave them utterance"; they were the mouthpieces of God, who spoke by the Spirit through them. What they said, God said through the Holy Spirit to the multitudes. The Holy Spirit was to bring all that Jesus had said to the remembrance of the apostles and to guide them "into all truth," and thus through inspired men he guided all who heeded the gospel call into all truth and all blessings which are in Christ. Those who received the words of the apostles received the words of God, the words of the Holy Spirit; those who obeyed, obeyed the commands of the Holy Spirit; and were added to the church. Hence, they were added to the church by the Holy Spirit, they were also added to the church by the Lord. (Acts 2: 47.) The Lord added them by their obeying the words of the Holy Spirit which were pronounced by Peter.

The greatest question ever asked by man was: "What must I do to be saved?" This question was asked on Pentecost and the Holy Spirit gave the answer. Hence, the greatest question asked by man has received an answer by the Holy Spirit. As man today asks the same question, the Holy Spirit gives the same answer today that was given on Pentecost. Man receives the richest blessings in the forgiveness of his sins as a promise made by the Holy Spirit.

BAPTISM OF HOLY SPIRIT

INTRODUCTION.

This a mooted question; the "who," the "when," and the "where" have all been disputed; which shall we say, "baptism *of, in* or *with* Holy Spirit"?

I. NOT THE SAME AS "FILLED WITH THE HOLY SPIRIT."

1. Zacharias, Elisabeth, and John the Baptist "filled with the Holy Spirit." (Luke 1: 15, 41, 67.)
2. Jesus filled with Holy Spirit. (Luke 4: 1.)
3. Peter. (Acts 4: 4, 8.)
4. Stephen. (Acts 7: 55.)
5. Paul. (Acts 9: 17; 13: 9.)
6. Barnabas. (Acts 11: 24.)

II. HOLY SPIRIT BAPTISM A FIGURE.

1. "Poured forth" the Spirit. (Acts 2: 17, 18, 33; 10: 45; Tit. 3: 6.)
2. The "living water." (John 4: 13, 14; 7: 37-39.)
3. "Baptism" in the Spirit. (John 1: 32, 33.)

III. HOLY SPIRIT BAPTISM A PROMISE.

1. By prophets. (Joel 2: 28-32.)
2. By John the Baptist. (Matt. 3: 11; Mark 1: 8; Luke 3: 16.)
3. By Christ. (John 1: 33; Acts 1: 5.)

IV. CHRIST THE ADMINISTRATOR.

1. John stated this.
2. Christ promised a Comforter. (John 14: 26; 15: 26.)
3. Christ promised it after his return to the Father. (John 16: 7; Acts 1: 4.)

V. TO WHOM THE BAPTISM PROMISED.

1. Jews—apostles. (Acts 1: 15; 2: 1-4, 33.)
2. Gentiles—house of Cornelius. (Acts 10: 44, 45.)

VI. EFFECTS OF HOLY SPIRIT BAPTISM.

1. Bear witness of Christ.
2. Spoke with tongues. (Acts 2: 4; 10: 46.)
3. Worked miracles. (Acts 3: 1-9; Heb. 2: 3, 4.)

BAPTISM OF HOLY SPIRIT

"I baptized you in water; but he shall baptize you in the Holy Spirit."
(Mark 1: 8.)

Possibly no phase of the Holy Spirit and his work in the redemption of man has been discussed more than "the baptism of the Holy Spirit"; it has been a mooted question for a long time and will possibly continue in this class until the Christ comes. No effort is made here to put at ease all minds on the question; an endeavor is made to present clearly the teachings of the New Testament on this subject. People who claim to be Christians believe in the Holy Spirit; some claim to have been baptized with the Holy Spirit often; others deny that they ever have been baptized with the Holy Spirit. Which claim is true? Some teach that *all* must be baptized with the Holy Spirit in order to be saved; they claim that baptism of the Holy Spirit and conversion are tantamount. Others claim that no one today is baptized with the Holy Spirit. Who is correct in the claim? So the "who" is baptized in the Holy Spirit is disputed; again just "when" one is baptized with the Holy Spirit is a matter of controversy; again just "where" one is baptized with the Holy Spirit has received its portion in debate.

Moreover, we have such expressions as "baptism *of* the Holy Spirit," "baptism *in* the Holy Spirit," and "baptism *with* the Holy Spirit." Some have attempted to make a distinction in the use of these prepositions; different translators of the New Testament have made such distinctions without any difference in meaning. The translators of the American Standard Version seem to have been in doubt. While they used the preposition "in," yet, in the marginal reading, they have placed the preposition "with." It does not matter which preposition is used, the content is the same in thought; hence, no distinction will be kept up in this study.

I. NOT THE SAME AS "FILLED WITH THE HOLY SPIRIT"

A distinction should be made between the "baptism of the Holy Spirit" and being "filled with the Holy Spirit." We read that the parents of John the Baptist were "filled with the Holy Spirit." It was prophesied of John that "he shall be filled with the Holy Spirit, even from his mother's womb." (Luke 1: 15.) This does not mean that John was baptized at birth or in infancy with the Holy Spirit. Again, we read that "Elisabeth was filled with the Holy Spirit" (Luke 1: 41), and this was before her son was born. Again, we read that "his father Zacharias was filled with the Holy Spirit, and prophesied." (Luke 1: 67.) Neither John, Elisabeth, nor Zacharias were baptized with the Holy Spirit, yet they were "filled with the Holy Spirit." Clearly a distinction is to be made between the baptism of the Holy Spirit and being filled with the Spirit.

Furthermore, we read that Jesus after his baptism in the Jordan by John the Baptist was "full of the Holy Spirit." (Luke 4: 1.) It is not understood that Jesus was baptized with the Holy Spirit, although the Holy Spirit came upon him at his baptism. The New Testament makes a clear distinction between Christ being full of the Holy Spirit and the baptism of the Holy Spirit which should come later. Even after Pentecost we read that "then Peter, filled with the Holy Spirit, said unto them." (Acts 4: 8.) Peter was not baptized the second time with the Holy Spirit; he was, like John, Zacharias, and others, filled with the Holy Spirit on this occasion. We also read that Stephen, "being full of the Holy Spirit," looked into heaven and related his vision to his hearers. (Acts 7: 55.) Stephen was not baptized in the Holy Spirit on this occasion, and yet he was full of the Holy Spirit.

Ananias, a disciple in Damascus, was sent to Saul that Saul might "be filled with the Holy Spirit." (Acts 9: 17.) Later we read: "But Saul, who is also called Paul, filled with the Holy Spirit" fastened his eyes on Elymas. (Acts 13: 9.) Also Barnabas is described as "a good man, and full of the Holy Spirit and of faith." (Acts 11: 24.) So we find that there were a number of disciples in the early church who were filled with the Holy Spirit, but were not baptized with the Holy Spirit; even some who served God before the church was established were filled with the Holy Spirit; this was before the fulfillment of the promise of the baptism of the Holy Spirit.

II. Holy Spirit Baptism a Figure

It is always wise to discriminate between plain, simple language and figures of speech; the figures are to be understood from the literal meaning of Scripture; an attempt to settle the meaning or interpret correctly the meaning of a word or phrase by means of its figurative use is absurd. The folly of such an effort is seen in a few illustrations. It is not the "word of God" that is a "lamp," but a "lamp" that is the "word of God"; neither is it "Christ" who is the "bright morning star," but according to this method of interpretation, it is the "bright morning star" that is "Christ." Such methods of attempting to give the meaning of a Scripture by its use of figures lead to errors and fallacies in conclusions. *Figurative* terms must be interpreted with *literal* terms; the *literal* meaning must be gained from the simple context, while the *figurative* terms must be understood in the light of the *literal* language.

In the prophecy of Joel as quoted by Peter on the day of Pentecost, we have the expression, "pour forth of my Spirit," used twice (Acts 2: 17, 18), and once by Peter in verse 33. Again, Peter used the expression, "poured out the gift of the Holy Spirit," at the household of Cornelius. (Acts 10: 45.) Paul used the expression, "renewing of the Holy Spirit, which he poured out upon us richly." (Tit. 3: 5, 6.) We are not to understand that there was a literal outpouring of the Holy Spirit; it was impossible for a person as the Holy Spirit to be literally poured out; the literal meaning of "poured out" leads to the idea of a liquid or fluid. There is some analogy or resemblance in the idea to be conveyed, but we must understand this to be a figurative expression. It is a gross misconception of the personality of the Holy Spirit to think of him being "poured out" like some liquid; such an idea is to mistake the figure used, and interpret the *literal* in terms of the *figurative,* instead of interpreting the *figurative* by the *literal.* When you hear people praying for "a Pentecostal shower" of the Holy Spirit, you may know that they do not understand the Scriptures.

Again, Jesus used figurative language in speaking of the Holy Spirit and the baptism of the Holy Spirit. In discussing "living water" with the Samaritan woman Jesus said: "Every one that drinketh of this water shall thirst again: but whosoever drinketh of the water that I shall give him shall never thirst; but the water that I shall give him shall become in him a well of water springing up into eternal life." (John 4: 13, 14.) At another time Jesus said: "If any man thirst, let him come unto me and drink. He that believeth on me, as the scripture hath said, from within him shall flow rivers of living water. But this spake he of the Spirit, which they that believed on him were to receive: for the Spirit was not yet given; because Jesus was not yet glorified." (John 7: 37-39.) The figure here is plainly designed to illustrate the blessings which should flow from him to others through the baptism of the Holy Spirit. There is no more propriety in thinking that the disciples were to drink literally of the Holy Spirit than to think that the Holy Spirit was literally poured out on the day of Pentecost.

So with respect to the "baptism" of the Holy Spirit, it is a figurative term as applied to the Holy Spirit. The first time that this figure was employed was used by the Father himself in giving to John the Baptist a criterion by which he might recognize the Messiah; he sent John to baptize in water and said to him: "Upon whomsoever thou shalt see the Spirit descending, and abiding upon him, the same is he that baptizeth in the Holy Spirit." (John 1: 33.) John then added: "I have seen, and have borne witness that this is the Son of God." It was thus made a distinguishing characteristic of the Messiah, that he should possess the power to baptize in the Holy Spirit. The baptism of John in water involved as its chief idea an overwhelming, a sudden and complete overpowering of the person submerged by water, and the entering into new conditions and relations, so the baptism of the Holy Spirit was to imply an equally entire subjugation and overmastery of the soul by the Spirit. It is in these obvious analogies that the appositeness of the figure may be seen, and its proper application understood. The same figurative use is made of the term baptism where Christ says of his sufferings and death: "I have a baptism to be baptized with; and how am I straitened till it be accomplished!" (Luke 12: 50.) The same use is found in Matt. 20: 22, 23; Mark 10: 38, 39. To carry out resemblances too far, or to mistake resemblances for identities, is to grossly misunderstand the word of God. We should understand that *literally* there is no such thing as a "pouring forth" of the Holy Spirit, or a "drinking" of the Spirit, or a "baptism" in the Holy Spirit; these are all figures designed by the resemblances they suggest, to present to the mind in various aspects and from various points of view the most lively and correct ideas of a fact.

III. Holy Spirit Baptism a Promise

The Holy Spirit baptism, both in the Old Testament and the New, is a promise. Joel uttered a promise when he said that the Holy Spirit would be "poured out" upon all flesh. Peter quoted on the day of Pentecost Joel 2: 28-32 as a promise and claimed that it was fulfilled, or being fulfilled, on Pentecost. The Holy Spirit baptism was a "gift"; Peter refers to it in reporting what occurred at the house of Cornelius as a "gift." "If then God gave unto them the like gift as he did also unto us, when we believed on the Lord Jesus Christ, who was I, that I could withstand God?" (Acts 11: 17.) Baptism of the Holy Spirit was promised, not only by the prophets, but by John the Baptist. (Matt. 3: 11; Mark 1: 8; Luke 3: 16.) The Christ, while he was here on earth, also promised the baptism of the Holy Spirit. "For John indeed baptized with water; but ye shall be baptized in the Holy Spirit not many days hence," said Jesus to his apostles just before he ascended to the Father. (Acts 1: 5.) This is what God had told John that Jesus would do. (John 1: 33.) So the baptism of the Holy Spirit was definitely a promise, and not a command; no one was ever commanded to be baptized in the Holy Spirit. Baptism in water was a command, but baptism in the Holy Spirit was a promise. It was a definite promise to certain individuals; the baptism of the Holy Spirit was a limited promise; it was not for all men, though it should bless "all flesh." It was made to certain individuals to take place within a few days after Christ ascended.

IV. Christ the Administrator

In giving the promise, John the Baptist said that Christ would be the administrator of the Holy Spirit baptism. The Father had said to John: "Upon whomsoever thou shalt see the Spirit descending, and abiding upon him, the same is he that baptizeth in the Holy Spirit." (John 1: 33.) Christ promised to send "the Comforter, even the Holy Spirit," to his disciples. (John 14: 26; 15: 26.) After his crucifixion, burial, and resurrection, and just before his ascension, Christ repeated the promise that he would send the Holy Spirit to them. (John 16: 7-14; Acts 1: 4.)

V. To Whom the Baptism Promised

Joel prophesied that the Holy Spirit would be poured forth upon "all flesh." Jews and Gentiles then constituted "all flesh." Those who were not Jews were Gentiles; the proselytes were considered as Jews. Peter, in quoting Joel on Pentecost, claimed a fulfillment of the prophecy of Joel. It was a fulfillment to the Jews, because through the Holy Spirit the apostles were enabled to speak the words of salvation to them. Peter had been committed with the keys of the kingdom of heaven, and he announced by the Holy Spirit on the day of Pentecost the terms of entrance into the kingdom of heaven. The apostles were baptized in the Holy Spirit on the day of Pentecost in fulfillment of Joel's prophecy. (Acts 1: 15; 2: 1-4, 33.) The Gentiles at the household of Cornelius a few years later received the baptism of the Holy Spirit. (Acts 10: 44, 45.)

VI. Effects of Holy Spirit Baptism

One of the effects which followed the Holy Spirit baptism was that it enabled the apostles to bear witness for Christ. He had taught them his Father's will; they were to repeat his teachings to others. They were to go and preach the gospel to "the whole creation," but they needed the Holy Spirit to guide them into all truth. The speaking with other tongues was another effect of the baptism of the Holy Spirit. The apostles on the day of Pentecost and the household of Cornelius, after receiving the baptism of the Holy Spirit, spoke with other tongues. (Acts 2: 4; 10: 44-46.) These tongues were for a sign; the speaking with other tongues by the apostles became a sign to those who heard that God was with them; the Gentiles at the house of

Cornelius by speaking with other tongues became a sign to Peter and other Jewish brethren that God had accepted the Gentiles. "God also bearing witness with them, both by signs and wonders, and by manifold powers, and by gifts of the Holy Spirit, according to his own will." (Heb. 2: 4.) Hence, the word spoken through Christ "was confirmed" to those who heard by these manifold powers and gifts of the Holy Spirit.   There is no record of anyone after the household of Cornelius as having been baptized with the Holy Spirit.   The baptism of the Holy Spirit never made anyone a Christian; it did not make the apostles Christians nor anyone else.

In every instance of a Holy Spirit baptism recorded in the New Testament a miracle was wrought in speaking with "other tongues" and other extraordinary things.   The Holy Spirit on Pentecost sanctioned only the preaching of the gospel; those who received the baptism were placed under obligation to preach Christ.   On Pentecost there were three classes which are mentioned by Luke.   Some were amazed and "marvelled," and looked at the work of the baptism of the Holy Spirit with mere curiosity and surprise; others "were in doubt" and "mocking," and were filled with skepticism and suspension; no evidences would satisfy and no truth convince them.   Others were inclined to hear Peter and believe; these are the ones who were added to the church and received the blessings of the baptism of the Holy Spirit upon the apostles.

CHAPTER V

BLASPHEMY AGAINST HOLY SPIRIT

INTRODUCTION.

"Blaspheme," from Greek "blapto," means "to hurt," and "phemi" means "to speak"; hence, to "blaspheme" means "to speak to hurt," "to speak against," "to speak irreverently, impiously"; it means to profane, to speak evil of good.

I. BLASPHEMY AGAINST GOD.

    1. In the Old Testament.
        a. The Egyptian. (Lev. 24: 11.)
        b. Penalty of death. (Lev. 24: 16.)
        c. Blasphemy among sins of Israel. (Isa. 65: 7.)

    2. In the New Testament.
        a. By the Gentiles. (Rom. 2: 24.)
        b. Name of God blasphemed. (Rev. 16: 9.)
        c. Word of God blasphemed. (Tit. 2: 5.)
        d. God and doctrine blasphemed. (1 Tim. 6: 1.)
        e. Paul once a blasphemer. (1 Tim. 1: 13.)

II. CHRIST CHARGED WITH BLASPHEMY.

    1. Speak blasphemous words. (Mark 2: 7.)
    2. Condemned as a blasphemer. (Matt. 26: 65.)

III. HOLY SPIRIT BLASPHEMED.

    1. Christ warned against it. (Matt. 12: 31, 32; Mark 3: 28, 29; Luke 12: 10.)
    2. This called "unpardonable sin."

IV. "SIN UNTO DEATH."

    1. "Unpardonable sin," the unrepented sin.
    2. Sins not unto death. (1 John 5: 16.)
    3. Sin willfully. (Heb. 6: 4-6; 10: 26-31.)

V. LIMITATIONS OF FORGIVENESS.

    1. No limit with God. (Matt. 9: 13; 28: 19.)
    2. No limit with Christ. (Matt. 12: 32.)
    3. Must be no limit with man. (Matt. 6: 12-14; 18: 21.)
    4. A limit with Holy Spirit. (Matt. 12: 32.)

BLASPHEMY AGAINST HOLY SPIRIT

"Whosoever shall blaspheme against the Holy Spirit hath never forgiveness, but is guilty of an eternal sin." (Mark 3: 29.)

"Blasphemy" comes from the two Greek words "blapto" and "phemi"; "blapto" means "to hurt," while "phemi" means "to speak," hence "to blaspheme" means "to speak to hurt," "to speak against." The full meaning of the term "blaspheme" means to speak irreverently, impiously; it primarily means defamation, or to speak evil. There is always the idea of "hurt" or "injury" in blasphemy; the speaker means to do harm or to speak evil of one. The term is broad enough to include blasphemy, or evil speaking against anything or any person. One man can blaspheme a theory or doctrine by speaking evil against it; one man can blaspheme another man by speaking words to hurt or injure him. In this study we are to consider blasphemy against the members of the Godhead and especially against the third member, the Holy Spirit.

When one attempts to injure by speech, either oral or written, God or any divine person, that one is guilty of blasphemy. To speak against any of the revealed attributes of God, Christ, or Holy Spirit is to blaspheme. When one speaks irreverently of the word of God, one is speaking blasphemously. When one profanes the worship of God by speaking against it, that one is guilty of the high crime of blasphemy. To rail upon, reject, refuse, misrepresent, and pervert the words or works of the Holy Spirit is to blaspheme against the Holy Spirit.

I. BLASPHEMY AGAINST GOD

Blasphemy is an old sin. For the creature to speak against the Creator has been condemned all down through the ages. God demands that his creatures respect him; to disrespect God is to lower one in the scale of God's favors granted to man. God has severely condemned the sin of blasphemy and has recorded examples of his condemnation as warnings to others. Soon after the law of Moses was given, there was the son of an

Israelitish woman by an Egyptian who "blasphemed the Name, and cursed." (Lev. 24: 11.) Moses did not know what to do with the case; he took the matter to Jehovah and received instructions that "he that blasphemeth the name of Jehovah, he shall surely be put to death; all the congregation shall certainly stone him: as well the sojourner, as the home-born, when he blasphemeth the name of Jehovah, shall be put to death." (Lev. 24: 16.) Blasphemy is always in word or deed, injury, dishonor, and defiance offered to God; its penalty has been the extreme penalty, death.

Many times some in the kingdom of Israel blasphemed Jehovah. Among the sins that Isaiah catalogued against Israel is found the sin of blasphemy. (Isa. 65: 7.) Sennacherib defied Jehovah and blasphemed the God of Israel. (2 Kings 19: 6-22.) David's sin gave occasion to the enemies of the Lord to blaspheme his name. (2 Sam. 12: 14.) See also Psalm 74: 10-18; Isa. 52: 5; Ezek. 35: 12. These are recorded as a warning to people today. Every Old Testament example of this sin sounds a note of warning to those who would speak against Jehovah, either against his name or his law. People must learn to reverence Jehovah and not blaspheme his character.

The warnings against the sin of blasphemy are frequently repeated in the New Testament. Paul, in writing to the church at Rome, said: "For the name of God is blasphemed among the Gentiles because of you, even as it is written." (Rom. 2: 24.) It is a fearful sin that rested upon the Jews and Christians to give occasion for others to blaspheme the name of God. In Revelation we read: "And men were scorched with great heat: and they blasphemed the name of God who hath the power over these plagues; and they repented not to give him glory." (Rev. 16: 9.) To blaspheme the word of God is to reject it and teach things contradicting God's word. Paul instructed Titus to teach Christians "to be sober-minded, chaste, workers at home, kind, being in subjection to their own husbands, that the word of God be not blasphemed." (Tit. 2: 5.)

There is a great responsibility on Christians to keep from furnishing occasion for others to blaspheme. "Let as many as are servants under the yoke count their own masters worthy of all

honor, that the name of God and the doctrine be not blasphemed."
(1 Tim. 6: 1.)   To blaspheme the doctrine of Christ is to pervert
the gospel, reject it, and substitute something else for the gospel.
No one can be saved while blaspheming the doctrine of Christ.
Paul, before his conversion, was a blasphemer.   He said of himself: "Though I was before a blasphemer, and a persecutor, and
injurious: howbeit I obtained mercy, because I did it ignorantly
in unbelief."   (1 Tim. 1: 13.)   Paul, in relating his experience
before Agrippa, said: "I strove to make them blaspheme; and
being exceedingly mad against them, I persecuted them even unto
foreign cities." (Acts 26: 11.)

II. Christ Charged with Blasphemy

The sin of blasphemy was considered the most grievous in the
catalog of sin.   If it could be proved on one that he had blasphemed, the death penalty was administered to the guilty one.
The enemies of Christ brought the serious charge against him
that he used blasphemous words.   Early in the ministry of Christ
he claimed to have the power to forgive sins; on one occasion
the scribes were sitting around and heard him say: "Son, thy
sins are forgiven."   They then charged him with the sin of
blasphemy.   "Why doth this man thus speak? he blasphemeth:
who can forgive sins but one, even God?"   (Mark 2: 5-7.)   Christ
claimed to be equal to God; he claimed the power to forgive sins.
These scribes were correct in their reasoning that none but
God could forgive sins, and if Christ did not have the power to
forgive sins, he was a blasphemer.   He was putting himself in
the place of God, and claiming all the power that God had; he
was robbing God of honor, if he be not the Son of God.   However,
as he was the Son of God, he was honoring God by exercising
the power that God gave him.   He was not speaking words of
blasphemy since his words and claims were true.

One of the sins charged against Christ in his trial before the
Jewish Sanhedrin was blasphemy.   Jesus was on trial and confessed that he was the Son of God, and "then the high priest
rent his garments, saying, He hath spoken blasphemy: what further need have we of witnesses? behold, now ye have heard the
blasphemy."   (Matt. 26: 65.)   This was a capital offense; blas-

phemy was punishable by death. These Jews were seeking an occasion to put Jesus to death; they thought that if they could prefer the charge of blasphemy against him, and sustain that charge, they would be justified in putting him to death. Hence, the charge of blasphemy against the Son of God. These Jews brought another charge against Christ when he was brought before Pilate.

III. HOLY SPIRIT BLASPHEMED

Sin has brought ruin to the race of man; it has caused man to speak against God and his laws. When Christ came and began his ministry, the devil assailed him with temptation in every form during his entire ministry. Men reviled him; they slandered and blasphemed him; at last they crucified him. They charged him with being in league with the devil. In reply to them he said: "Every sin and blasphemy shall be forgiven unto men; but the blasphemy against the Spirit shall not be forgiven. And whosoever shall speak a word against the Son of man, it shall be forgiven him; but whosoever shall speak against the Holy Spirit, it shall not be forgiven him, neither in this world, nor in that which is to come." (Matt. 12: 31, 32.) Mark records this warning of Christ: "All their sins shall be forgiven unto the sons of men, and their blasphemies wherewith soever they shall blaspheme: but whosoever shall blaspheme against the Holy Spirit hath never forgiveness, but is guilty of an eternal sin." (Mark 3: 28, 29.) Luke records the same emphatic warning against blaspheming the Holy Spirit. (Luke 12: 10.) This warning is a danger signal. The sin of blasphemy began in the heart; it grew in purpose; it was completed in a deliberate, overt act. It was the final rejection of the Holy Spirit. This sin has been called the "unpardonable sin."

IV. "SIN UNTO DEATH"

Many are deeply concerned about the "unpardonable sin." The only sin that is "unpardoned" or "unpardonable" is the sin that is not repented of. The unpardonable sin is the unrepented sin. God has been willing to forgive man's sin if man would repent; man has oftentimes refused to repent, and there is no forgiveness of sins to that one who is not penitent. Under the next topic will be found a discussion on the limitations of forgiveness, but here we are to consider the "sin unto death." John says: "If any man see his brother sinning a sin not unto death, he shall ask, and God will give him life for them that sin not unto death. There is a sin unto death: not concerning this do I say that he should make request. All unrighteousness is sin: and there is a sin not unto death." (1 John 5: 16, 17.) Here John makes a simple division of sin—sin not unto death, and sin unto death. What is this sin which results in certain and hopeless death? It is the sin that has been terribly designated as that of willfully rejecting the testimony of the Holy Spirit as to the true nature and Messiahship of Christ; no one need pray for forgiveness of this sin. To pray for its forgiveness would be to pray for salvation outside of Christ and the Holy Spirit; there can be no true spirit of prayer in behalf of one who rejects the Holy Spirit.

To sin willfully is put in the class of rejecting the Holy Spirit; the Hebrew letter discusses willful sin. (Heb. 6: 4-6; 10: 26-31.) To be made partakers of the Holy Spirit is a blessing that belongs to all Christians; the world cannot receive the Holy Spirit. (John 14: 17.) It is possible, as here taught, that one may have been enlightened, and tasted of the heavenly gift, and made partaker of the Holy Spirit, and turn away from Christ and fall away beyond the reach of recovery. The one who blasphemes the Holy Spirit cannot be saved in such a condition; so long as he remains a blasphemer of the Holy Spirit, there is no hope of his salvation. If the Holy Spirit is rejected, there are no other heavenly means for man's salvation. The Holy Spirit dispensation is the last; a rejection of the Holy Spirit is a rejection of heaven.

"For if we sin wilfully after that we have received the knowledge of the truth, there remaineth no more a sacrifice for sins." To sin willfully after one has received the knowledge of the truth is the same as to apostatize from Christ. To sin willfully is to sin willingly and deliberately and persist in that sin; it is a sin that is committed with a high hand and is open violation and contempt for the words spoken by the Holy Spirit. The one who so sins willfully shuts himself out from the grace and mercy of God which may be enjoyed only through the Holy Spirit. If the Holy Spirit is rejected, then there is no grace, mercy, hope, or salvation.

V. Limitations of Forgiveness

It should be remembered that God has had his dispensation with man, that Christ has had his dispensation, and now the Holy Spirit has his dispensation. The dispensation of Christ on earth continued only a few years during his personal ministry. One could live under God's dispensation, the latter days of it, and continue living through Christ's dispensation, and into the dispensation of the Spirit. There was no limit with God as to the forgiveness of sin. All the sins of God's people before the cross were pretermitted through the forbearance of God. (Rom. 3: 25.) Sins during Christ's dispensation were *pretermitted,* but sins under the Spirit dispensation are *remitted.* Absolute forgiveness of sin was postponed until after the shedding of the blood of Christ or until the Spirit's dispensation. One could sin against God, and then sin against Christ, and yet have an opportunity to be saved. The sins against God during his dispensation and the sins against Christ during his dispensation could be pretermitted, and finally under the Spirit dispensation be remitted. (Matt. 9: 13; 12: 32; 28: 19.)

Man should have no limit in his forgiveness of his fellow man. (Matt. 6: 12-14; 18: 21.) It seems that in the wisdom of God there is a limitation of the forgiveness of sins under the Spirit dispensation. It has been a mooted question as to whether blasphemy against the Holy Spirit shows a condition of heart that renders one unable to repent, or whether it produces an unwillingness on God's part to forgive. Putting it another way, does blasphemy against the Holy Spirit come from a heart that is unable to repent? Does blasphemy against the Holy Spirit so grieve God that he is unwilling to forgive? Is a heart that blasphemes the Holy Spirit so degenerate that it is unable to repent or is the sin of blasphemy against the Holy Spirit such a crime against God that he will not forgive it? It seems that the heart that is so wicked and degenerate that it will blaspheme the Holy Spirit is unable to repent. God cannot forgive an unrepented sin, and if a heart is so degenerate that it cannot repent, there can be no forgiveness of that sin.

It is a fearful thing for man to reject God or his truth. Man sins against his own intelligence and soul when he turns aside from any truth. All truth that pertains to the redemption of man came through the Holy Spirit. For man to pervert the truth of God is to pervert the words of the Holy Spirit; for man to reject the teachings of the New Testament is to reject the Holy Spirit. To speak a word against the truth of the gospel is to speak a word against the power of God to save—it is to blaspheme the words of the Holy Spirit. The word of God may be blasphemed. (Tit. 2: 5.) Paul before his conversion blasphemed the word of God. (1 Tim. 1: 13.) The name of God may be blasphemed. "And they blasphemed the name of God who hath the power over these plagues; and they repented not to give him glory." (Rev. 16: 9.)

SINS AGAINST HOLY SPIRIT

INTRODUCTION.

Man may sin against God (Psalm 51: 3, 4); man sinned against Christ; they crucified him; so man may sin against Holy Spirit.

I. BLASPHEMING HOLY SPIRIT.

1. Christ revealed this. (Matt. 12: 31, 32; Mark 3: 28, 29; Luke 12: 10.)
2. No New Testament example of this sin.

II. DESPISING HOLY SPIRIT.

1. Turning from Holy Spirit. (Heb. 6: 4-6.)
2. "Done despite unto the Spirit." (Heb. 10: 21-29.)

III. LYING TO HOLY SPIRIT.

1. Ananias lied to Holy Spirit. (Acts 5: 3.)
2. Sapphira lied also. (Acts 5: 9.)

IV. RESISTING HOLY SPIRIT.

1. Stephen's hearers. (Acts 7: 51.)
2. They rejected the truth.

V. DEFILING TEMPLE OF HOLY SPIRIT.

1. Defiling the body. (1 Cor. 6: 19, 20.)
2. Defiling the church. (1 Cor. 3: 16, 17.)

VI. QUENCHING HOLY SPIRIT.

1. Some Christians do this. (1 Thess. 5: 19.)
2. Hinder work of Holy Spirit.

VII. GRIEVING HOLY SPIRIT.

1. Any sin of Christians. (Eph. 4: 30.)
2. An unholy life.

SINS AGAINST HOLY SPIRIT

"Peter said, Ananias, why hath Satan filled thy heart to lie to the Holy Spirit?" (Acts 5: 3.)

The Godhead, God the Father, the Word, Christ, and the Holy Spirit constitute the divine family. Each member of the Godhead has had his dispensation on earth with man. Man sinned against God during his dispensation; in fact, every sin that man committed was sin against God. David confessed and said: "For I know my transgressions; and my sin is ever before me. Against thee, thee only, have I sinned, and done that which is evil in thy sight." (Psalm 51: 3, 4.) Even when David sinned against Uriah, it was a sin against God also.

While Christ was on earth, man sinned against him. Man contradicted his word; man perverted his teachings; man persecuted him; man bore false witness against him; man crucified him. Nearly every form of sin was committed against Christ. "For hereunto were ye called: because Christ also suffered for you, leaving you an example, that ye should follow his steps: who did no sin; neither was guile found in his mouth: who, when he was reviled, reviled not again; when he suffered, threatened not; but committed himself to him that judgeth righteously: who his own self bare our sins in his body upon the tree, that we, having died unto sins, might live unto righteousness; by whose stripes ye were healed." (1 Pet. 2: 21-24.)

In like manner man may sin against the Holy Spirit. In this study we are to examine the number of ways by which man may sin against the Holy Spirit. Every form of sin that man may commit against God may be committed against the Holy Spirit; every sin, except the sins against the body of Christ, that man committed against Christ may be committed against the Holy Spirit. The relationship of the members of the Godhead is such that to sin against any one member is to sin against the other members. Hence, the sins committed today against the Holy Spirit may be committed against the other members of the

Godhead. However, in a particular way, the New Testament describes certain sins that are against the Holy Spirit.

I. Blaspheming Holy Spirit

In a former chapter we have discussed the sin of blasphemy against the Holy Spirit, but since we are listing all of the sins that may be committed against the Holy Spirit, this sin comes up for further review. It was possible for one to live in the latter days of God's dispensation, and continue through the short period of the dispensation of Christ on earth, and into the dispensation of the Holy Spirit. One could blaspheme God, and repent of it and accept Christ; one could reject Christ during his dispensation, and accept the teachings of the Holy Spirit on Pentecost and thereafter. However, if one rejected or rejects the Holy Spirit, there is not another dispensation. It is either accept the Holy Spirit or be damned; no other dispensation will appear, and man who rejects the Holy Spirit dispensation rejects the last opportunity. "Verily I say unto you, All their sins shall be forgiven unto the sons of men, and their blasphemies wherewith soever they shall blaspheme: but whosoever shall blaspheme against the Holy Spirit hath never forgiveness, but is guilty of an eternal sin." (Mark 3: 28, 29.) See also Matt. 12: 31, 32 and Luke 12: 10.

We have no New Testament example recorded of blasphemy against the Holy Spirit. However, it is possible for man to commit this sin or else Jesus would not have warned against it. The Pharisees had accused Christ of being in league with Beelzebub, the prince of devils, and by his Satanic agency casting out devils from men; Christ recognized this as blasphemy against himself; it was a malignant rejection of Christ against their own reason; it was devilish imputation to Christ; it was attributing to Christ a hellish purpose against the clearest evidence to the contrary. Apply the same principles to blasphemy against the Holy Spirit and we have the correct definition of this sin; it is a malignant, persistent, willful rejection of the Holy Spirit linked with an imputing to the Holy Spirit hellish purposes against reason and conclusive evidence.

II. Despising Holy Spirit

The sin of despising the Holy Spirit is clearly set forth in the Hebrew letter. These Hebrew Christians had been converted; they were inclined to return to Judaism. This letter was written to show them the folly of going back to the law of Moses. "For as touching those who were once enlightened and tasted of the heavenly gift, and were made partakers of the Holy Spirit, and tasted the good word of God, and the powers of the age to come, and then fell away, it is impossible to renew them again unto repentance; seeing they crucify to themselves the Son of God afresh, and put him to an open shame." (Heb. 6: 4-6.) If these Christians return to the law of Moses, it would demand the crucifixion. He had already been crucified once according to the law, but if they went back to keeping the law, they must demand his crucifixion again; they must "crucify to themselves the Son of God afresh, and put him to an open shame."

This sin is further described as despising the Holy Spirit. "For if we sin wilfully after that we have received the knowledge of the truth, there remaineth no more a sacrifice for sins, but a certain fearful expectation of judgment, and a fierceness of fire which shall devour the adversaries. A man that hath set at nought Moses' law dieth without compassion on the word of two or three witnesses: of how much sorer punishment, think ye, shall he be judged worthy, who hath trodden under foot the Son of God, and hath counted the blood of the covenant wherewith he was sanctified an unholy thing, and hath done despite unto the Spirit of grace?" (Heb. 10: 26-29.) The word "despite" is from the Greek "enubrizo" which is a verb denoting to treat with contumely, to give insult to; it is a powerful word for insulting the Holy Spirit after receiving his blessings. This is a fearful sin. "It is a fearful thing to fall into the hands of the living God." (Heb. 10: 31.)

III. Lying to Holy Spirit

We have an example of lying to the Holy Spirit in the New Testament. Against two of the early members of the church in Jerusalem was made the charge of lying to and tempting the Holy Spirit. The swift execution of divine judgment reveals the estimate God places upon this sin.   Evidently Ananias and his wife, Sapphira, voluntarily made a covenant with the church to give their possessions to it as did Barnabas. (Acts 4: 36, 37.)   This husband and wife attempted to practice gross deception, thinking that no one would know the truth; they coveted that which they had pledged to God, and then sought to mislead the apostles by seeming to keep the covenant which they made. But Peter said: "Ananias, why hath Satan filled thy heart to lie to the Holy Spirit, and to keep back part of the price of the land?" (Acts 5: 3.)   Peter further said to Ananias: "Thou hast not lied unto men, but unto God." (Acts 5:4.)   The word "lie" here is from the Greek "pseuasthai" and means to deceive; the design of Satan was to deceive the Holy Spirit; Satan filled the heart of Ananias to deceive; the result of the attempt was merely to lie.   While the devil filled Ananias' heart, Ananias responded voluntarily to the sin of lying.

Sapphira was not present when Ananias lied to the Holy Spirit; she did not know the penalty that had been visited upon her husband; so about three hours afterwards she came in and Peter asked her about the price of the land which they had sold, and she made the same statement that Ananias had made. Peter then asked her: "How is it that ye have agreed together to try the Spirit of the Lord?" (Acts 5: 9.)   The same penalty was meted out to her.   To "try the Spirit of the Lord" was tantamount to lying to the Holy Spirit.   It was close to the unpardonable sin.   The penalty visited upon these two members of the church shows the severity of condemnation that God has placed upon this sin.

IV. Resisting Holy Spirit

Another sin against the Holy Spirit is recorded in Acts 7: 51. Here we have it stated that Stephen charged his hearers as being "stiffnecked and uncircumcised in heart and ears, ye do always resist the Holy Spirit."   "Resist" here is from the Greek "antipiptete," which is a word that means to fall against, to rush against; this is the only time it is used in the Greek New Testament.   This is a very strong expression made by Stephen and it implies *active* resistance.   This sin of resisting the Holy Spirit led

Stephen's hearers to commit a great crime; they put Stephen to death. This sin may not take on the malignant features of blasphemy; neither may it take the fearful and ungrateful attitude of despising the Holy Spirit, but it does place the sinner in open antagonism to God's love. It causes one to reject the truth, and may cause one to reject the final opportunity of salvation.

V. Defiling Temple of Holy Spirit

The next sin that we mention against the Holy Spirit is that of defiling the temple. "Temple of Holy Spirit" may mean our bodies. "Know ye not that your body is a temple of the Holy Spirit which is in you, which ye have from God? and ye are not your own; for ye were bought with a price: glorify God therefore in your body." (1 Cor. 6: 19, 20.) When Christians defile their bodies, they are sinning against the Holy Spirit; this calls for an observance of all the laws of hygiene and requires one to live a pure life. The second use of "temple of the Holy Spirit" refers to the church. "Know ye not that ye are a temple of God, and that the Spirit of God dwelleth in you? If any man destroyeth the temple of God, him shall God destroy; for the temple of God is holy, and such are ye." (1 Cor. 3: 16, 17.) This has reference to the church. In both of these Scriptures Paul is emphasizing the sacredness of the temple of the Holy Spirit. The destruction or defilement is substantially the same in both; it is the perversion of the temple from a holy to an unholy use. Any sin against the members of the church is a sin against the church, and a sin against the Holy Spirit which abides in the church. It is a crime against the Holy Spirit to sin against the temple in which the Holy Spirit dwells.

VI. Quenching Holy Spirit

Paul, in writing to the church at Thessalonica, commanded them to stop quenching the Holy Spirit; some of them were trying to put out the fire of the Holy Spirit, and were growing indifferent toward the work of Christians as taught by the Holy Spirit. The reference here is to the work of the Holy Spirit in a general way, and not specially to his guidance in prayer or prophecy. "Pray without ceasing; in everything give thanks: for this is the will of God in Christ Jesus to you-ward. Quench not the Spirit." (1 Thess. 5: 17-19.) Indifference, lukewarmness, and idleness all hinder the work of the Holy Spirit. To discourage the work of the Lord is to quench the Holy Spirit who prompts and guides in this work.

VII. Grieving Holy Spirit

A final sin against the Holy Spirit is that presented by Paul when he said: "Grieve not the Holy Spirit of God, in whom ye were sealed unto the day of redemption." (Eph. 4: 30.) One may grieve the Holy Spirit by speaking impure language, using bitter and angry words against others, and doing anything that is displeasing to the Holy Spirit. The precepts enjoined by Paul here are practical; the Christian is to walk an exemplary life before men and imitating the life of Christ. The Holy Spirit is grieved when unholy actions, wicked deeds, or anything that is contrary to the teachings of Christ are done. Christians should love one another and help each other in living the Christian life.

We have now presented seven distinct sins against the Holy Spirit. Each one of the sins carries with it its own penalty. To sin against God the Father has been grievous enough, since such sin has ruined the race of man; to sin against Christ who died for us and gave himself for us is still greater as it embodies enmity with deepest ingratitude; but to sin against the Holy Spirit is greater still, since it not only includes all the others, but adds to these transgressions against all truth. Every soul should learn the enormity of sinning in any way against the Holy Spirit.

The ascription of grief to the Holy Spirit is an assumption of his personality; grief is an attitude which does not belong to an attribute, but can be exercised only by a person. The truth of the personality of the Holy Spirit is taken for granted throughout the Bible. The nature of grief is understood by all from universal experience of it; grief is a portion of the inheritance of humanity; it is common to infancy, childhood, youth, manhood, and age; none need have it explained; every heart knows its own bitterness.

When we ascribe grief to the Holy Spirit, it is in accommodation to the weakness of our minds and the poverty of our language. In the absolute sense the Holy Spirit is incapable of grief; when grief is ascribed to the Holy Spirit, it is to teach us that, as we grieve over that which is contrary to our desires, so there are actions contrary to the will of the Holy Spirit. The Holy Spirit is grieved by everything that is contrary to holiness; he is holy himself, and he demands holiness in all intelligent beings.

The Bible warns us concerning our treatment of the Holy Spirit. Three terms express our duty negatively: "resist not," "quench not," and "grieve not." "Resist," "quench," and "grieve" express the three perils of men in relation to the Holy Spirit. "Resisting" the Holy Spirit is in opposition to his approach and entrance into the lives of people; resistance to the Holy Spirit is not only the peril but practice of the impenitent. To "quench" suggests the presence of the Spirit; to quench the Holy Spirit is to drive him away. To "grieve" the Holy Spirit means to do that which is contrary to the Spirit; it implies that the Holy Spirit dwells in one.

CHAPTER VII

GIFTS OF HOLY SPIRIT

INTRODUCTION.

Difference between Holy Spirit as a gift and gifts of Holy Spirit; also difference between baptism of Holy Spirit and gifts of Holy Spirit.

I. EXTRAORDINARY GIFTS.

1. Baptism of Holy Spirit.
   a. This a promise. (Matt. 3: 11; Luke 24: 49; Acts 1: 5.)
   b. Fulfillment of the promise. (Acts 2: 4; 10: 46-48; 11: 15-18.)
   c. What followed the fulfillment? (Acts 2: 4; 10: 46.)

2. Gifts bestowed by laying on of hands.
   a. By the apostles. (Acts 8: 14-24; 19: 6.)
   b. By others. (1 Tim. 4: 14.)

3. Diversities of gifts. (1 Cor. 12: 4-11.)
   a. Gifts which are to be referred to the intellectual powers.
   b. Gifts which are exhibitions of faith.
   c. Gifts of tongues.
   d. These should cease. (1 Cor. 13: 8.)

II. ORDINARY GIFTS.

1. These were to be permanent.
2. As a Comforter. (John 14: 15-17.)
3. World could not receive Holy Spirit as a Comforter.
4. All comfort from Holy Spirit. (1 Thess. 4: 18.)
5. Difference in comforting God's people and reproving the world.

GIFTS OF HOLY SPIRIT

"Now concerning spiritual gifts, brethren, I would not have you ignorant."
(1 Cor. 12: 1.)

No discussion of the Holy Spirit would be complete without an investigation of the gifts of the Holy Spirit as taught in the New Testament. It should be remembered that there is a clear and definite distinction to be made between the Holy Spirit as a gift and the gifts of the Holy Spirit. The Holy Spirit, when received, may be spoken of as a gift. In fact, Peter so speaks of the Holy Spirit as a gift. When the Holy Spirit came on the household of Cornelius, "on the Gentiles also was poured out the gift of the Holy Spirit." (Acts 10: 45.) Later Peter, referring to this, said: "If then God gave unto them the like gift as he did also unto us." (Acts 11: 17.) "The gift of the Holy Spirit" here was the Holy Spirit. The gifts of the Holy Spirit are those gifts which came from the Holy Spirit.

The gifts of the Holy Spirit are many and are distributed individually and selectively to various Christians on the sovereign authority of the Holy Spirit himself. There is to be made a distinction between the baptism of the Holy Spirit and the gifts of the Holy Spirit. The baptism of the Holy Spirit may be a "gift," but the "gifts" of the Holy Spirit are many. "The gift of the Holy Spirit" as a phrase is found only twice in the New Testament. (Acts 2: 38 and 10: 45.) However, it seems to have a different connotation in each use of the phrase. In Acts 2: 38 the apostle seems to have in mind that gift that belongs to all Christians, while in Acts 10: 45 he has reference to the baptism of the Holy Spirit. Many think that Acts 2: 38 has reference to the miraculous measure of the Holy Spirit; others think that it means the baptism of the Holy Spirit; still others think that it means the ordinary gift of the Holy Spirit which is promised to all Christians. "Because the love of God hath been shed abroad in our hearts through the Holy Spirit which was given unto us." (Rom. 5: 5.) It seems clear that Acts 2: 38 does not mean the baptism of the Holy Spirit; hence, we are left to determine whether it means a miraculous gift or the ordinary gift. All agree that miraculous gifts were bestowed in the early days of the church, and all agree that every Christian received an ordinary measure of the Holy Spirit, for "because ye are sons, God sent forth the Spirit of his Son into our hearts, crying, Abba, Father." (Gal. 4: 6.)   So it matters very little as to whether we can determine which the apostle meant.

I. EXTRAORDINARY GIFTS

As we study the general subject of gifts of the Spirit, and make a survey of the complete teaching of the New Testament, we find that they may be divided into two general classes.   First, we study the "Extraordinary Gifts."   The first subdivision of these is the baptism of the Holy Spirit.   In a former chapter we have studied the baptism of the Holy Spirit; it was a promise. (Matt. 3: 11; Luke 24: 49; Acts 1: 5.)   This promise was fulfilled in due time.   (Acts 2: 4; 10: 46-48; 11: 15-18.)   Christ was the administrator. as he was the one who made the promise of the baptism of the Holy Spirit.   John the Baptist knew that Christ would do this, hence he spoke of Christ fulfilling this promise.   Christ told his apostles that they should "wait for the promise of the Father, which, said he, ye heard from me."   (Acts 1: 4.)   Jesus said: "But when the Comforter is come, whom I will send unto you from the Father, even the Spirit of truth, which proceedeth from the Father, he shall bear witness of me." (John 15: 26.)   The baptism of the Holy Spirit was not a command, but a promise; it had been fulfilled.   The speaking of tongues followed the baptism of the Holy Spirit.   (Acts 2: 4; 10: 46.)   This baptism of the Holy Spirit was the advent of the Holy Spirit into the world as the divine executive for all time.

Among the extraordinary gifts of the Holy Spirit are found gifts which were bestowed by the laying on of hands.   These gifts differ from the baptism of the Holy Spirit in that they had some human agency through whom they were given.   The baptism of the Holy Spirit came direct from God, but these special gifts came through human agency.   After the gospel had been preached to the Samaritans, and many of them had heard it, believed it, and were baptized, Peter and John went down there and "prayed for them, that they might receive the Holy Spirit: for as yet it was fallen upon none of them: only they had been baptized into the name of the Lord Jesus. Then laid they their hands on them, and they received the Holy Spirit. Now when Simon saw that through the laying on of the apostles' hands the Holy Spirit was given, he offered them money, saying, Give me also this power, that on whomsoever I lay my hands, he may receive the Holy Spirit." (Acts 8: 15-19; see also Acts 19: 6.)

It seems that others had power to bestow these gifts of an extraordinary measure. Timothy had some special gift. Paul said to him: "Neglect not the gift that is in thee, which was given thee by prophecy, with the laying on of the hands of the pres-bytery." (1 Tim. 4: 14.) This gift was bestowed upon Timothy through "the laying on of the hands of the presbytery." Again, it seems that Timothy had another gift as Paul said: "For which cause I put thee in remembrance that thou stir up the gift of God, which is in thee through the laying on of my hands." (2 Tim. 1: 6.) Either Timothy had two gifts which were bestowed on him by the laying on of hands or Paul was one of the "pres-bytery." It is better to think of Timothy as having two or more gifts. It may be urged that Paul was an apostle; this is true, but the "presbytery" was not composed of apostles; hence, here is a gift bestowed upon Timothy by the laying on of hands of others than apostles. Some claim that Timothy had power to bestow a spiritual gift; they based their conclusion on the state-ment made by Paul to Timothy when he said: "Lay hands hastily on no man, neither be partaker of other men's sins." (1 Tim. 5: 22.) Others claimed that this Scripture has reference to the manner of *ordaining* one into some office.

There is another Scripture which seems to teach that others besides the apostles had power or the gift to bestow miraculous gifts on others. In listing the spiritual gifts, Paul said: "And to another workings of miracles." (1 Cor. 12: 10.) MacKnight says that this means that one of the gifts was the gift to bestow on others the power to work miracles; hence, he translates this as "and to another the inworkings of powers, that is, an ability to work in others the spiritual gifts and miraculous power." If this be the meaning of 1 Cor. 12: 10, then others had the power to bestow miraculous gifts besides the apostles; that in the church at Corinth there were those who could bestow on others a gift to work miracles.

There were "diversities of gifts" by the Holy Spirit. (1 Cor. 12: 4-11.) Here the apostle names nine distinct gifts which he classifies under three heads. The first class includes those gifts which are to be referred to the intellectual powers—"the word of wisdom," "the word of knowledge," and "faith." (1 Cor. 12: 8, 9.) The second class are the gifts which exhibit the faith of the one that possesses them—"gifts of healings," "workings of miracles," "prophecy," and "discernings of spirits." (1 Cor. 12: 9, 10.) The third class are the gifts of tongues—"divers kinds of tongues" and "interpretation of tongues." (1 Cor. 12: 10.) This enumeration of gifts is preceded by the emphatic statement of the principle that "to each one is given the manifestation of the Spirit to profit withal." (1 Cor. 12: 7.) This statement enables us to understand 1 Cor. 14, in which Paul discusses the *violation* of this principle. It was possible for those who possessed these extraordinary gifts to neglect them or to abuse the proper use of them. The possessor of these gifts had the same power over them that he had over his natural gifts, hence he could neglect or misuse his gift. All of these gifts were to be used for the general edification, and not for the self-glorification of the one who possessed the gift. "But now, brethren, if I come unto you speaking with tongues, what shall I profit you, unless I speak to you either by way of revelation, or of knowledge, or of prophesying, or of teaching?" (1 Cor. 14: 6.) The chief end of the use of all of these gifts was "that the church may receive edifying." (1 Cor. 14: 5.) The general admonition is: "Let all things be done unto edifying." (1 Cor. 14: 26.) It should be noted further that the gift of speaking in tongues is in the lowest bracket of ministrations; Paul thought it better to speak one word with the understanding than ten thousand words in a tongue. He counsels the Christians at Corinth, and through them every Christian, to covet the best gifts, and to show a more excellent way in that search than in the seeking of tongues.

These extraordinary gifts of the Holy Spirit were to cease. Jesus had promised these extraordinary gifts in giving the commission. (Mark 16: 20.) The preaching of the gospel under the commission was *confirmed* "by the signs that followed." These signs followed the preaching of the word for its confirmation at its first proclamation. Before Paul had visited Rome he wrote: "I long to see you, that I may impart unto you some spiritual gift, to the end ye may be established." (Rom. 1: 11.) Here we see again the purpose of these spiritual gifts. He wrote to the church at Corinth that his speech and preaching "were not in persuasive words of wisdom, but in demonstration of the Spirit and of power: that your faith should not stand in the wisdom of men, but in the power of God." (1 Cor. 2: 4, 5.) How long were these gifts to continue? Paul wrote to the church at Ephesus that they should continue "till we all attain unto the unity of the faith, and of the knowledge of the Son of God, unto a fullgrown man, unto the measure of the stature of the fulness of Christ: that we may be no longer children, tossed to and fro and carried about with every wind of doctrine, by the sleight of men, in craftiness, after the wiles of error." (Eph. 4: 13, 14.) Again Paul wrote: "Whether there be prophecies, they shall be done away; whether there be tongues, they shall cease; whether there be knowledge, it shall be done away." (1 Cor. 13: 8.)

We have a perfect record of these gifts which were bestowed to help confirm the preaching of the word; there was no need for a continuation of them after the full gospel had been revealed and confirmed and a record made to preserve it. The church is older than the New Testament; it was some years after the church was established before the first line of the New Testament was written. The early stages of the church, before there was a written copy of the word, needed these spiritual gifts. However, after the early stage of the church, they were not needed, hence they ceased. All claims to miraculous spiritual gifts today are false, and contradict the New Testament in its claim that the word has been confirmed. The writer of the Hebrew letter says that we ought to give "the more earnest heed to the things that were heard," and that the word "was confirmed unto us by them that heard; God also bearing witness with them, both by signs and wonders, and by manifold powers, and by gifts of

the Holy Spirit, according to his own will." (Heb. 2: 1-4.)
These spiritual gifts as recorded, like the signs of Jesus, "are
written, that ye may believe that Jesus is the Christ, the Son of
God; and that believing ye may have life in his name." (John
20: 31.)

II. Ordinary Gifts

The ordinary gifts of the Holy Spirit were promised to all
and accompany all who faithfully follow the Lord. We live in
the Spirit dispensation; his blessings or gifts in the ordinary
measure abide with us. The Holy Spirit abides with Christians.
"Ye are not in the flesh but in the Spirit, if so be that the Spirit
of God dwelleth in you. But if any man hath not the Spirit of
Christ, he is none of his. . . . But if the Spirit of him that raised
up Jesus from the dead dwelleth in you, he that raised up Christ
Jesus from the dead shall give life also to your mortal bodies
through his Spirit that dwelleth in you." (Rom. 8: 9-11.)
The "indwelling of the Spirit" will be treated in another chapter.
It is mentioned here to emphasize the ordinary gifts of the Holy
Spirit.

It would be impossible to live in a spiritual dispensation without receiving the common gifts of the Holy Spirit. The law is
declared to be spiritual (Rom. 7: 14); our services are declared to be spiritual (12: 1); the teaching of the gospel is declared to be spiritual (1 Cor. 9: 11); Christians partake of spiritual food (1 Cor. 10: 3); newborn babes in Christ "long for
the spiritual milk" (1 Pet. 2: 2); Christians are said to be "a
spiritual house" (1 Pet. 2: 5); Christians are said to be "a
temple of the Holy Spirit" which is in them (1 Cor. 6: 19); the
church is also declared to be "a temple of God" in which "the
Spirit of God dwelleth" (1 Cor. 3: 16).

It should be remembered that the Holy Spirit performs the
same office in the spiritual realm that he does in the material
realm. It has been observed that the Holy Spirit took up his
abode in the laws governing the material world and continues his
work with material things through these laws. Likewise the
Holy Spirit took up his abode in Christians and continues his work
through the spiritual laws. The Holy Spirit came on Pentecost
and began to speak through the apostles the word of God. Those

who received those words received the words of the Holy Spirit. Those who hear the same words as were spoken on Pentecost are hearing the words of the Holy Spirit.   Hence, the Holy Spirit is guiding and blessing God's people today and every blessing that Christians receive today is a gift of the Holy Spirit. The New Testament was given by the Holy Spirit, and every blessing that comes to us today through the New Testament is a gift of the Holy Spirit.   There is not a spiritual truth today except that which came through the Holy Spirit; there is not a blessing received through spiritual truth that is not a gift of the Holy Spirit.   These gifts of the Holy Spirit are permanent so long as the present order of things remains.   Through faith in Christ we become heirs of these spiritual gifts, and the more faithful we are to God the richer are these blessings to us.

The work of the Holy Spirit in its various departments reveals a remarkable variety of activities.   The Holy Spirit works through the laws of nature in keeping the universe intact, and he works through the truth of God in carrying out the will of God in the salvation of souls.   There was a multiplicity of gifts of the Holy Spirit in the "extraordinary" list; there is a great number of gifts of the Holy Spirit in the ordinary workings of individual Christians.   The comforting of the Holy Spirit gives encouragement to God's people; the reproving of the world through the truth of the gospel brings it under condemnation.

Chapter VIII

SPEAKING WITH OTHER TONGUES

Introduction.

Nine spiritual gifts listed in 1 Cor. 12: 4-11; Holy Spirit author of order, never of confusion; this gift claimed today.

I. Scope of New Testament Teaching.
    1. Eight writers of the New Testament.
    2. Paul alone mentions gift of tongues.
    3. He mentions it to only one church.

II. Only Five Groups of References.

    1. Acts 2: 4, 6, 11.
        a. "Other tongues" used, not "unknown tongues."
        b. Purpose: to prove gospel of Christ fulfillment of prophecy.

    2. Acts 10: 46.
        a. Power given to Gentiles.
        b. Purpose: to convince Jewish Christians that Gentiles had a right to the blessings of the gospel.

    3. Acts 19: 6.
        a. These twelve baptized into Christ.
        b. Purpose: to enable them to teach or prophesy.

    4. 1 Cor. 12: 1-10, 30.
        a. Nine gifts of Holy Spirit here mentioned.
        b. "Divers kinds of tongues" one of them.
        c. Speaking with other tongues never universal in the church.
        d. Only a special gift to a limited number. (Verse 30.)

    5. 1 Cor. 14: 2, 26-32.
        a. Use of the gift limited.
        b. If no interpreter present, it is not to be used.

III. Abuse of the Gift.

    1. The claim that it continue.
    2. Not accompanied by prostration.
    3. Gift of tongues in lowest bracket of ministrations.
    4. Unable to control the gift.

CHAPTER VIII

SPEAKING WITH OTHER TONGUES

"For to one is given through the Spirit the word of wisdom; . . . to another divers kinds of tongues; . . . but all these worketh the one and the same Spirit, dividing to each one severally even as he will." (1 Cor. 12: 8-11.)

The nine spiritual gifts listed in 1 Cor. 12: 4-11 have called for much study; they have been variously classified and defined. It is thought wise to give one chapter to one of these gifts. This is done because the gift of speaking with tongues is claimed by many modern teachers today. There is such a confusion in the minds of people because of these modern teachers that the space may be used profitably in the study of it.

The Holy Spirit is the author of order; God is a God of order; Christ is a teacher of order; so the Holy Spirit is a teacher of order, never of confusion. This should be remembered as we study what is revealed in the New Testament on the gift of speaking with other tongues. It is clear that the Holy Spirit is slandered by the modern claimants to this gift. Furthermore, it should be remembered that the New Testament reveals a difference between the *experiences* of the apostles and the *teachings* of the apostles. The apostles had power and wisdom that others did not have; they did things that others were not permitted to do. If these facts are kept in mind, the subject may be treated with more clearness. Hence, the perplexing problem with many today will be solved.

I. Scope of New Testament Teaching

There are eight writers of the New Testament—Matthew, Mark, Luke, Peter, Paul, James, John, and Jude. There are twenty-seven books of the New Testament; there are twenty-one books or letters written to individual Christians, churches, and groups of churches. Paul wrote thirteen or fourteen of these letters. There are twenty-seven churches mentioned by name in the New Testament. Paul is the only writer who discussed the gift of speaking with other tongues. He wrote not a word on the subject of tongues to the church at Rome, Ephesus, Colosse, Thessalonica, Philippi, or the churches in Galatia. He wrote a letter or letters to all of these churches, but said nothing about the gift of speaking in tongues. Neither did he mention the subject in his Epistles to Timothy, Titus, or Philemon. James did not mention the speaking of tongues in his general Epistles; John, who wrote five books of the New Testament, does not mention the subject. Even Peter, the spokesman on the day of Pentecost, who evidently had the gift of speaking with tongues, did not mention the subject in writing his two letters. It is a strange omission indeed if the gift of tongues was an essential part of the Christian experience or if it was to be perpetuated in the church of the Lord's people.

Paul is not only the only writer of the New Testament 'who discusses the matter, but he discusses it with only one church, Corinth. Luke, the writer of the Acts, mentions the speaking with tongues as a historical fact; he is interested only in the historicity of the subject, but not in the discussion of it. Acts is a record of some of the acts of some of the apostles; Luke records by the Holy Spirit such things as in the wisdom of God it was thought wise and best for man to know. In the Acts we have a history of the ever-increasing number of disciples of Christ who constitute the body of Christ. It is vital that the gift of the Holy Spirit is the fact of essential and constant interest in the book of Acts. The gift of the Holy Spirit is important in that it is central, vital, essential. Also the "gifts" of the Holy Spirit are simple testimonies of the presence of the Holy Spirit. As Christ is the Son of God, so the Holy Spirit is the gift of God; the Holy Spirit, the Father's gift, on behalf of Christ, becomes the giver of many graces and gifts. The speaking with tongues is only one of these gifts.

II. Only Five Groups of References

There are five and only five groups of passages in the New Testament which have reference to the Holy Spirit's gift of "tongues." They are presented here for our study in sequence of narration; we should have no difficulty in learning the teachings of these Scriptures on this very sadly abused subject. We take them in order:

1. Acts 2: 4, 6, 11. This reference is to the speaking of tongues on the day of Pentecost. We know that this was a gift of the Holy Spirit; that is, the Holy Spirit enabled the apostles to speak with "other tongues"; they spake "as the Spirit gave them utterance." (Verse 4.) This is the first reference or occasion of anyone's speaking in tongues after the ascension of Christ. The New Testament does not use the expression "unknown tongues"; it uses the term "other tongues" or "kinds of tongues," but never "unknown tongues." The Holy Spirit had come upon the apostles on this Pentecost, and "they were all filled with the Holy Spirit, and began to speak with other tongues, as the Spirit gave them utterance." The speech of Peter and the other apostles on this day could be understood; it was perfectly intelligible. The amazement of the multitude was that "we hear them speaking in our tongues the mighty works of God." (Verse 11.) This act is interpreted as "every man heard them speaking in his own language." (Verse 6.) This gift of speaking in other tongues was proof that the gospel of Christ was the fulfillment of the prophecy. The employment of languages which were perfectly intelligible to the hearers was in itself a fulfillment of prophecy; the languages used on the day of Pentecost were understood by those who were addressed. Hence, the first employment of the gift of "other tongues" was proof that the gospel was the fulfillment of Jewish prophecy.

The second reference to the speaking of tongues is found in Acts 10: 46. "For they heard them speak with tongues, and magnify God." This was another supernatural occurrence; it was an exercise of the gift of speaking in tongues. The household of Cornelius was an assembly of Gentiles. Peter had hardly finished preaching to the company assembled when the Holy Spirit came upon them. On the day of Pentecost the gift of speaking with tongues was used by the Jews in the presence of Jews and proselytes only, but here it is used by Gentiles in the presence of Jewish Christians. This is just the reverse of the conditions on Pentecost. This use of the speaking of tongues seems to have been given in proof that God approved the giving of the gospel to the Gentiles. The kingdom of heaven is to be composed of citizens of a new race; it is to include the Gentiles. The speaking with tongues at Jerusalem by the apostles and the household of Cornelius at Caesarea was significantly different; at Pentecost the sign was given to the disciples to convince the unbelieving Jews; in the house of Cornelius the Gentiles speak with other tongues to convince Jewish Christians that the door of the gospel is open to the Gentiles.

Acts 19: 6. "And when Paul had laid his hands upon them, the Holy Spirit came on them; and they spake with tongues, and prophesied." These twelve Ephesian disciples of John the Baptist had been baptized with John's baptism unto repentance; but when Paul preached to them Jesus, they believed and were baptized in the name of the Lord Jesus with the baptism of the commission. The gift of tongues here was for the purpose of prophesying, or, as we would say, of preaching. The gift of tongues to the twelve Ephesians was in proof of their acceptance to God, which emphasized that John's baptism at that date was not valid. For some reason, we are not told why, these twelve were used to convince others of the importance of being baptized "into the name of the Lord Jesus."

1 Cor. 12: 1-10, 30. In this chapter Paul discusses nine spiritual gifts; in this chapter and chapter 14, we have the fullest discussion of the gift of tongues that may be found in the New Testament. "There are diversities of gifts, but the same Spirit." He enumerated as gifts of the Spirit the following: "The word of wisdom," "the word of knowledge," "faith," "healings," "workings of miracles," "prophecy," "discernings of spirits," "divers kinds of tongues," and "the interpretation of tongues." The "tongues" are different languages or dialects; they are not confused jabberings, gibberish chatterings, or indistinct and unintelligible gabblings as we hear manifested today by those who claim to "speak with tongues." The gift of tongues here is only one of the gifts of the Holy Spirit. The "tongues" might be one language in one place and another language in another place; the gift of tongues was not always the same, and was always subject to interpretations. This gift was not to be exercised unless there was an interpreter present. In verse 30 it is clearly stated that the gift of tongues is not, neither was it ever intended to be, universal in the church. It was a specific gift to

a limited number. "Do all speak with tongues?" This is a denial of the universality of the gift; it was a limited gift to a limited few; it passed when all other spiritual gifts ceased.

1 Cor. 14: 2, 26-32. The use of the gift of tongues is further limited, when the language employed is unknown to any person present, to communion with God, and it has significance only between the speaker and God, to whom he speaks. "For he that speaketh in a tongue speaketh not unto men, but unto God; for no man understandeth; but in the spirit he speaketh mysteries." (1 Cor. 14: 2.) Again, "he that speaketh in a tongue edifieth himself; but he that prophesieth edifieth the church." (Verse 4.) In verses 26-32 Paul discounts and discourages the use of "tongues" unless there is an interpreter. This shows that the gift of speaking with tongues was of secondary importance and should be carefully guarded lest it become a snare and a temptation to the one to whom it is given; it should never be used to confuse the public worship nor anyone not in worship. It was a vain accomplishment to speak with tongues if the interpreter was not present. "Tongues are for a sign, not to them that believe, but to the unbelieving: but prophesying is for a sign, not to the unbelieving, but to them that believe." (1 Cor. 14: 22.) Paul further regulates this gift and points out the confusion that might result from it. He said: "If therefore the whole church be assembled together and all speak with tongues, and there come in men unlearned or unbelieving, will they not say that ye are mad? But if all prophesy, and there come in one unbelieving or unlearned, he is reproved by all, he is judged by all; the secrets of his heart are made manifest; and so he will fall down on his face and worship God, declaring that God is among you indeed." (1 Cor. 14: 23-25.)

III. ABUSE OF THE GIFT

The gift of speaking in tongues was abused in the church at Corinth. Paul rebuked those who so abused this gift. "The spirits of the prophets are subject to the prophets." (1 Cor. 14: 32.) The final injunction of the Holy Spirit concerning this gift is: "If any man speaketh in a tongue, let it be by two, or at the most three, and that in turn; and let one interpret: but if there be no interpreter, let him keep silence in the church; and let him speak to himself, and to God." So the confusion which has so often in many places brought reproach upon this gift would be avoided, and God will be exalted if it should be properly used, for "God is not a God of confusion, but of peace." In this way Paul regulates this gift. He has written more to regulate this gift than the other eight gifts mentioned.

There are certain modern cults in religion that claim to have the power of speaking with tongues; they claim to exercise this gift of the Holy Spirit. Their claim is false, as all of these gifts, as we have seen in a former chapter, have ceased. They claim that their speaking with tongues is an evidence of "a second work of grace"; this further work of grace is claimed to be an evidence of a new and higher relation to Christ; it is made a test of one's spiritual growth and one's fellowship with Christ. Those who make this modern claim are often found to throw themselves prostrate on the floor, and then arise and give a demonstration of the speaking in tongues. No interpreter is present; sometimes they claim that even the speaker does not know what is said, and no one else knows. Even if the claim was true, and they actually exercised the gift of speaking in tongues, they are violating Paul's injunction for them to keep silent if there is not an interpreter present. No modern claimant has ever advanced a single new idea or thought; they are not edified; no one is edified; but God and his truth are blasphemed by such false claims.

The falling prostrate by the seeker is claimed to be a part of the formula for obtaining the gift of speaking in tongues. The public demonstration of altars of seeking and witnessing by tongues has been the occasion of confusion and of disgrace. Many contend that they are unable to control even themselves, their tongues, or the Spirit moving upon them. Paul teaches otherwise: "Let all things be done unto edifying." (1 Cor. 14: 26.) These modern teachers and claimants of this gift do not edify anyone; hence, they violate this Scripture, even if they possess the spiritual gift of speaking in tongues. Again, Paul said: "And the spirits of the prophets are subject to the prophets; for God is not a God of confusion, but of peace." (Verse 32.) Hence, Paul through the Holy Spirit has hedged the use of the gift of speaking with tongues about and placed limitations upon the use of this gift, which are violated by every claimant in modern times of this gift. Usually those who make the claim to exercise this gift are ignorant people; they are not only ignorant of the Bible, but ignorant of the common affairs of life. They have not added anything new to the teachings of the Holy Spirit; they have not brought an unbeliever to Christ. They have deceived some by their claims; those who are deceived are in their own class of illiterates. In spite of their illiteracy, they assume a superiority complex and claim to know more than anyone else; they claim to have some special marks of favor from the Holy Spirit. Needless to say they are deceived or they are deceivers; there is no truth to their claims.

The Holy Spirit gave power to the early disciples to speak "with other tongues." This was one phase or aspect of the work of the Holy Spirit. There was a definite use for the speaking with tongues; like all other miracles, it was to confirm the truth spoken by the inspired speaker. We now have this word confirmed and a record of it; there is no further need for the speaking of tongues any more than there is a need to heal the cripple, open the eyes of the blind, cause the dumb to speak, and to raise the dead. All these miracles have ceased.

HOLY SPIRIT AND WORD OF GOD

INTRODUCTION.

Holy Spirit has various relations to God, to Christ; these are important; his relation to word of God.

I. **HOLY SPIRIT USED WORDS.**

  1. Prophets spoke by Holy Spirit. (2 Sam. 23: 1, 2; Isa. 1: 1, 2.)
  2. Holy men spoke by Holy Spirit. (2 Pet. 1: 21.)
  3. Holy Spirit speaks through New Testament. (1 Tim. 4: 1.)
  4. Holy Spirit spoke through apostles. (Matt. 10: 20; Acts 2: 4.)
  5. Holy Spirit took words of Christ. (John 16: 13-15.)

II. **DISPENSATION OF HOLY SPIRIT.**

  1. Law spiritual. (Rom. 7: 14.)
  2. Teaching spiritual. (1 Cor. 9: 11.)
  3. Our service spiritual. (Rom. 12: 1.)
  4. Christians a spiritual house. (1 Pet. 2: 5.)
  5. Spiritual food. (1 Cor. 10: 3.)
  6. Spiritual milk. (1 Pet. 2: 3.)

III. **SPIRIT AND WORD INSEPARABLE.**

  1. Words, spirit, and life. (John 6: 63.)
  2. Word living and active. (Heb. 4: 12.)

IV. **IDENTICAL IN ACTION.**

		Holy Spirit	*Word*
1.	In creation	Gen. 1: 2; Job 33: 4	Heb. 1: 3; 2 Pet. 3: 5
2.	Gives life	2 Cor. 3: 6	James 1: 18
3.	Born of	John 3: 8	1 Pet. 1: 23-25
4.	Salvation	Tit. 3: 5	James 1: 21
5.	Sanctification	1 Cor. 6: 11; 2 Thess. 2: 13	John 17: 17
6.	Dwells in	Rom. 8: 11	Col. 3: 16
7.	Spirit is truth	1 John 5: 7	John 17: 17
8.	Power. of	Rom. 15: 13	Heb. 1: 3

HOLY SPIRIT AND WORD OF GOD

"Our gospel came not unto you in word only, but also in power, and in the Holy Spirit, and in much assurance." (1 Thess. 1: 5.)

The third member of the Godhead sustains about the same relations to all things in the universe that God and Christ do; his relation to God is expressed as a member of the Godhead. We have seen that the Holy Spirit had a part in the creation of the material universe; the Holy Spirit perpetuates or continues the material universe through the laws given for its government. We have also observed in a former chapter the relation of the Holy Spirit to Christ. We only know his relation to God and to Christ in so far as it is revealed to us. No interest is manifested here or elsewhere in any speculative theory about the mysteries of the Holy Spirit in conjunction with God and Christ. Much space is given in "theology" to the speculations about the relation of the different members of the Godhead; it is unfortunate that men have spent so much time in formulating theories about these relationships. Such questions respecting them never can be answered, and they are of no moment, or else they would have been clearly revealed to us in the Bible.

It is important to view the Holy Spirit in all his relations that are revealed in the Bible. This is especially true with respect to his relation to all that pertains to the redemption of man. The Bible was written because man needed to know and to have God's wisdom on these things. The relation of the Holy Spirit and the word of God is an important one. Perhaps no relation is more clearly demonstrated in the Bible than the relation of the Holy Spirit and the word of God. We are to see that the Holy Spirit has his instrumentalities or means by which he works in the salvation of souls and the redemption of the race of man. God was not limited in exercising his power in the creation of the material universe; however, he chose Christ, the Word, as his agent in the creation. He has exercised the power of his *fiat* at times, but more often has he worked through divinely chosen agents. The Christ while on earth chose to work through the

use of agents.   He chose his apostles and trained them for work
in saving the world.   The Holy Spirit came to earth and has
done his work through divinely chosen agents.   The most common instrumentality through which the Holy Spirit works is the
truth of God; he works through no other agent in the conversion
of sinners and the sanctification of saints.   The relationship of the
Holy Spirit to the word of God should be clearly understood;
much of the teachings of the word of God may be easily misinterpreted if this is not clear to religious teachers.   Many theories
concerning the direct operation of the Spirit have arisen from a
lack of understanding the relationship existing between the Holy
Spirit and the word of God.

I. Holy Spirit Used Words

Since the Holy Spirit is to work *through* man and *for* man,
he has chosen to use words.   The vehicle of thought from the
mind of the Spirit to the mind of man is words.   The formula of
the prophets was: "Thus saith the Lord."   The prophets spoke
through the Holy Spirit.   What Jehovah said is the word of
God; this was spoken by the prophets through the Holy Spirit.
"Now these are the last words of David.   David the son of
Jesse saith, And the man who was raised on high saith, The
anointed of the God of Jacob, and the sweet psalmist of Israel: the
Spirit of Jehovah spake by me, and his word was upon my
tongue." (2 Sam. 23: 1, 2.)   Again David said: "For ever,
O Jehovah, thy word is settled in heaven."   (Psalm 119: 89.)
"The vision of Isaiah the son of Amoz, which he saw concerning
Judah and Jerusalem. . . . Hear, O heavens, and give ear, O
earth; for Jehovah hath spoken." (Isa. 1: 1, 2.)   The word
of God as an instrument of the Holy Spirit is at one time a lamp
to the feet of the wanderer, and a light shining in a dark place;
then again it is a voice from heaven that cries at the gates of the
cities; it is also the rod of God's mouth and the song of the weary
pilgrim; again, it is an incorruptible seed and the engrafted word.
Using martial language it is the sword of the Spirit, sharper than
any two-edged sword; it is a helmet, a shield, a buckler.   Goads,
nails, fire, a hammer are its symbols; it breaks the flinty rock
and is mighty to the pulling down of strongholds.

The prophets in Old Testament times spoke by the Holy Spirit. "For no prophecy ever came by the will of man: but men spake from God, being moved by the Holy Spirit." (2 Pet. 1: 21.) Jesus, speaking to the Jews, said: "David himself said in the Holy Spirit." (Mark 12: 36.) Peter, later speaking to those who had assembled in the upper room, said: "Brethren, it was needful that the scripture should be fulfilled, which the Holy Spirit spake before by the mouth of David concerning Judas, who was guide to them that took Jesus." (Acts 1: 16.) Paul said to the Jews who had assembled in Rome to hear him: "Well spake the Holy Spirit through Isaiah the prophet unto your fathers." (Acts 28: 25.) Hence, the New Testament bears witness through Christ, Peter, and Paul that the Holy Spirit *spoke;* that is, used words through the prophets. The words of the prophets are the words of the Holy Spirit. David, Isaiah, Jeremiah, Ezekiel, Daniel, and a long catalog of those ancient worthies all spoke by the Holy Spirit; their words were the words of the Holy Spirit.

The Holy Spirit used words in speaking through the New Testament. "But the Spirit saith expressly, that in later times some shall fall away from the faith." (1 Tim. 4: 1.) Here we have the Spirit speaking through Paul to Christians. If the words of the Old Testament are the words of the Holy Spirit, much more are the words of the New Testament. If men spoke by the Holy Spirit before the Holy Spirit came to earth, much more would men speak by the Holy Spirit when he came; or, if men spoke by the Holy Spirit during God's dispensation, much more would they speak by the Holy Spirit during the Spirit's dispensation. Jesus preached by the Spirit (Luke 4: 18); he gave commandment by the Holy Spirit (Acts 1: 2); and forbade his disciples to preach until they should receive the Spirit (Acts 1: 5). He assured his disciples that the Spirit would come and would teach them what to say. "For it is not ye that speak, but the Spirit of your Father that speaketh in you." (Matt. 10: 20.) "Be not anxious beforehand what ye shall speak: but whatsoever shall be given you in that hour, that speak ye; for it is not ye that speak, but the Holy Spirit." (Mark 13: 11.) Hence, the words of the apostles were the words of the Holy Spirit. The apostles received the Holy Spirit on Pentecost and "began to speak with other tongues, as the Spirit gave them utterance." (Acts 2: 4.) Later Paul made the claim for himself that "my speech and my preaching were not in persuasive words of wisdom, but in demonstration of the Spirit and of power: that your faith should not stand in the wisdom of men, but in the power of God." (1 Cor. 2: 4, 5.) Christ declared that the Holy Spirit would come *speaking*. He also predicted what the Holy Spirit would say. "Howbeit when he, the Spirit of truth, is come, he shall guide you into all the truth; for he shall not speak from himself; but what things soever he shall hear, these shall he speak: and he shall declare unto you the things that are to come. He shall glorify me: for he shall take of mine, and shall declare it unto you. All things whatsoever the Father hath are mine: therefore said I, that he taketh of mine, and shall declare it unto you." (John 16: 13-15.) The revelation of God's will that Christ revealed to his apostles was taken up by the Holy Spirit and reiterated through the apostles of the world. The Holy Spirit used the words of Christ in guiding the apostles to preach the gospel to the whole creation.

II. Dispensation of Holy Spirit

Time and again reference has been made to the dispensation of the Holy Spirit. Each member of the Godhead has had his dispensation with man. God's dispensation began with the creation of man and continued until Christ began his personal ministry. The dispensation of Christ began with his baptism and continued until Pentecost; the dispensation of the Holy Spirit began with the first Pentecost after the resurrection of Christ and will continue until Christ comes again. We are living in the dispensation of the Holy Spirit. The laws governing Christians were given by the Holy Spirit; in that sense they are spiritual laws. (Rom. 4: 14.) The teachings of the Holy Spirit as given to Christians are spiritual. (1 Cor. 9: 11.) The service that we render is a spiritual service because it is guided by the Holy Spirit. (Rom. 12: 1.)

The church is a spiritual kingdom; it is called a spiritual house. "Ye also, as living stones, are built up a spiritual house, to be a holy priesthood, to offer up spiritual sacrifices, acceptable to God through Jesus Christ." (1 Pet. 2: 5.) Not only are Christians called a "spiritual house," but they live upon "spiritual food" and "spiritual drink." (1 Cor. 10: 3, 4.) As babes in Christ young Christians are to live upon the "spiritual milk." Everything pertaining to the Christian life may be designated as being spiritual. Christians live under the dispensation of the Holy Spirit, governed by spiritual laws, and guided by spiritual teaching; their service is a spiritual service and their lives sustained by spiritual food and spiritual milk; they constitute a spiritual house and are in the spiritual kingdom.

III. Spirit and Word Inseparable

So far as the instructions of the Holy Spirit concern man, the Holy Spirit and the word of God are inseparable. Jesus said: "It is the spirit that giveth life; the flesh profiteth nothing: the words that I have spoken unto you are spirit, and are life." (John 6: 63.) The Holy Spirit and the word of God are inseparable in the conversion of the sinner. "Of his own will he brought us forth by the word of truth, that we should be a kind of firstfruits of his creatures." (James 1: 18.) The psalmist declared: "The law of Jehovah is perfect, restoring the soul." (Psalm 19: 7.) The entire burden of Psalm 119 is a tribute to the word of God as an instrument to accomplish God's purposes. Paul declared: "For I am not ashamed of the gospel: for it is the power of God unto salvation to every one that believeth." (Rom. 1: 16.) The word of God is declared: "For the word of God is living, and active, and sharper than any two-edged sword, and piercing even to the dividing of soul and spirit, of both joints and marrow, and quick to discern the thoughts and intents of the heart." (Heb. 4: 12.) The Holy Spirit has never dispensed of the agency of truth in renewing the hearts of men and in guiding Christians in their every walk of life.

IV. Identical in Action

The Holy Spirit and the word of God are inseparable and also identical in their action on the hearts of men. Whatever is affirmed of the Spirit in the redemption of man is also affirmed of the word of God. Some of the important actions of the Holy Spirit are here listed with scriptural reference showing that the same actions are affirmed of the word of God. The scriptural references for the action of the Holy Spirit are placed in the first column and those of the word of God in the third column, with the action placed in the middle column.

Holy Spirit	Action	Word of God
Gen. 1: 2; Job 33: 4	In creation	Heb. 1: 3; 2 Pet. 3: 5
2 Cor. 3: 6	Gives life	James 1: 18
John 3: 8	Born of	1 Pet. 1: 23-25
Tit. 3: 5	Salvation	James 1: 21
1 Cor. 6: 11; 2 Thess. 2: 13	Sanctification	John 17: 17
Rom. 8: 11	Dwells in	Col. 3: 16
1 John 5: 7	Spirit is truth	John 17: 17
Rom. 15: 13	Power of	Heb. 1: 3

Whatever is declared of the Holy Spirit is also declared of the word of God. The Holy Spirit was present in creation and so was the word of God; by divine fiat God brought into existence the material creation. The Spirit gives life and the word of God gives life; we are born of the Spirit and born of the word of God. There are not two births, but one. We are saved by the Holy Spirit; we are saved by the word of God; there are not two salvations mentioned here, but it is one action; the Holy Spirit saves through the word of God. Christians are sanctified through the Holy Spirit; they are sanctified through the word of truth; the Holy Spirit dwells in Christians; the word of Christ dwells in us richly. The Spirit is the Spirit of truth; the word of God is the truth. There is power in the Holy Spirit; there is power in the word of God. The Holy Spirit in no instance has dispensed with the truth, whether it be in the new birth or in the sanctification of saints. No man can intelligently and successfully affirm himself to be conscious of a divine fiat of the Holy Spirit that is not expressed by the word of God. The power of the Holy Spirit, both in conversion and sanctification, is so blended with the force of the word of God that no intelligent mind can separate them. No one can logically express an article of faith that does not come through the word of God. The Holy Spirit and the word of God are inseparable.

The Holy Spirit is the Spirit of truth; he is given this title because he has revealed the truth to man and uses the truth of the gospel to convert and save man. The Holy Spirit is never called a teacher in the Bible, but in many Scriptures his functions as a teacher are clearly indicated. While the word "teacher" is never used as applied to the Holy Spirit, yet the verb "teach" and similar expressions are used. Jesus said that the Holy Spirit would "guide you into all the truth" (John 16: 13), and "he shall declare unto you the things that are to come. He shall glorify me: for he shall take of mine, and shall declare it unto you." All these expressions describe the function of the Holy Spirit as a teacher of the word of God. He has all the qualifications of a teacher, and has the truth which man needs to be taught.

It seems natural that since the Holy Spirit is the author of the Bible, or that the Bible was given by the Holy Spirit, he is also the best interpreter of it. The author of a book is best prepared to give the meaning of any paragraph that he has written; so the Holy Spirit may interpret the Bible. The Holy Spirit teaches by· revealing the truth that pertains to the salvation of souls and the redemption of the race. The Holy Spirit is called the Spirit of truth (John 14: 17; 15: 26; 16: 13; 1 John 4: 6); this means the truth as it is revealed in Christ Jesus—the truth concerning his becoming a man, his life and teaching, his death, resurrection, ascension, glorification, mediatorial reign, his teaching concerning the church, its mission, ministry, message, everything which he taught concerning man, his duty, and destiny.

CHAPTER X

HOLY SPIRIT IN CONVERSION

INTRODUCTION.

This another mooted question; the battleground of religious dispute; no conversion without having begun, continued, and consummated by Holy Spirit.

I. MEANING OF CONVERSION.

1. Names for conversion.
    a. Those given by man.
    b. Those given by the Bible.
        (1) Born of water and Spirit. (John 3: 5.)
        (2) A new heart. (Ezek. 36: 26.)
        (3) Quickened with Christ. (Eph. 2: 5.)

2. Necessity of conversion.
    a. Must turn to God.
    b. Cannot be saved without it.

3. A change or turning.
    a. A change or purification of heart by faith. (Acts 15: 9.)
    b. Change of life by repentance. (Luke 13: 5.)
    c. Change of state or relation by baptism. (Rom. 6: 3; Gal. 3: 27.)

II. HOW HOLY SPIRIT CONVERTS.

1 Through word of God. (Psalm 19: 7; John 6: 44, 45.)
2. By the gospel. (Rom. 1: 16; 1 Cor. 4: 14, 15.)
3. By word of truth. (James 1: 18; 1 Pet. 1: 22, 23.)

III. EXAMPLES OF CONVERSION.

1. The Pentecostians. (Acts 2.)
2. The Samaritans. (Acts 8.)
3. The eunuch. (Acts 8.)
4. Saul of Tarsus. (Acts 9.)
5. Cornelius. (Acts 10.)
6. The jailer. (Acts 16.)
7. The Corinthians. (Acts 18.)

HOLY SPIRIT IN CONVERSION

"But according to his mercy he saved us, through the washing of regeneration and renewing of the Holy Spirit, which he poured out upon us richly, through Jesus Christ our Saviour." (Tit. 3: 5, 6.)

This brings us to another mooted question with respect to the Holy Spirit. Much theorizing and speculation have been done with respect to the work of the Holy Spirit in conversion. So much superstition has clustered around conversion that it is difficult to get people to receive the teachings of the New Testament on this question. There are many who cling to their presentiments, their irrational impressions, their apocryphal revelations, their ridiculous prodigies, and their outrages upon common sense and scriptural teaching until they are blinded to the simple teaching of the Holy Spirit on the subject of conversion. Many are ready to relate their marvelous excitements that have no significance and no foundation except in their own imaginations and claim such as conversion. They are deluded; they deceive themselves and others.

Many have been the debates on the work of the Holy Spirit in conversion; extreme claims and foolish experiences have been given as a proxy for conversion. There is but little difference among religious people about how to live the Christian life, but there is a wide difference as to how people become Christians. Some say that we become Christians at one point and others at another point; some say that the Holy Spirit operates one way in conversion and others in another way. What is the truth pertaining to conversion? Let it be understood now that since the church was established there has never been a genuine case of conversion that was not begun, carried on, and consummated by the Holy Spirit. The discussions have been on *how* the Holy Spirit works in conversion; all admit that the Holy Spirit has something to do with conversion. It is wise to pause at this point long enough to inquire the meaning of conversion.

I. Meaning of Conversion

With the understanding that the Holy Spirit operates upon the heart of the sinner in conversion, we proceed to investigate the Bible meaning of conversion. There are different names given to the process called conversion. Man has invented and applied names to that which he calls conversion. Sometimes it is called "joining the church," "getting religion"; these convey human conceptions of conversion. The Bible also calls it "born of water and the Spirit," "washing of regeneration and renewing of the Holy Spirit," "made us alive together with Christ" (Eph. 2: 5), "obedient to the faith," "added unto the Lord."

Man is a sinner; his sins have come between him and God; by sin man lost that primal state and relation with God. Christ came to earth to re-establish that broken relationship; his work was to redeem and restore, to bring man back to his former state and relation with God. Christ's mission presupposes a disturbance in the relationship between God and man, a dislocation and a degeneracy through apostasy. Man is lost; he needs a Savior. He must be converted to God. The absolute necessity of conversion is clearly set forth in the New Testament; man cannot be saved until he turns from his sins. "Except ye turn, and become as little children, ye shall in no wise enter into the kingdom of heaven." (Matt. 18: 3.) So long as man loves the pleasures of sin and continues in the practice of sin, he cannot be saved. The necessity of conversion lies partly in man and partly in God. Man is depraved by sin and cannot have fellowship with God in such a condition. God's nature is such that he cannot fellowship sin; hence, from the nature of man in his sinful condition and the nature of God in his holiness, we view the necessity of conversion.

Conversion is a turning about; it is turning from sin and turning to God; there is a turning *from* something and a turning *to* God in conversion. Paul wrote: "For they themselves report concerning us what manner of entering in we had unto you; and how ye turned unto God from idols, to serve a living and true God." (1 Thess. 1: 9.) These Christians at Thessalonica *turned* first from their sins and idolatry and then *turned* unto God; they were converted. There are three important and basal changes wrought in conversion. The first change is a purification of heart. This is brought about by faith. The Holy Spirit said through Peter that God "made no distinction between us and them, cleansing their hearts by faith." (Acts 15: 9.) God made no distinction in the conversion of the Jews and Gentiles; their hearts were cleansed by faith. Later Peter wrote: "Seeing ye have purified your souls in your obedience to the truth." (1 Pet. 1: 22.) By faith the heart is purified. The second change that is wrought in conversion is the change of life; this is done by repentance. "Except ye repent, ye shall all likewise perish." (Luke 13: 5.) The goodness of God leads to repentance, and godly sorrow precedes repentance. The life is not changed until it ceases to love and practice sin. A repentance brings about a change in mind and results in a reformation of life. The third change in conversion is a change of state or relation. This is done by baptism. One is baptized *into* Christ. "All we who were baptized into Christ Jesus were baptized into his death." (Rom. 6: 3.) "For as many of you as were baptized into Christ did put on Christ." (Gal. 3: 27.) Baptism changes the state or relation. With a purified heart and a changed life one is ready to be translated into Christ Jesus; conversion includes all of these changes. In conversion there is produced a new attitude, new emotions, new actions, a new creature. What part has the Holy Spirit in these three changes?

II. How Holy Spirit Converts

One of the functions of the Holy Spirit is to convert sinners. How does he do this? It has been observed that the Holy Spirit in the redemption of man uses the truth of God. The Holy Spirit and the word of God are never separate in conversion and sanctification. The instrumentality of truth in conversion is a fact abundantly substantiated in the New Testament. The instrumentality of truth in conversion is invariable; the same truth is used in every conversion by the Holy Spirit. This is the same that all are converted by the Holy Spirit with the same instrumentality of truth, and the same truth used by the Holy Spirit in every conversion. While there is no conversion without the Holy Spirit, there is no operation of the Holy Spirit in conversion independent of God's word. "The law of Jehovah is perfect, restoring the soul." (Psalm 19: 7.) No one can come to God who is not converted; no one can come to God except the Holy Spirit brings him. How does the Holy Spirit bring people to God? "No man can come to me, except the Father that sent me draw him: and I will raise him up in the last day. It is written in the prophets, And they shall all be taught of God. Every one that hath heard from the Father, and hath learned, cometh unto me." (John 6: 44, 45.) No one can come to God except he be converted; no one can be converted except by the Holy Spirit; the Holy Spirit uses the truth of God in converting people; hence, when people hear and learn of God, they can come to him. They must be taught of God before they can come to him; they must be taught by the Holy Spirit in order to come to God; the Holy Spirit uses the gospel or the truth of God in teaching people.

The gospel is declared to be the power of God unto salvation. "For I am not ashamed of the gospel: for it is the power of God unto salvation to every one that believeth." (Rom. 1: 16.) The Holy Spirit wrote through Paul to the church at Corinth and said: "For though ye have ten thousand tutors in Christ, yet have ye not many fathers; for in Christ Jesus I begat you through the gospel." (1 Cor. 4: 15.) The gospel was the means by which the Holy Spirit begot these Christians; there is no difference in their conversion and the conversion of one today. The Holy Spirit used the gospel in converting Christians then, and he uses the gospel now in converting people. This is why it is declared to be the power of God unto salvation. Again emphasizing further the use of the word of God in conversion, James wrote: "Of his own will he brought us forth by the word of truth, that we should be a kind of firstfruits of his creatures." (James 1: 18.) Peter emphasizes the same thought when he wrote: "Having been begotten again, not of corruptible seed, but of incorruptible, through the word of God, which liveth and abideth." (1 Pet. 1: 23.) From these Scriptures we learn that "this is the word of good tidings which was preached unto you." (1 Pet. 1: 25.) Furthermore, it is clear that the Holy Spirit always operates upon the heart of the sinner in conversion through the truth, and that truth is the gospel.

The New Testament does not teach that the Holy Spirit operates directly upon the heart of the sinner; there is no teaching that the Holy Spirit comes *directly, immediately, independently* into the hearts of sinners and converts them.   There is no case on record in the New Testament where anyone was converted who did not first hear the truth, believe in Christ, repent of sin, and was baptized into Christ.   The gospel is preached and people hear the gospel; they believe it.   "So belief cometh of hearing, and hearing by the word of Christ."   (Rom. 10: 17.)   "The word of God" is "the sword of the Spirit."   (Eph. 6: 17.)   The Spirit still wields and thrusts this sword into the heart of the sinner in conversion.   Jesus taught: "Ye shall know the truth, and the truth shall make you free."   (John 8: 32.)   If the theory of the *direct* influence of the Holy Spirit in conversion is true, why are not all converted?   If the sinner càn do nothing, and must wait until the Holy Spirit comes directly into his heart and converts him, are not the Holy Spirit, God, and Christ all responsible if one is not converted?   How can a sinner be responsible for his unsaved state, if the Holy Spirit without any means independently and miraculously must convert him?   It is pious nonsense to talk about the Holy Spirit's converting one independent of the truth.

III. EXAMPLES OF CONVERSION

All the examples in the New Testament of conversion reveal the fact that the gospel as God's power to save is heard, believed, and obeyed.   The conversion of about three thousand on Pentecost as recorded in Acts 2 emphasizes that the gospel was preached by the Holy Spirit through Peter, that the people heard, believed, and obeyed.   They were thus converted and added to the church.   When the disciples were scattered from Jerusalem as recorded in Acts 8, Philip "went down to the city of Samaria, and proclaimed unto them the Christ."   (Acts 8: 5.)   The people "gave heed with one accord unto the things that were spoken by Philip, when they heard, and saw the signs which he did."   (Verse 6.)   "When they believed Philip preaching good tidings concerning the kingdom of God and the name of Jesus Christ, they were baptized, both men and women."   (Verse 12.)   Here we see that they heard the gospel, believed it, and obeyed it; they were converted.

A typical case of conversion is recorded in Acts 8, known as the conversion of the Ethiopian eunuch. He was returning from Jerusalem, "sitting in his chariot, and was reading the prophet Isaiah." (Verse 28.) The Holy Spirit directed Philip to "go near, and join thyself to this chariot. And Philip ran to him, and heard him reading Isaiah the prophet, and said, Understandest thou what thou readest?" The eunuch answered: "How can I, except some one shall guide me?" He then asked Philip to "come up and sit with him." The eunuch asked Philip the meaning of the prophecy which he was reading. "And Philip opened his mouth, and beginning from this scripture, preached unto him Jesus." (Verse 35.) The eunuch heard, believed, and was baptized. He went on his way rejoicing as a converted man. Again we see that the Holy Spirit used the gospel, the word of God, in the conversion of the eunuch.

Saul of Tarsus is another typical case of conversion. There are three records in the book of Acts of the conversion of Saul; they are found in Acts 9, 22, and 26. There are certain miraculous elements that accompanied Saul's conversion; these miraculous elements were not a part of his conversion; they were not essential to his conversion; they were for an entirely different purpose. Saul heard Jesus; he was convinced that he was the Christ; he repented of his sins; he was baptized. Saul was converted. The Holy Spirit used the gospel or the truth of God in his conversion. In the case of Cornelius as recorded in Acts 10, Peter preached the gospel to the household of Cornelius; they heard the gospel; they believed it; they repented of their sins; they were baptized into Christ. They were converted the same as all others. The conversion of the jailer as recorded in Acts 16 is cumulative evidence that the Holy Spirit used the truth of God or the gospel of Christ in converting the jailer. Paul and Silas preached the gospel to him; he believed it with all of his house; they were penitent of their sins; they were all baptized into Christ. They were converted. Again, in Acts 18, we have a record of the conversion of the Corinthians. The brief record states that "many of the Corinthians hearing believed, and were baptized." (Acts 18:8.) No one would deny that these Corinthians were converted; they, like all the rest of the cases recorded in the New Testament, heard the truth, believed and obeyed it. The Holy Spirit operated on the hearts of all of these through the truth of God. They were all converted by the Holy Spirit.

The preaching of the gospel worked a wonderful effect on the city of Corinth. Of course it produced this effect only on those who heard it. Corinth was a wicked city; it was given to idolatry. The truth of the gospel was preached to them; they heard this truth; it convinced them; they believed what was preached; "so belief cometh of hearing, and hearing by the word of Christ." (Rom. 10: 17.) They not only heard, believed the gospel, but they obeyed the commands of the gospel; they repented of their sins and were baptized into Christ. The Corinthians did the same thing that all others were commanded to do; they were taught the truth by the Holy Spirit through Paul. As a result, a church of Christ was established in this idolatrous city. The church at Corinth and all other churches of New Testament times were the results of the work of the Holy Spirit.

CHAPTER XI

INDWELLING OF HOLY SPIRIT

INTRODUCTION.

Holy Spirit converts sinners; dwells in Christians; comforted the apostles; abides as a Comforter.

I. SOME DISTINCTIONS.

1. Indwelling not incarnation—different from conception of Christ.
2. Not omnipresence of God—Holy Spirit, like God, everywhere. (Psalm 139: 7, 8.)
3. Not spiritual gifts—these belonged to early church.
4. Not word of God—New Testament instrument which Holy Spirit employs; should not mistake *instrument* for the *agent*.

II. CHRISTIANS HAVE HOLY SPIRIT.

1. Holy Spirit given to the obedient. (Acts 5: 32.)
2. Holy Spirit sent into hearts. (Gal. 4: 6.)
3. Bears witness with our spirits. (Rom. 8: 16.)
4. Must have Spirit to be Christ's. (Rom. 8: 9.)
5. Promised to dwell in us. (Rom. 8: 11.)
6. Spirit dwells in Christians. (1 Cor. 3: 16; 2 Tim. 1: 14.)

III. HOW HOLY SPIRIT DWELLS IN CHRISTIANS.

1. How our spirit dwells in our body.
2. God dwells in us. (2 Cor. 6: 16; 1 John 4: 12, 15.)
3. Christ dwells in us. (Eph. 3: 17; Col. 3: 16.)
4. How do God and Christ dwell in us? (Gal. 3: 2.)
5. Neither dwells personally in us.
6. Likewise Holy Spirit. (1 Cor. 3: 16; James 4: 5.)
7. Holy Spirit dwells in us through his agent, the word.

IV. EXAMPLES OF INDWELLING OF HOLY SPIRIT.

1. Miraculous indwelling.
   a. Five Scriptures of "full of the Spirit." (Luke 4: 1; John 3: 34; Acts 6: 5; 7: 55; 11: 24.)
   b. Only three persons.
      (1) Jesus. (Luke 4: 1.)
      (2) Stephen. (Acts 6: 5; 7: 55.)
      (3) Barnabas. (Acts 11: 24.)
   c. "Filled with the Spirit."
      (1) Zacharias.
      (2) Elisabeth.
      (3) John the Baptist.
      (4) Peter.
      (5) Paul and others.
2. Ordinary measure of Holy Spirit.

INDWELLING OF HOLY SPIRIT

"Know ye not that ye are a temple of God, and that the Spirit of God dwelleth in you?" (1 Cor. 3: 16.)

"But ye are not in the flesh but in the Spirit, if so be that the Spirit of God dwelleth in you." (Rom. 8: 9.)

It has clearly been demonstrated that we live under the dispensation of the Holy Spirit; that the church is a spiritual kingdom, that Christians are subjects of a spiritual law and live upon spiritual food. The Holy Spirit operates in conversion through the truth of God. Every phase of man's experience in the Christian religion is begun, carried on, and completed by the Holy Spirit. The Holy Spirit does not leave one when the act of conversion is completed; he remains with Christians. He dwells in God's people. God uses means in the preaching of the gospel; faithful men are commanded to teach the word of God to others. The Holy Spirit, both in conversion and in sanctification, uses the truth of God as an instrument or agent for his work. "Sanctify them in the truth: thy word is truth." (John 17: 17.) Christians are encouraged to "grow in the grace and knowledge of our Lord and Saviour Jesus Christ." (2 Pet. 3: 18.) Newborn babes are encouraged to "long for the spiritual milk which is without guile," that they "may grow thereby unto salvation." (1 Pet. 2: 2.) Conversion is followed by sanctification; both are accomplished by the Holy Spirit through the word of God.

The Holy Spirit was promised to the apostles as a guide and a comforter. Jesus said just before his crucifixion: "I will pray the Father, and he shall give you another Comforter, that he may be with you for ever, even the Spirit of truth." (John 14: 16, 17.) Again he said: "Howbeit when he, the Spirit of truth, is come, he shall guide you into all the truth." (John 16: 13.) When the Holy Spirit came, he was to remain on earth; his dispensation began when the dispensation of Christ ended. It should be kept in mind that the sanctification of saints is the work of the Holy Spirit; no one can sanctify himself in the sense of a process affecting his spiritual life more than one can save himself. It should be

remembered that the Holy Spirit and the word of God are inseparable in the conversion of sinners and the sanctification of saints.
The Holy Spirit comforts God's people through the hope and
promises of God which are revealed in the word of God. All of
life's details, so far as Christians are concerned, need no other
wisdom, guidance, and comfort than that which are written in
the book of God.

I. SOME DISTINCTIONS

The indwelling of the Holy Spirit should be made clear before
we proceed to a further discussion of it; there are certain distinctions that should be observed in order for the subject to be clear
in the mind of the reader. The indwelling of the Holy Spirit is
one thing and the "incarnation" or the manifestation of God in the
flesh in the person of Christ is another thing. Furthermore, it
is to be distinguished from the "omnipresence of God." "Whither
shall I go from thy Spirit? or whither shall I flee from thy presence? If I ascend up into heaven, thou art there: if I make my
bed in Sheol, behold, thou art there. If I take the wings of the
morning, and dwell in the uttermost parts of the sea; even there
shall thy hand lead me, and thy right hand shall hold me."
(Psalm 139: 7-10.) God is omnipresent and the Holy Spirit in
his dispensation has the characteristic of omnipresence, but the
omnipresence of the Holy Spirit is one thing and his dwelling in
Christians is another thing.

Moreover, the indwelling of the Holy Spirit in Christians is to
be distinguished from "spiritual gifts," which belonged to the
early church. Those miraculous gifts which were used to confirm the preaching of the gospel passed with the infancy of the
church. However, the Holy Spirit abides; he remains with
Christians. There is a wide difference between the miraculous
gifts of the Holy Spirit and the indwelling of the Spirit. A
further distinction should be made between the word of God and
the indwelling of the Holy Spirit. The word of God, the New
Testament, the word of truth, is the instrument which the Holy
Spirit employs. We should not mistake the *instrument* for the
agent; it would be folly to make no distinction between the instrument of a man that he may use in his work and the man himself.

Perhaps some have made the gross error in concluding that the indwelling of the Holy Spirit is nothing more than the presence of the word of God in the mind or memory of the Christian. It may be that we cannot tell the difference so that others may see or understand it; however, there is a difference between our words and our spirits. In like manner there is a difference in the Holy Spirit and the words of the Holy Spirit.

II. Christians Have Holy Spirit

The New Testament abundantly teaches that Christians have the Holy Spirit. Peter said: "We are witnesses of these things; and so is the Holy Spirit, whom God hath given to them that obey him." (Acts 5: 32.) Christ had said: "But this spake he of the Spirit, which they that believed on him were to receive: for the Spirit was not yet given; because Jesus was not yet glorified." (John 7: 39.) The world cannot receive the Holy Spirit (John 14: 17); he comes to those who obey the gospel; those who love God and keep his commandments are given the Holy Spirit. The believer owes his salvation to the Holy Spirit. Christians are called the temple of the Holy Spirit. A group of Christians is called the temple of God and the individual Christian is called the temple of God. The Holy Spirit dwells in the temple of God. As the presence of God dwelt in the ancient tabernacle and the temple, so the Holy Spirit dwells in the church, the temple of God; in like manner he dwells in each faithful member of the church. "Know ye not that ye are a temple of God, and that the Spirit of God dwelleth in you?" (1 Cor. 3: 16.) Again, we have the language: "Or know ye not that your body is a temple of the Holy Spirit which is in you, which ye have from God? and ye are not your own, for ye were bought with a price: glorify God therefore in your body." (1 Cor. 6: 19, 20.) Paul said to the Christians in Galatia: "Because ye are sons, God sent forth the Spirit of his Son into our hearts, crying, Abba, Father." (Gal. 4: 6.)

The Holy Spirit bears witness with Christians that they are the children of God. "The Spirit himself beareth witness with our spirit, that we are children of God." (Rom. 8: 16.) In fact, if we do not have the Spirit of Christ, we are not Christians.

"But ye are not in the flesh but in the Spirit, if so be that the Spirit of God dwelleth in you. But if any man hath not the Spirit of Christ, he is none of his." (Rom. 8: 9.) Here Paul makes the possession of the Holy Spirit on the part of the believer to be the test of genuine discipleship. The possession of the Holy Spirit brings a feeling of assurance to the Christian; hence, he is an abiding guest with God's people. This feeling of assurance is increased by the communion of the Holy Spirit. "The grace of the Lord Jesus Christ, and the love of God, and the communion of the Holy Spirit, be with you all." (2 Cor. 13: 14.) This was a prayer that Paul prayed for the church at Corinth. In writing to Timothy as a faithful disciple, Paul recognized that the Holy Spirit dwelt in him. "That good thing which was committed unto thee guard through the Holy Spirit which dwelleth in us." (2 Tim. 1: 14.) So it is clear that the Holy Spirit dwells in Christians. It should be remembered that the Holy Spirit is never separated from the word of truth in his work of conversion and sanctification; but how does the Holy Spirit dwell in Christians?

III. How Holy Spirit Dwells in Christians

From the Scriptures quoted above it is clear that the Holy Spirit was promised to Christians, and that he came and was given to those who obeyed the will of God. It is also clear that he dwells in Christians; there are many scriptural references that emphasize the fact of the indwelling of the Holy Spirit; we are now to inquire *how* the Holy Spirit dwells in Christians. It is granted that there is mystery connected with the indwelling of the Holy Spirit. Our spirits dwell in our bodies; we cannot tell how our spirits dwell in our bodies; there is some mystery connected with this. We may know much about our spirits and more about our bodies; we can know that there is a union between the spirit and the body. We know when the spirit leaves the body the death is the result. So with the indwelling of the Holy Spirit in Christians. We do not profess to know all the mysteries connected with the indwelling of the Holy Spirit, yet we can know that he dwells in Christians. We can know what the New Testament teaches about this, but nothing else.

There is a mystery as to how God dwells in us. However, there is the emphatic declaration that he does dwell in us. "And what agreement hath a temple of God with idols? for we are a temple of the living God; even as God said, I will dwell in them, and walk in them; and I will be their God, and they shall be my people." (2 Cor. 6: 16.) Again we have the statement: "No man hath beheld God at any time: if we love one another, God abideth in us, and his love is perfected in us. . . . Whosoever shall confess that Jesus is the Son of God, God abideth in him, and he in God." (1 John 4: 12-15.) It is also said that Christ dwells in us. "That ye may be strengthened with power through his Spirit in the inward man; that Christ may dwell in your hearts through faith." (Eph. 3: 16, 17.) Again, "Let the word of Christ dwell in you richly." (Col. 3: 16.) How does God and Christ dwell in us? This question is answered with the following Scripture: "Whosoever goeth onward and abideth not in the teaching of Christ, hath not God: he that abideth in the teaching, the same hath both the Father and the Son." (2 John 9.) Neither God nor Christ dwells personally in us. God is in his heavens and Christ is at the right hand of God; Christ has ascended back to the Father, so he does not dwell in us in person. He dwells in us through his representative. The Holy Spirit represents God and Christ on the earth. When the Holy Spirit dwells in Christians, God and Christ dwell in them. The Holy Spirit dwells in Christians. "Know ye not that ye are a temple of God, and that the Spirit of God dwelleth in you? If any man destroyeth the temple of God, him shall God destroy; for the temple of God is holy, and such are ye." (1 Cor. 3: 16, 17.) So God dwells in Christians through the Holy Spirit. "Or think ye that the scripture speaketh in vain? Doth the spirit which he made to dwell in us long unto envying?" (James 4: 5.) As God and Christ dwell in us through the Holy Spirit, so the Holy Spirit dwells in us through his agent, the word of truth. "My little children, of whom I am again in travail until Christ be formed in you." (Gal. 4: 19.) For Christ to be "formed" in us is the development of the spiritual life; this life is developed by the Holy Spirit through his agency, the word of God. All growth of the regenerated life and character conforms to the laws of the Holy Spirit in all of his workings. When the word of Christ dwells in Christians, the Holy Spirit dwells in them. The Holy Spirit and the word of God are inseparable; the word of God is the word of the Holy Spirit. "Let the word of Christ dwell in you richly" (Col. 3: 16) is the way for Christ to dwell in us; it is the way for the Holy Spirit to dwell in us.

IV. EXAMPLES OF INDWELLING OF HOLY SPIRIT

The Holy Spirit has dwelt in believers in different measures. In the early days of the church he dwelt in them in a miraculous way. There are five Scriptures which use the expression "full of the Spirit" or its equivalent. They are as follows: Luke 4: 1; John 3: 34; Acts 6: 5; 7: 55; 11: 24. There are only three persons of whom it is affirmed that they were "full of the Holy Spirit." These persons were Jesus (Luke 4: 1), Stephen (Acts 6: 5; 7: 55), and Barnabas (Acts 11: 24). These are the only references in which the adjective "full" is used to indicate the fullness of the Spirit. There are ten passages which use the expression "filled with the Spirit"; these are Luke 1: 15, 41, 67; Acts 4: 8, 31; 6: 3; 9: 17; 13: 9, 52; Eph. 5: 18. The following persons are said to have been filled with the Holy Spirit: Zacharias, Elisabeth, John the Baptist, Peter, and other believers. There are eleven passages in the New Testament in which we find the expression "receiving the Spirit."

It may be difficult to distinguish the difference between all of the terms which are found in the New Testament concerning the indwelling of the Holy Spirit in his miraculous manifestations. It is difficult to distinguish the difference between "being full of the Spirit" and being "filled with the Spirit." These expressions seem to have been limited to the early days of the church. The Samaritan Christians, upon whom Peter and John laid their hands, "received the Holy Spirit"; they had already been converted, and received the Spirit in a miraculous way. The same is true with the household of Cornelius, to whom Peter preached and upon whom "the Holy Spirit fell on all them that heard the word."

There is a sense in which the Holy Spirit in the "ordinary measure" dwelt with all Christians; in this measure he dwells with Christians today. In this sense all of the references to the indwelling of the Spirit in Christians find their application. The more faithful a Christian is the more of the Spirit of Christ he has; the more consecrated Christians are the richer and fuller are the blessings of the Holy Spirit. "I beseech you therefore, brethren, by the mercies of God, to present your bodies a living sacrifice, holy, acceptable to God, which is your spiritual service. And be not fashioned according to this world: but be ye transformed by the renewing of your mind, that ye may prove what is the good and acceptable and perfect will of God." (Rom. 12: 1, 2.) "Seeing that his divine power hath granted unto us all things that pertain unto life and godliness, through the knowledge of him that called us by his own glory and virtue; whereby he hath granted unto us his precious and exceeding great promises; that through these ye may become partakers of the divine nature, having escaped from the corruption that is in the world by lust." (2 Pet. 1: 3, 4.)

The church is called the temple of God. "Know ye not that ye are a temple of God, and that the Spirit of God dwelleth in you? If any man destroyeth the temple of God, him shall God destroy.; for the temple of God is holy, and such are ye." (1 Cor. 3: 16, 17.) Each Christian is also a temple for the indwelling of the Holy Spirit. "Or know ye not that your body is a temple of the Holy Spirit which is in you, which ye have from God? and ye are not your own; for ye were bought with a price: glorify God therefore in your body." (1 Cor. 6: 19, 20.) "And be not drunken with wine, wherein is riot, but be filled with the Spirit." (Eph. 5: 18.)

HOLY SPIRIT IN SANCTIFICATION

INTRODUCTION.

Work of Holy Spirit has a wide range; covers conversion of sinner and sanctification of saint; the divine side of man's redemption.

I. MEANING OF SANCTIFICATION.

1. Hebrew, "gadeash"; Greek, "Hagiazo," "set apart"; Latin, "sanctus," holy; and "facio," to make.
2. "Sanctification" process by which God makes us holy.
3. "Sanctification" synonymous with "holy." (Acts 20: 32; 26: 18; Rom. 15: 16.)
4. "Set apart" for a holy purpose.
5. Times, places, objects, and people sanctified.

II. HOLY SPIRIT AGENT IN SANCTIFICATION.

1. Only believers sanctified.
2. Spirit dwells in Christians. (Rom. 8: 9.)
3. We walk by the Spirit. (Gal. 5: 16.)
4. Filled with Spirit. (Eph. 5: 18, 19.)

III. SEALED BY HOLY SPIRIT.

1. Christ anointed and sealed. (Luke 4: 18; John 6: 27; Acts 4: 27; 10:38.)
2. Christians anointed and sealed. (2 Cor. 1: 21; Eph. 1: 13; 4: 30.)
3. Earnest of the Spirit. (2 Cor. 1: 21, 22; 5: 5; Eph. 1: 13, 14.)

IV. MEANS USED BY HOLY SPIRIT.

1. The word of God.
2. The truth. (John 17: 17.)
3. The gospel.
4. Prayer. (Eph. 6: 18.)

HOLY SPIRIT IN SANCTIFICATION

"God chose you from the beginning unto salvation in sanctification of the Spirit and belief of the truth." (2 Thess. 2: 13.)

"According to the foreknowledge of God the Father, in sanctification of the Spirit, unto obedience and sprinkling of the blood of Jesus Christ." (1 Pet. 1: 2.)

The work of the Holy Spirit covers a wide range in the redemption of man. It begins with the conversion, regeneration of the sinner and continues through the perfection of saints; the work of the Holy Spirit begins with the preaching of the gospel to the alien and continues to the salvation of souls in glory. In fact, the work of the Holy Spirit covers the entire divine side of man's redemption. The Holy Spirit fills the dispensation of the Spirit; no one is able to take the dimensions or measure the scope of the Holy Spirit in his various relations and multiforms of work.

It would be natural for the Holy Spirit, not only to begin the work of grace with the aliens, but to continue that work through the development and perfection of Christians into the likeness of Christ. The primary result of conversion is a proper adjustment of the converted soul to God's will; the Christian begins the spiritual life as a babe in Christ; all of the laws of spiritual growth and development are carried on by the Holy Spirit through the truth of God. The babe in Christ is a new creature; old things have passed away and all things have become new. There is needed a new adjustment in the family of God. Just as there is needed an "orientation" of the freshman in college to the new surroundings, so there is needed an adjustment of heart and life with the babe in Christ to his new environments. The work of the Holy Spirit through the truth of the gospel makes this adjustment. The whole process of adjustment to the new surroundings in the spiritual kingdom is called "sanctification."

I. Meaning of Sanctification

It is well to get the meaning of the terms of a discussion before proceeding with the investigation. Time and labor may be saved by a thorough understanding of the meaning of the subject. There has been some discussion as to the proper translations of the various terms which have been applied to the growth and development of the Christian life. We need to understand the meaning of "sanctification," "holy," and "divine." The meaning of "holy" in the Old Testament should be understood, because from it we get the meaning in the New Testament. As the Old Testament was first written in Hebrew, we are forced to go back to the Hebrew word for its meaning in the Old Testament. "Gadeash" and "gadosh" are the root words for the idea and the meaning of "separate," "apart." We are not so much interested in the etymology of these words as we are the usage or meaning of them. Their primary significance was "holy"; thus God was esteemed holy because of his ethical uniqueness, his utter aloofness from all evil. Men and places and objects were esteemed holy because they were set apart and consecrated to the service of God. Since God was "separate," "holy," the things used in his service were considered holy. "Holy, holy, holy, is the Lord God, the Almighty, who was and who is and who is to come." (Rev. 4: 8.) This expresses the absolute "separateness" of God from all sin.

The Greek "hagiazo" and "hagios" correspond to the Old Testament "holy" at its highest significance; it is raised and purified by the superior spirituality of the dispensation of the Holy Spirit. The characteristic name of the Spirit in the New Testament is "holy"; his characteristic work is that of sanctification; hence, Christians are "saints," holy ones. The idea of "set apart" or "separateness" is carried into the New Testament with a deeper significance than it had in the Old Testament. It seems that Christians have not understood their aloofness to all that is evil; they are "set apart" or "sanctified" in Christ; they have his sanctification.

The English "sanctification" comes from two Latin words— "sanctus" which means "holy" and "facio" which means "to make." Hence, "sanctification" is the process by which the Holy Spirit makes us holy; therefore, sanctification is the process by which the Holy Spirit through the truth of God makes people partakers of the holiness of God. It is a progressive work begun in the conversion of the sinner and is carried on in the life of the Christian unto perfection. No one ever reaches the high hope and great goal of perfection in the flesh; this is attained in glory. Sanctification is the process by which God through the Holy Spirit makes people holy. The love that Christ had for his disciples is expressed in his sanctification. "And for their sakes I sanctify myself, that they themselves also may be sanctified in truth." (John 17: 19.) In this same prayer Jesus prayed that his disciples should be sanctified. "Sanctify them in the truth: thy word is truth." (John 17: 17.) Christ while on earth was holy and separate from sinners. Christians are baptized into Christ; in Christ they are new creatures. They have the sanctification that Christ had.

"Sanctification" is synonymous with "holiness." "And now I commend you to God, and to the word of his grace, which is able to build you up, and to give you the inheritance among all them that are sanctified." (Acts 20: 32.) Paul's mission among the Gentiles was to "open their eyes, that they may turn from darkness to light and from the power of Satan unto God, that they may receive remission of sins and an inheritance among them that are sanctified by faith in me." (Acts 26: 18.) Again Paul wrote: "That I should be a minister of Christ Jesus unto the Gentiles, ministering the gospel of God, that the offering up of the Gentiles might be made acceptable, being sanctified by the Holy Spirit." (Rom. 15: 16.) Paul was the minister of the gospel to the Gentiles that they might be sanctified by the Holy Spirit; the sanctification of the Gentiles was brought about by the Holy Spirit through the gospel. Paul reminds the Corinthian Christians that they are "sanctified in Christ Jesus." (1 Cor. 1: 2.) In writing to the Romans, Paul exhorted them: "By the mercies of God, to present your bodies a living sacrifice, holy, acceptable to God." (Rom. 12: 1.) The thought is kept before Christians that they are dedicated, consecrated, set apart to the worship and service of God. Sanctification has reference to the process which affects the spiritual life; the spiritual state of the Christian is that he is a "saint"; that is, one who has been sanctified. Times, places, objects, and people are said to be sanctified, as these are all used in the service of God.

II. Holy Spirit Agent in Sanctification

Only believers can be sanctified with the sanctification of the Holy Spirit. It is impossible for the sinner to be set apart to the service of God so long as he remains in sin; sanctification is the process which takes place after regeneration. The Holy Spirit dwells in us (Rom. 8: 9), and we are to walk by the Spirit (Gal. 5: 16), and Christians are to be filled with the Spirit (Eph. 5: 18). Moreover, the Holy Spirit bears witness with our spirit that we are children of God. (Rom. 8: 16.) While the Holy Spirit is the one who sanctifies Christians, his agent is the truth of God. We find the word "holy" applied to the Spirit more frequently in the New Testament than in the Old Testament. There appears to be a higher degree of holiness set forth in the Spirit's dispensation. Even Christ in his mediatorial prayer addressed God as "Holy Father" and "Righteous Father." (John 17: 11, 25.) Christ himself was the holy Son and servant in perfect harmony with the Father's will of righteous goodness, discerned by his disciples to be the "Holy One of God." So marked and characteristic did the name become that "Holy Spirit" is the normal expression for God at work among men; his main object seems to be the manifestation of the highest conceivable spiritual excellence and the transformation of men into his adorable likeness.

The term "spirit of holiness" (Rom. 1: 4) is used only one time in the New Testament; here Christ is said to have been "declared to be the Son of God with power, according to the spirit of holiness." As Christ on the side of his human flesh was of the seed of David, so was he marked out as the Son of God in the most potent and impressive way by the resurrection; it seems that the purpose of Christ was to impart the "spirit of holiness" to men in and through the presence of his holy and sanctifying Spirit. The New Testament teaches the whole Christian life to be one process of sanctification. It is to be regretted that "sanctification" has for many modern teachers been perverted in its meaning; the term "saint" needs to be redeemed and given its New Testament meaning. In the New Testament it describes what the Christians in Rome and Corinth were by way of status and privilege; it sets forth what they ought to be, what every one of them in Christ might be. Every member of the body of Christ is holy or a saint in the sense of having been redeemed by Christ and brought into a new relation with God in Christ; Christians have been changed; they are consecrated ones, living dedicated lives. The modern, maudlin sentiment that some religious teachers have given to "sanctification" should be discarded and the New Testament meaning of the term restored to its proper dignity and influence.

III. Sealed by Holy Spirit

Sanctification is distinguished from conversion as growth is distinguished from birth; sanctification is the perfecting of the saint; it is the bringing of the newborn babe up into the measure of the stature of the fullness of Christ. Sanctification presents two aspects—a putting off and a putting on. "That ye put away, as concerning your former manner of life, the old man, that waxeth corrupt after the lusts of deceit; and that ye be renewed in the spirit of your mind, and put on the new man, that after God hath been created in righteousness and holiness of truth." (Eph. 4: 22-24.) "Let us walk becomingly, as in the day; not in revelling and drunkenness, not in chambering and wantonness, not in strife and jealousy. But put ye on the Lord Jesus Christ, and make not provision for the flesh, to fulfil the lusts thereof." (Rom. 13: 13, 14.)

Christ was anointed by the Holy Spirit. "The Spirit of the Lord is upon me, because he anointed me to preach good tidings to the poor." (Luke 4: 18.) The term "anoint" in the Bible was used for a variety of purposes; we are interested here in the "anointing" for consecration and destination. The idea of "destination" is close akin to "sealing"; it is prominent in anointing. When the oil was applied to Aaron and his sons, it was a sign that they were set apart to the priesthood and qualified therefor; when Samuel took oil and poured it upon the head of Saul, the act designated him as Jehovah's choice for the kinship; when Samuel took the horn of oil and anointed David in the midst of his brethren, it was the token of his divine appointment to be king; Elijah was directed to anoint Elisha as his successor in the prophetic office, so men were invested with authority and sanctity by anointing. It is clearly seen how the custom of sealing and anointing lend themselves to spiritual uses. "Howbeit the firm foundation of God standeth, having this seal, The Lord knoweth them that are his." (2 Tim. 2: 19.) This includes the idea of ownership, authentication, security, and destination. So Christ was anointed and sealed for his special work. (John 6: 27; Acts 4: 27; 10: 38.)

In like manner Christians are anointed and sealed in their sanctification by the Holy Spirit. "Now he that establisheth us with you in Christ, and anointed us, is God; who also sealed us, and gave us the earnest of the Spirit in our hearts." (2 Cor. 1: 21, 22.) "In whom ye also, having heard the word of the truth, the gospel of your salvation,—in whom, having also believed, ye were sealed with the Holy Spirit of promise, which is an earnest of our inheritance, unto the redemption of God's own possession, unto the praise of his glory." (Eph. 1: 13, 14.) "And grieve not the Holy Spirit of God in whom ye were sealed unto the day of redemption." (Eph. 4: 30.) "Now he that wrought us for this very thing is God, who gave unto us the earnest of the Spirit." (2 Cor. 5: 5.) "Earnest" is a first payment to secure a transaction, to bind a bargain; it thus becomes a pledge of further payment until the whole purchased value is in hand. It is a pledge that God will continue to give that which is needed for complete sanctification.

IV. Means Used by Holy Spirit

It has been cited again and again that the Holy Spirit and the word of God are inseparable; the Holy Spirit uses the instrumentality of truth to accomplish his work. Sanctification is accomplished by the Holy Spirit through the truth. "Sanctify them in the truth: thy word is truth," said Christ. (John 17: 17.) This "word of truth" is the gospel. "In whom ye also, having heard the word of the truth, the gospel of your salvation,—in whom, having also believed, ye were sealed with the Holy Spirit of promise, which is an earnest of our inheritance, unto the redemption of God's own possession, unto the praise of his glory." (Eph. 1: 13, 14.) So the Christian life which begins in a crisis called conversion is completed in a process called sanctification; this is brought about through a continued obedience to the truth of God. Prayer may be considered a means of our sanctification; through prayer we open the door of the soul for the truth of God to have its way with us; we are taught to pray for all men (1 Tim. 2: 1); we are encouraged to pray always "with all prayer and supplication" in the Spirit (Eph. 6: 18.) It was while Peter was praying on the housetop that he found the will of God with respect to preaching to the Gentiles, so we may also find it greatly to our sanctification if we live in the spirit of prayer at all times.

Only the believer in Christ can be sanctified in him; sanctification by the Holy Spirit belongs to Christians. The more consecrated in prayer one may be, the more complete is that one's sanctification. The Holy Spirit helps God's sanctified people in praying. The Spirit instructs *how* to pray, for *what* to pray, *when* to pray. "And in like manner the Spirit also helpeth our infirmity: for we know not how to pray as we ought; but the Spirit himself maketh intercession for us with groanings which cannot be uttered; and he that searcheth the hearts knoweth what is the mind of the Spirit, because he maketh intercession for the saints according to the will of God." (Rom. 8: 26, 27.)

BORN OF WATER AND THE SPIRIT

INTRODUCTION.

We begin Christian life as a new creature; to be a Christian implies a new life; hence, born again.

I. LOGICAL APPROACH.

1. Must have reverence for truth.
2. Must expect difficulties and mysteries.
3. These may be removed.

II. ABSOLUTE NECESSITY.

1. Cannot enter kingdom without it. (John 3: 5.)
2. Cannot enter church without it.
3. Church and kingdom synonymous.

III. "BORN AGAIN."

1. Tantamount to conversion, obedience to gospel, regeneration, and translation.
2. "Born anew," "born of water and the Spirit."
3. Some theories answered.
   a. Born of water means natural birth (this makes two births).
   b. Born of water means baptism, and born of Spirit when raised from the dead.

IV. WHAT IS A BIRTH?

1. Two necessary actions.
   a. A begetting.
   b. A delivery.
2. Begetting process similar to natural.
3. God begets through Holy Spirit.
   a. Word of God the seed. (Luke 8: 11; 1 Cor. 4: 15; James 1: 18; 1 Pet. 1: 23.)
   b. Begotten when one believes. (John 1: 11, 12; 1 John 5: 1.)
   c. Spirit gives life. (John 6: 63, 64; 2 Cor. 3: 6.)
4. Deliverance in baptism.
   a. Life not imparted by deliverance.
   b. Birth passes the pre-existence life into a new and favorable state for further growth and development.

BORN OF WATER AND THE SPIRIT

"Except one be born anew, he cannot see the kingdom of God. . . . Except one be born of water and the Spirit, he cannot enter into the kingdom of God." (John 3: 3-5.)

The "new birth" has been the subject of much controversy; it is still the battleground of many theological conflicts. "Birth" is the beginning of a new life; it is the beginning of life in a new environment. The Christian life is begun as "a new creature," as "newborn babe," "a regenerated soul." To be a Christian implies a new life; it implies that old things have passed away; that an old life has ceased, and that a new life has begun. This new life implies a new birth, being born again, "born anew," "born from above." It is sometimes called conversion, regeneration, "alive together with Christ." (Eph. 2: 5.) Sometimes it is spoken of as a "new creation." It is nowhere in the New Testament called "a new birth," but this is clearly implied in New Testament language.

Christ came to establish a new kingdom; this kingdom is called the church. There never had been a kingdom like it. The kingdom of Israel was familiar to his generation, but this new kingdom was uniquely new; it was difficult even for the disciples of Jesus to understand its nature. With the beginning of this kingdom the Holy Spirit was to begin his dispensation on earth. This kingdom was to be a spiritual kingdom; its laws were to be spiritual laws; its blessings were spiritual blessings; its subjects were to be spiritual subjects. Entrance into this kingdom required such radical changes that one who entered it had to be "born anew."

I. LOGICAL APPROACH

Since there is so much misunderstanding and misconception of the meaning of the "new birth," it is necessary to approach the subject in an intelligent way. First, the investigation should be conducted with due reverence for divine truth; one should let the New Testament guide him in all of his efforts to understand and teach this subject. One should listen to the dictates of sober judgment, a pure conscience, and unbiased mind; one should want to know the truth of God on this subject. The New Testament must be the guide and the source of all instructions. It is confessed that there are mysteries connected with this subject; there may be insoluble mystery; not absurdities, but mysteries; not contradictions, but mysteries. We may not understand these mysteries, but the simple and practical truths may be understood. This investigation, like all others, is followed on the principle that whatever is necessary *for man to understand has been clearly revealed.* There is not a fact, principle, or truth essential to man's salvation for man to know, but that has been expressed clearly in language that may be easily understood.

Furthermore, in this investigation we should be governed by the principle which the wisest men have acknowledged in respect to other things than religion; that is, the perplexities and mysteries which arise should never be allowed to confuse us in the practical affairs of life. People have believed in the processes of digestion, and many have never understood them, yet people have gone on and have eaten as though they understood perfectly well all that pertained to digestion. There are mysteries connected with sleep, and many do not know how the body is rebuilt in sleep, yet they go on and enjoy sleep as though they understood full well all that takes place during slumber. So the mysteries concerning the "new birth" may never be understood, yet people are being born into the family of God in spite of the mysteries. There is a practical side to eating, sleeping and being "born anew"; we may understand the practical things and receive the full blessings that belong to the act. In this study we shall ignore the theological questions that attempt to probe into the mysteries of the spiritual birth; we shall be content to deal with the simple and practical things which are clearly revealed in the New Testament.

II. ABSOLUTE NECESSITY

Christ, in his conversation with Nicodemus that night, made it clear that one *must be born anew.* If it should be claimed that he did not make clear the process of being born again, he did make it emphatic that it was absolutely necessary to be born again before one could enter his spiritual kingdom. First, we are to notice that the Holy Spirit has to do with the "new birth." The work of the Holy Spirit is not within the realm of human agency or power. Man can employ the means, but cannot impart life; man can cultivate, but he cannot create; he can repair and mend old things, shape and fashion things which are already in existence, but he cannot in the absolute *make* new things. No man can *generate* himself; neither can any man *regenerate* himself. However, there are some things that man *can do;* these he *must do* if he is ever "born anew." Why must man be born again?

There are two emphatic reasons why conversion, regeneration, or the new birth is necessary. First, we may consider the reason for this necessity on the part of man. When we look at man's lost condition, we can see a reason for a new birth. Man has been separated from God; his sins have come between him and God. (Isa. 59: 2.) The Bible represents man as a sinner; he is blind and dead through his "trespasses and sins." (Eph. 2: 1.) Man is degenerated and desperately wicked in heart; man is represented in this unregenerate state as at enmity with God. Man is unfit in this state to dwell in the spiritual kingdom of God; he is unfitted for the holy relationship of a child of God. The guilt and stain of sin are such that man needs a regeneration; he needs to be born again, he *must be born anew* before he can enjoy the spiritual blessings which are in Christ. Hence, the "new birth" is the one absolute necessity for all who would enter the kingdom of God, and "the new birth" is accomplished by the Holy Spirit communicating the germ of a new life through the truth of God; it is necessary in order that man may become a citizen of the kingdom of God.

The second reason for the necessity of the new birth is viewed from the nature of God. God is holy. "Ye shall be holy; for I Jehovah your God am holy." (Lev. 19: 2.) "Ye shall be holy; for I am holy." (1 Pet. 1: 16.) Holiness is a characteristic of the nature of God. Man is unholy in his sinful condition; God and Christ are always holy. Unholy man must become holy before he can associate with God and Christ. Unholy man becomes holy by virtue of being "born anew" "born of water and the Spirit," by being made partakers of a new nature. Peter speaks of our partaking of the divine nature. (1 Pet. 1: 4.) Some claim that this "divine nature" is not the nature of God, but a nature which is from God. Man must be changed before he is to receive the full and rich blessings that come from God in Christ Jesus. "That which is born of the flesh is flesh; and that which is born of the Spirit is spirit." (John 3: 6.) Since one cannot enter the kingdom of God without being born again, and the kingdom and church are synonymous, one cannot enter the church without being born "of water and the Spirit."

III. "BORN AGAIN"

Since we see the absolute necessity of being born again, we are now to examine more closely the nature of this "new birth." It is tantamount to conversion, obedience to the gospel, regeneration, and translation into the kingdom. People who have been converted have been "born anew"; all who have "obeyed the gospel of God" have been "born of water and the Spirit"; all who have been delivered out of the power of darkness, and translated "into the kingdom of the Son of his love" (Col. 1: 13) have been "born of the Spirit." When one has been "born of water and the Spirit," that one is in Christ; he is a citizen of the kingdom of God. Hence, the process of translating one from "darkness" into "the kingdom" of God's Son is the process of being born anew. The process of being "born anew" is the process of being added to the church. No one has ever become a member of the church of the Lord who was not added by the Lord to the church. Hence, becoming a member of the church of the Lord is tantamount to being "born of water and the Spirit." The process of being "born anew" is the process of being regenerated; it is the same as being saved "through the washing of regeneration and renewing of the Holy Spirit." (Tit. 3: 5.)

There are many theories that have confused people with respect to the process of being "born again." Many have been blinded to the truth because their minds have been beclouded by the doctrines taught by men. Some have grossly misinterpreted the nature of the new birth; they have been confused as to the meaning of being "born of water and the Spirit." They have claimed that there are two births mentioned here—being born of water as one and being born of the Spirit as the other. This would make three births—the fleshly birth, the birth of water, and the birth of the Spirit. Christ told Nicodemus, a well-developed man, that he—everyone—must "be born of water and the Spirit." It seems fortunate that Nicodemus was so slow to understand Christ; this gave Christ the occasion to clear the matter. Nicodemus understood that Christ was talking about only one birth; the language of Christ cannot be fairly interpreted to mean anything else. He has no reference here to the physical birth or fleshly birth, but is discussing the birth that is necessary to enter his kingdom.

Still others have claimed that one is born of water when that one is baptized, and that one is not born of the Spirit until one is raised from the dead. Again, this theory would make two births of the phrase "born of water and the Spirit." Again, it would violate the teachings of Jesus, since he is emphasizing that one birth is essential to entrance into his kingdom. It is sinful to pervert the language of Christ to sustain a false theory. The language of Christ means the same now as it did when Christ spoke to Nicodemus; since it did not mean two births when Christ used it, this language cannot mean two births now.

IV. WHAT IS A BIRTH?

There are two necessary and essential actions in a birth—a begetting and a delivery. This is true whether we have reference to a natural birth or a spiritual birth. The Holy Spirit is the divine agent in both of these actions in the spiritual birth. The word of God is the seed of the kingdom. "The seed is the word of God." (Luke 8: 11.) Paul wrote to the church at Corinth: "For in Christ Jesus I begat you through the gospel." (1 Cor. 4: 15.) He had preached the gospel at Corinth, "and many of the Corinthians hearing believed, and were baptized." (Acts 18: 8.) By the preaching of the gospel through the Holy Spirit, by the Corinthians hearing and obeying it, they were begotten by the gospel. Again, James wrote: "Of his own will he brought us forth by the word of truth, that we should be a kind of firstfruits of his creatures." (James 1: 18.) So Christians are brought forth "by the word of truth" which is the gospel. Peter emphasized the same when he wrote: "Having been begotten again, not of corruptible seed, but of incorruptible, through the word of God, which liveth and abideth. . . . And this is the word of good tidings which was preached unto you." (1 Pet. 1: 23-25.)

One is begotten by the word of God when that one believes. "But as many as received him, to them gave he the right to become children of God, even to them that believe on his name: who were born, not of blood, nor of the will of the flesh, nor of the will of man, but of God." (John 1: 12, 13.) "Whosoever believeth that Jesus is the Christ is begotten of God: and whosoever loveth him that begat loveth him also that is begotten of him." (1 John 5: 1.) The gospel is preached; people hear the gospel; they believe it, and in believing it they are begotten of God. The Holy Spirit imparts the life; life is imparted in the process of begetting. "It is the spirit that giveth life; the flesh profiteth nothing: the words that I have spoken unto you are spirit, and are life." (John 6: 63.) The apostles were made "ministers of a new covenant; not of the letter, but of the spirit: for the letter killeth, but the spirit giveth life." (2 Cor. 3: 6.)

The second necessary action in a birth is the delivery; this is done in baptism. "For in one Spirit were we all baptized into one body." (1 Cor. 12: 13.) The entire process is directed and accomplished by the Holy Spirit. One function of the Holy Spirit is to "convict the world in respect of sin, and of righteousness, and of judgment: of sin, because they believe not on me; of righteousness, because I go to the Father, and ye behold me no more; of judgment, because the prince of this world hath been judged." (John 16: 8-11.) The word of God is "the sword of the Spirit." (Eph. 6: 17.) The Holy Spirit convicts the sinner with gospel truth. The sinner hears the truth, believes it, and is begotten by it. Through the instructions of the Holy Spirit he is commanded to obey it. He turns in penitence from his sins, and is then baptized into Christ. All this is done through the teaching of the Holy Spirit. This last act of being buried in baptism and raised to "walk in newness of life" (Rom. 6: 4) is the deliverance. Birth passes the pre-existent life into a new and favorable state and environment for further growth and development.

Baptism as was seen in the study on conversion puts one into Christ. It is the last act of the translation from darkness into the kingdom of the Son of his love. "Or are ye ignorant that all we who were baptized into Christ Jesus were baptized into his death?" (Rom. 6: 3.) And again: "For ye are all sons of God, through faith, in Christ Jesus. For as many of you as were baptized into Christ did put on Christ." (Gal. 3: 26, 27.) If one is in Christ, that one is a new creature. "Wherefore if any man is in Christ, he is a new creature: the old things are passed away; behold, they are become new." (2 Cor. 5: 17.) If one is a "new creature," that one has been born anew, "born of water and the Spirit."

The new life in Christ comes after one has been born again; no one can experience this life who has not been "born of water and the Spirit." The life began when the gospel was preached and one believed it and repented of sin; then the believing penitent is baptized into Christ; here the new life is enjoyed. One may fail or neglect to take the spiritual nourishment, exercise and breathe the spiritual atmosphere, and fail to develop this new life. Many church members do not grow; they let the cares of the world hinder their growth. No one can enjoy the fullness of the Christian life without developing to the fullest of one's capacity.

CHAPTER XIV

FRUIT OF THE SPIRIT

INTRODUCTION.

Spirit operates in conversion; dwells in Christians; Christian conduct the "fruit of the Spirit."

I. THE CHRISTIAN LIFE.

1. Church members may live on two levels.
   a. The lower, carnal, "works of the flesh."
   b. The higher, spiritual, "fruit of the Spirit."
2. Test of our profession.
3. Christians to bear fruit. (John 15: 2-8.)

II. "WORKS OF THE FLESH."

1. Fifteen kinds mentioned. (Gal. 5: 19-21.)
2. "Such like"—too many to mention.
3. Cannot enter heaven with these.
4. Cannot abide in Christ with these.

III. KINDS OF FRUIT.

1. Must have Spirit to bear his fruit.
2. Nine different kinds. (Gal. 5: 22.)
   a. Love; b, joy; c, peace; d, long-suffering; e, kindness; f, goodness; g, faithfulness; h, meekness; i, self-control.
3. Not "fruits," but "fruit."
4. All bear the same kind.
5. We become like Christ.

CHAPTER XIV

FRUIT OF THE SPIRIT

"But the fruit of the Spirit is love, joy, peace, longsuffering, kindness, goodness, faithfulness, meekness, self-control; against such there is no law." (Gal. 5: 22, 23.)

The work of the Holy Spirit covers such vast, intimate, and such intricate ranges of action, association, and attitudes as to make it impossible in one brief chapter to make a complete survey. The Holy Spirit enters into all of the details of the conversion of the sinner; he dwells in Christians and bears fruit in the Christian life. The Christian sojourns in a spiritual kingdom with a spiritual king, in a spiritual body with Christ as head, and is subject to the will of God in all activities as a child of God. The Christian is to be developed into the likeness of Christ; he is to grow in grace and in the knowledge of the truth of God day by day. All of this is under the supervision of the Holy Spirit. Let it be kept in mind that the Holy Spirit and the word of God are never separated in the redemption of man. Whatever the Spirit does in his work with man, either in regeneration or in sanctification, he does it through the word of truth, the gospel. The word of God is the instrumentality that the Holy Spirit always uses in his work.

The chief work that the Holy Spirit has with Christians is to develop them into the likeness of Christ; the primary objective of the Holy Spirit in dwelling in Christians is to reproduce in men the beauty and glory of the personality of Christ. It is significant that the Holy Spirit has an important work throughout the sanctification of saints. People are not machines in the hands of the engineer to be made of service by moving so many levers; they are not lumps of clay in the hands of a potter molded without their volition; men are made a little lower than the angels, endowed with reason, will, judgment, memory; they possess faculties implying intelligence and natural power of action, plan, purpose, and desire. The Holy Spirit recognizes this nature of man in dealing with men, and places upon them the responsibility of cooperation with his work and response to his holy influences.

I. The Christian Life

There are two levels of life or two planes upon which church members may live—a lower and a higher, a carnal and a spiritual. The Christian who enjoys the Christian life and develops most nearly into the likeness of Christ must live upon the higher plane. Those who live upon the lower plane live as the world does. They are those who live after the flesh. "For they that are after the flesh mind the things of the flesh; but they that are after the Spirit the things of the Spirit. For the mind of the flesh is death; but the mind of the Spirit is life and peace: because the mind of the flesh is enmity against God; for it is not subject to the law of God, neither indeed can it be: and they that are in the flesh cannot please God." (Rom. 8: 5-8.) It is said to find so many who have been converted, but are living upon this low level.

The higher, spiritual level is where the fruit of the Spirit is manifested. The lower level of life is the fleshly, the carnal level, the level of the world; the higher level of life is the spiritual, the Christian level. There are just these two ways of living—"in the flesh" and "in the Spirit." The carnal nature and the spiritual are sometimes both in the same person; some claim these two natures are always in the same person. There is a conflict between the two—which shall prevail? (Rom. 7: 14-24.) To bear fruit is the supreme and ultimate purpose of the Christian life. "Every branch in me that beareth not fruit, he taketh it away: and every branch that beareth fruit, he cleanseth it, that it may bear more fruit. . . . I am the vine, ye are the branches: He that abideth in me, and I in him, the same beareth much fruit: for apart from me ye can do nothing. . . . Herein is my Father glorified, that ye bear much fruit; and so shall ye be my disciples." (John 15: 2-8.) One cannot live a faithful Christian life without bearing the fruit of the Holy Spirit. No one can bear the fruit of the Spirit without having the Spirit; the Holy Spirit must dwell in Christians before the fruit of the Spirit can be manifested.

The test of the Christian life is "the fruit of the Spirit." It is as easy to recognize the fruit of the Spirit as it is the works of the flesh. "By their fruits ye shall know them. Do men gather grapes of thorns, or figs of thistles? Even so every good tree bringeth forth good fruit; but the corrupt tree bringeth forth evil fruit. A good tree cannot bring forth evil fruit, neither can a corrupt tree bring forth good fruit. Every tree that bringeth not forth good fruit is hewn down, and cast into the fire. Therefore by their fruits ye shall know them." (Matt. 7: 16-20.) So faithful Christians are known by the fruit of the Spirit. The Christian life is a practical life; every principle of the teaching of Christ may be practiced in the life of his disciples. Jesus did not deal with theories or speculations; he revealed the Father's will in simple and practical living.

II. "Works of the Flesh"

Those who are living on the lower plane of the flesh are minding the things of the flesh. They do the works of the flesh. "Now the works of the flesh are manifest, which are these: fornication, uncleanness, lasciviousness, idolatry, sorcery, enmities, strife, jealousies, wraths, factions, divisions, parties, envyings, drunkenness, revellings, and such like." (Gal. 5: 19-21.) There are fifteen specific works of the flesh mentioned here; the phrase "and such like" may include all other works of the flesh; hence, all the catalog of sins is here mentioned. Those who practice such things live on a very low level as church members, and can never develop into the likeness of Christ, and "shall not inherit the kingdom of God."

"Works of the flesh" may mean the frailty of human nature and its corruption by sin. These "works" make a very black list, fifteen in number, with the language sufficient to include every work of the flesh. Sensuality and uncleanness in their enticing and debasing forms are included in this list. Idolatry, which sums all evils which arise from putting anything *before* or in *place* of God, is included; again, selfishness as a root which produces a coarse rank crop of "enmities, strife, jealousies, wraths, factions, divisions, parties, envyings" is mentioned in this dark list. Intemperance which stands for self-indulgence is not omitted in the catalog of "the works of the flesh." These "works of the flesh" are very similar to "the works of the devil." (1 John 3: 8.) "The mind of the flesh is enmity against God" (Rom. 8: 7) and "the mind of the flesh is death" (Rom. 8: 6). So "the works of the flesh" are tantamount to "the works of the devil."

This is why those who do the works of the flesh cannot be pleasing to God.

Church members who do the works of the flesh cannot abide in Christ; such works are far out of harmony with the Spirit of Christ. The wide contrast between "the works of the flesh" and "the fruit of the Spirit" stands out so prominent that the dark background of the works of the flesh makes the fruit of the Spirit more attractive. Paul has sketched in detail the works of the flesh so that he could emphasize the fruit of the Spirit. In modern life a partial list of the ordinary works of the flesh may be seen in the social life of many church members today. The strife, physical force, wealth, luxury, lust, drunkenness, gambling, poverty, gossip, divorces, remarriages, and a host of others are manifestly works of the flesh. It is a sad fact that membership in a local church bearing the name of Christ is not what it should be, a guarantee of regeneration, "born of water and the Spirit." Many who claim membership are still in the world and doing the works of the flesh. Some who have been "born anew" do not bear the fruit of the Spirit because they live on the lower level of a church member life.

III. Kinds of Fruit

The glory of Christianity is the fruit of the Holy Spirit. When Jesus said, "My Father worketh even until now, and I work" (John 5: 17), he did not exclude the work of the Holy Spirit, but rather included his work. Time and again it has been emphasized that the Father works through the Son (John 3: 14-18; Rom. 5: 6-11), and the Son works through the Holy Spirit (John 3: 5, 6; Rom. 5: 1, 5; 8: 5-10), and the Holy Spirit works through the word of God or the gospel (John 16: 8-14; James 1: 18; 1 Pet. 1: 22, 23). It follows that both the Father and the Son work through the Holy Spirit (Rom. 8: 14-17), and that the three members of the Godhead now work through the gospel. Since God and Christ are eternal workers, so the Holy Spirit is an eternal worker. (Heb. 9: 14.) It should be observed that spiritual growth and development of Christians conform to the laws of the Holy Spirit's working. No one can bear the fruit of the Spirit who does not have the Spirit.

In Gal. 5: 22, 23 there are nine different kinds of fruit mentioned. This fruit of the Holy Spirit in the lives of faithful Christians is put in contrast with the fifteen different "works of the flesh" "and such like." It should further be noted that Paul did not speak of the "fruits" of the Spirit, but "the fruit of the Spirit." This implies that there is unity in all fruit of the Spirit; there is a harmonious blending of the nine different kinds of fruit mentioned. It is not to be understood that the nine different kinds mentioned are the only fruit of the Holy Spirit. The fruit of the Spirit is sometimes called the Christian graces. Peter mentions eight of the Christian graces. (2 Pet. 1: 5-7.) Paul begins with love in enumerating his list and Peter ends with love.

"Love" as a fruit of the Spirit includes love for God, Christ, his church, his people, his worship, and all that came from God. "God gave us not a spirit of fearfulness; but of power and love and discipline." (2 Tim. 1: 7.) This love goes out to God (Matt. 22: 37), to our neighbors (Matt. 22: 39), to our brethren in Christ (John 13: 34; 15: 12), and to our enemies (Luke 6: 27-35). This love of God is shed abroad in our hearts by the Holy Spirit. (Rom. 5: 5.) The next fruit of the Spirit mentioned is "joy." "The kingdom of God is not eating and drinking, but righteousness and peace and joy in the Holy Spirit." (Rom. 14: 17.) "These things have I spoken unto you, that my joy may be in you, and that your joy may be made full." (John 15: 11.) "Ask, and ye shall receive, that your joy may be made full." (John 16: 24.) Christians are to rejoice in the Lord always. (Phil. 4: 4.)

The third fruit mentioned is "peace." This peace is that inner tranquillity which Christians possess. "Peace I leave with you; my peace I give unto you." (John 14: 27.) "Being therefore justified by faith, we have peace with God through our Lord Jesus Christ." (Rom. 5: 1.) "The peace of God, which passeth all understanding, shall guard your hearts and your thoughts in Christ Jesus." (Phil. 4: 7.) "Longsuffering" is another fruit of the Spirit. "I therefore, the prisoner in the Lord, beseech you to walk worthily of the calling wherewith ye were called, with all lowliness and meekness, with longsuffering, forbearing one another in love." (Eph. 4: 1, 2.) "Kindness" is another fruit of the Spirit; Christians must be kind to one another and to all. "Kindness" here means being kindly disposed toward others; it means sweetness of disposition. Paul mentions this fruit in recounting his afflictions and persecutions; "in longsuffering, in kindness, in the Holy Spirit, in love unfeigned" is his language. (2 Cor. 6: 6.) "Goodness" is next in order in this list; the fruit of the Spirit is goodness. Kindness in action is goodness of heart. "Forbearing one another, and forgiving each other, if any man have a complaint against any; even as the Lord forgave you, so also do ye." (Col. 3: 13.) Another fruit is "faithfulness"; faithfulness is faith continued in the life; it is faith in God, in his Word, in his Son, and in his love for us as wrought by the Holy Spirit in our lives. "Meekness" and "self-control" are the last two mentioned in this list. "Meekness" means mildness as opposed to anger and contention; it implies submissiveness to God. "Blessed are the meek: for they shall inherit the earth." (Matt. 5: 5.) "Self-control" implies a control over all of the powers of one's being; these are brought under the guidance of the Holy Spirit.

All faithful Christians bear the same kind of fruit; hence, all Christians are like Christ. Some church members are such driveling believers that they do not let the Holy Spirit produce fruit in their lives. Christians may "quench" the Holy Spirit (1 Thess. 5: 19), and are warned against such. They may "grieve" the Holy Spirit (Eph. 4: 30), and are warned against this. Those who grieve the Holy Spirit and quench the Spirit cannot bear the fruit of the Spirit. The Holy Spirit who dwells in Christians through the word of God does not create a new element of mind, neither introduces any new principle of mental action; his work is done through the word of God by operating on the powers of the soul in a normal way. The fruit of the Spirit is no shock of spasmodic piety; the fruit of meekness and peace are a check on the vibrations of emotions between extremes. The Christian development advances in the line of Christian duties; the fruit of the Spirit is born in the normal Christian life; as Christians obey the truth of God and live faithful to his word, the fruit of the Spirit is the natural result.

All the graces of soul culture in the service of God may be considered fruit of the Spirit. It is through the guidance of the truth that one becomes a Christian, and through the continued guidance of the truth of God does one develop the Christian life; it is through the truth of God that one may become like Christ and polished and adorned by the graces of the fruit of the Spirit. One must have the Spirit dwelling in one before that one can bear the fruit of the Spirit. One may imitate the Christian life and cultivate some of the habits of a Christian, but one cannot bear the fruit of the Spirit without having the Spirit dwell in him. The Holy Spirit is the Spirit of love, joy, peace, long-suffering, kindness, goodness, faithfulness, meekness, self-control; hence, those in whom the Holy Spirit dwells may bear this fruit.

There is great diversity in fruit bearing; the plenary power of the Holy Spirit can produce in a Christian those graces that make one like Christ. One member of the church may have graces developed to a higher degree than others; this depends on some of the natural traits of the individual and the emphasis that may be put on any one aspect of the Christian life. It would seem easy to bear the fruit of the Spirit, since one has the Holy Spirit. This is true; it is natural for growing Christians to bear more fruit year by year. Someone has said, "Sow a thought and reap an act; sow an act and reap a habit; sow a habit and reap a character; sow a character and reap a destiny." Sow an evil thought and one reaps an evil act; sow good thoughts and reap good acts; sow to the Spirit and one will reap eternal life.

CHAPTER XV

THE LEADING OF THE HOLY SPIRIT

INTRODUCTION.

This the Spirit dispensation; Holy Spirit prominent and dominant; guides in all spiritual activities.

I. THE LEADING OF THE GODHEAD.

1. How God led during his dispensation.
   a. Led Noah to build the ark. (Heb. 11: 7.)
   b. Led Abraham out of Ur. (Gen. 12: 1; Heb. 11: 8, 9.)
   c. Led Israel out of Egypt. (Deut. 8: 15; 29: 5; Psalm 77: 20.)
2. How Christ led.
   a. Led his disciples by teaching them.
   b. To lead others same way. (John 6: 44, 45.)
   c. Instrumentality of truth used.
3. How Holy Spirit leads.
   a. Led Christ. (Luke 4: 1, 29.)
   b. Leads others. (Rom. 8: 14.)
   c. Speaks through apostles. (Matt. 10: 20.)

II. THEORY OF DIRECT OPERATION.

1. Not taught in the Bible.
2. Makes God responsible if any unsaved.
3. Why operated on certain ones:
4. No conversions where gospel not preached.
5. If theory true, why send missionaries?

III. EXAMPLES OF HOLY SPIRIT'S LEADING.

1. How he leads alien sinners.
   a. At Pentecost. (Acts 2: 4, 14-38.)
   b. By speaking through Peter.
2. How he leads saints.
   a. By speaking to them. (1 Tim. 4: 1.)
   b. He speaks in New Testament to Christians.
3. To follow New Testament is to follow Holy Spirit.
4. Spirit leads all same way.

THE LEADING OF THE HOLY SPIRIT

"For as many as are led by the Spirit of God, these are sons of God."
(Rom. 8: 14.)

The operations of the Holy Spirit are various under the dispensation of the Spirit; it is important that we have a clear conception of all of these operations. Religious teachers have gone to two extremes—one is that the Holy Spirit has nothing to do in conversion and sanctification; the other is that the Holy Spirit does everything in conversion and sanctification. Be it remembered that the Holy Spirit is prominent and dominant in both; however, there is a happy medium between these extremes. In all of his work and operations in conversion and sanctification the Holy Spirit uses the instrumentality of truth. The burden of Psalm 119 is a tribute to the adoration of truth as the word of God; over and over in this Psalm the importance of the word of God as an instrument in divine purposes is emphasized; throughout the New Testament teachings the instrumentality of truth is stressed in the work of the Holy Spirit.

A distinction should be drawn between the miraculous and extraordinary manifestations of the Holy Spirit and the common or ordinary manifestations. The Holy Spirit in some extraordinary way led Jesus. "Then was Jesus led up of the Spirit into the wilderness to be tempted of the devil." (Matt. 4: 1; Luke 4: 1.) Paul in some way was led by the Holy Spirit. "And they went through the region of Phrygia and Galatia, having been forbidden of the Holy Spirit to speak the word in Asia; . . . they assayed to go into Bithynia; and the Spirit of Jesus suffered them not." (Acts 16: 6, 7.) Paul and his company may not have understood the guidance of the Holy Spirit at the time, but subsequent events made the leadership of the Spirit so plain that they could not doubt it. If one is interested in tracing the leadership of the Holy Spirit in the life of Paul further, one will find numerous examples in Acts 21, 22, and 23. Peter, by the miraculous manifestations of the Holy Spirit, was led to the household of Cornelius; Philip was guided by the Holy Spirit in his extraordinary way to the eunuch. However, we are interested here in the ordinary work of the Holy Spirit.

I. THE LEADING OF THE GODHEAD

Each member of the Godhead—God, the Creator; the Word, the Christ; and the Holy Spirit—has had his dispensation among men. Each has manifested his guidance of men during his dispensation. We are to investigate the guidance of each as he dealt with men. First, we look at the leadership of God during his dispensation. There are numerous examples of God's leading men. First, God led Noah to build the ark. "By faith Noah, being warned of God concerning things not seen as yet, moved with godly fear, prepared an ark to the saving of his house." (Heb. 11: 7.) In the record found in Genesis, Jehovah spoke to Noah and told him just how to build the ark. "And God said unto Noah, . . . Make thee an ark of gopher wood. . . . And this is how thou shalt make it." (Gen. 6: 13-15.) "And Noah did according unto all that Jehovah commanded him." (Gen. 7: 5.) God led Noah by speaking to him the language that he understood and Noah did just what God commanded him.

God led Abraham out of Ur of the Chaldees. "By faith Abraham, when he was called, obeyed to go out unto a place which he was to receive for an inheritance; and he went out, not knowing whither he went. By faith he became a sojourner in the land of promise." (Heb. 11: 8, 9.) "So belief cometh of hearing, and hearing by the word of Christ." (Rom. 10: 17.) God spoke to Abraham and told him what to do. Abraham did this, and in this way God led him. "Now Jehovah said unto Abram, Get thee out of thy country, and from thy kindred, and from thy father's house, unto the land that I will show thee. . . . So Abram went, as Jehovah had spoken unto him." (Gen. 12: 1-4.) So God led Abraham by speaking to him and Abraham's obeying God.

Another clear example of *how* God led people during his dispensation is found in the history of the deliverance of Israel from Egyptian bondage. God sent Moses to deliver Israel; Moses went and demanded of Pharaoh that he let the people go. Pharaoh refused for a time, and God visited upon him and the

Egyptians the ten plagues. He finally let them go and Moses led them out of Egypt into the wilderness, down to the foot of Mount Sinai, and finally through their wanderings in the wilderness. God led them. "Then thy heart be lifted up, and thou forget Jehovah thy God, who brought thee forth out of the land of Egypt, out of the house of bondage; who led thee through the great and terrible wilderness." (Deut. 8: 14, 15.) Again, Jehovah is said to have led them through the wilderness. "But Jehovah hath not given you a heart to know, and eyes to see, and ears to hear, unto this day. And I have led you forty years in the wilderness." (Deut. 29: 4, 5.) God had led the people by instructing Moses what to do. Many years later the psalmist wrote: "Thou leddest thy people like a flock, by the hand of Moses and Aaron." (Psalm 77: 20.) So Jehovah led people by speaking to them, by their hearing him, and by their obeying him.

Next we come to the dispensation of Christ and ask how he led people. The first disciples that Jesus made were made by teaching. "On the morrow he was minded to go forth into Galilee, and he findeth Philip: and Jesus saith unto him, Follow me." (John 1: 43.) Jesus commanded and people obeyed; he taught them what to do and they did as he directed. In this way he led people to do the will of God. There was no mysterious influence or supernatural power exercised over them to get them to do what he commanded. This was not the way that Jesus led his disciples. He said: "No man can come to me, except the Father that sent me draw him: and I will raise him up in the last day. It is written in the prophets, And they shall all be taught of God. Every one that hath heard from the Father, and hath learned, cometh unto me." (John 6: 44, 45.) Jesus used the instrumentality of truth in leading people. He spoke to them in their own language; he taught them so that they could understand; those who learned followed him. Christ led people while on earth as God led them in the former dispensation.

The third member of the Godhead also leads people. This is the dispensation of the Holy Spirit. The Holy Spirit led Christ. (Luke 4: 1.) He leads God's people today. "For as many as are led by the Spirit of God, these are sons of God." (Rom. 8: 14.) How does the Holy Spirit lead people? If he led them in a different way from that which God and Christ led them, some instruction would be given. We are forced to believe that this third member of the Godhead leads people during his dispensation as did God and Christ. The entire teaching of the Christ concerning the Holy Spirit leads us to believe that he would operate on people as did God and Christ. Since the Holy Spirit is a speaking, intelligent being, he speaks to people, they hear, and obey. Christ said to his apostles: "But when they deliver you up, be not anxious how or what ye shall speak: for it shall be given you in that hour what ye shall speak. For it is not ye that speak, but the Spirit of your Father that speaketh in you." (Matt. 10: 19, 20.) So the Holy Spirit leads people by speaking to them. He speaks to people in the New Testament. When people follow the New Testament, they are following the Holy Spirit. When they do what the Holy Spirit teaches, they are being led by the Holy Spirit.

II. Theory of Direct Operation

Many minds are so cluttered with the useless rubbish and plunder of traditions and superstitions that it is difficult for them to understand and appreciate the New Testament teaching on the guidance of the Holy Spirit. They have been taught by religious leaders that in some mysterious way the Holy Spirit operates independent of the instrumentality of the truth. They have never learned that the Holy Spirit uses the truth of God, the gospel, in regeneration and in sanctification; that the Holy Spirit dwells in Christians through the truth of God, and that he leads people by speaking to them through the gospel as revealed in the New Testament. Truth, as an instrument of God's will, is used at one time as a lamp to the feet of the wanderer, at another time it is a light shining in a dark place. It is the voice from heaven at one time and the rod of God's mouth at another time; it is the message of the Holy Spirit and guides God's people in all the meanderings of Christian service. This truth is revealed to us in the New Testament.

There is no such a thing as the "occasionalism" of piety inspired by the Holy Spirit in a direct way with Christians; neither is there "the intermittency of devout affections" which gives to anyone the "intrinsic grandeur" of religious experience. Wise is that one who has learned the value of truth and its instrumentality by the Holy Spirit. The immediate, direct, mysterious, superstitious, and traditional impact or contact of the Holy Spirit with the soul or spirit of man is not taught in the New Testament. A little thought and analysis of the claims of those who have been operated on in a direct way by the Holy Spirit will soon manifest the folly of such a claim. If the Holy Spirit operates in a direct way, independent of truth, why does he not operate on all? God wants all to be saved. Why does he not send the Holy Spirit and convert all? Why will such a claim be made by a poor, ignorant, superstitious person and not be made by a more intelligent person? The theory of the direct operation of the Holy Spirit has the Spirit operating quicker on a superstitious person than a more thoughtful and intelligent person. Why do we not find conversion where the truth is not known? Among heathen where Christ is not known, where the gospel is not preached, we never hear of a conversion. Some missionaries must carry the truth of the gospel before heathens are converted. Neither do we find the Holy Spirit leading anyone where the truth of the gospel is not known.

III. Examples of Holy Spirit's Leading

It may be clearly pointed out as to how the Holy Spirit leads the alien in becoming a Christian. On the day of Pentecost, when the Holy Spirit came to the apostles in his miraculous manifestation, the multitude was drawn together to observe the phenomenal manifestations. Some thought that the apostles were drunken; others were confused in their reasonings. Peter stood up with the eleven and began to speak as the Holy Spirit gave utterance. The Holy Spirit spoke through Peter to the multitude; Peter presented Jesus to them. His arguments were so convincing that they were caused to ask Peter and the rest of the apostles, "What shall we do?" The Holy Spirit still speaking through Peter told these believers who had been convinced that Jesus was the promised Messiah, the Son of God, and the Savior of man, that they should repent and be baptized every one of them "in the name of Jesus Christ" unto the remission of their sins, that they should "receive the gift of the Holy Spirit." (Acts 2: 38.)

About three thousand on this day did exactly what the Holy Spirit told them to do; they were led by the Holy Spirit to become Christians.

In like manner the Holy Spirit leads saints. The Commission as recorded by Matthew is: "Go ye therefore, and make disciples of all the nations, baptizing them into the name of the Father and of the Son and of the Holy Spirit: teaching them to observe all things whatsoever I commanded you: and lo, I am with you always, even unto the end of the world." (Matt. 28: 19, 20.) The baptized believers were to be taught how to live the Christian life; the guidance of the Holy Spirit is as important in the Christian life as it is in the leading of alien sinners into the service of God. The guidance of saints by the Holy Spirit is through the teachings of the Holy Spirit. "But the Spirit saith expressly, that in later times some shall fall away from the faith, giving heed to seducing spirits and doctrines of demons, through the hypocrisy of men, that speak lies, branded in their own conscience as with a hot iron." (1 Tim. 4: 1, 2.) The Holy Spirit speaks through the New Testament to Christians.

It cannot be emphasized too often that the Holy Spirit in all of his work uses the instrumentality of truth. The Holy Spirit employs in conversion *truth* as distinct from error. There is not a shadow of evidence in the Bible that a human heart was ever changed from sin to holiness by the force of error; no man was ever moved aright by wrong. No soul ever thrived on error. Profound and honest belief of his faults can never save a man; neither can one be led aright by error. A warning has echoed down through the ages of inspiration "that they all might be judged who believed not the truth, but had pleasure is unrighteousness." (2 Thess. 2: 12.) Furthermore, the Holy Spirit not only uses truth, but the truth of the gospel in conversion and in sanctification. The Holy Spirit does not use the axioms of mathematics, the truth of science, philosophy, or even morality, but the truth that came through Christ. Christ said: "I am the way, and the truth, and the life." The gospel "is the power of God unto salvation to every one that believeth."

The Holy Spirit has never dispensed with the agency of truth in the guidance of Christians. No doctrine of God has been promulgated except by teaching the truth. Faith comes by hearing the word of Christ. (Rom. 10: 17.) This faith that blesses comes through the hearing of the gospel, and the gospel is expressed in terms of the truth by the Holy Spirit. The only evidence any man can have from experience that he has been converted is the evidence of actual exercises of heart in view of truth; divine power in the change of any man is wrought by the agency of the truth. This is why Christ has commanded the truth of the gospel to be preached; he has condemned all who preach not his gospel. By the truth of the gospel people are led to become Christians and are guided in the Christian life.

The New Testament was given by inspiration; it is the teachings of the Holy Spirit. We have a record of the teachings of Christ through the Holy Spirit in the New Testament. To follow the New Testament is to follow the Holy Spirit; to do what the Holy Spirit teaches one to do is to do what the New Testament requires. To be guided by the New Testament is to be guided by the Holy Spirit. The Holy Spirit leads all the same way; he does not lead one man into one church and another into another church; he leads all into the church of our Lord. The Holy Spirit does not lead one Christian one way and lead another still another way. What the New Testament says to one it says to everyone. What the Holy Spirit says to one he says to everyone in that condition. Hence, all Christians are led the same way; they are led to wear the same name, to worship the same way, and to develop into the likeness of Christ. All should yield to the simple teachings of the New Testament, for in doing so they are led by the Holy Spirit.

HOLY SPIRIT AND THE CHURCH

Introduction.

This a double subject; Holy Spirit and the church; both are great and important subjects; Holy Spirit addressed letters to the church.

I. Relation of Holy Spirit to the Church.

    1. Relation in the early days of the church.
        a. Guide the apostles in teaching.
        b. Confirm the spoken word. (Heb. 2: 1-4.)
        c. Full revelation now recorded. (1 Cor. 13: 9-11.)

    2. Relation today.
        a. A different relationship today.
        b. No miraculous manifestation.
        c. All truth now confirmed.
        d. Church perfected today. (Eph. 4: 11-16.)

II. Church the Body of Christ.

    1. Frequently so declared. (Rom. 12: 4, 5; 1 Cor. 12: 14; Eph. 1: 22; Col. 1: 24.)
    2. Christ the head of the body. (Eph. 5: 23; Col. 1: 18.)
    3. Only one body, hence one church. (Eph. 4: 4.)
    4. Holy Spirit dwells in the body.
    5. Body without Spirit dead. (James 2: 26.)

III. Church the Kingdom of Christ.

    1. God appointed a kingdom to him. (Luke 22: 29.)
    2. Christ the King.
    3. He continues to reign. (1 Cor. 15: 24-28.)
    4. The meaning of kingdom. (Rom. 14: 17.)

IV. Church Temple of God.

    1. Church house of God. (1 Tim. 3: 15.)
    2. Church a spiritual house. (1 Pet. 2: 5.)
    3. Church dwelling place of Spirit. (1 Cor. 3: 16, 17.)
    4. Christians temple of Holy Spirit. (1 Cor. 6: 19.)

V. Christ the True Vine.

    1. Christians are branches. (John 15: 1-5.)
    2. Must abide in Christ.
    3. Must have Spirit of Christ. (Rom. 8: 9.)
    4. All fruit bearing in Christ.
    5. All life comes through Christ.

HOLY SPIRIT AND THE CHURCH

"For in one Spirit were we all baptized into one body, whether Jews or Greeks, whether bond or free; and were all made to drink of one Spirit." (1 Cor. 12: 13.)

The theme of this chapter is a double one—the Holy Spirit and the church. Either of these subjects requires much space, but since the Holy Spirit is treated throughout these discussions, emphasis is placed here on the church. There is a definite and prominent relation between the Spirit and the church. In fact, there are two abiding monuments of the work of the Holy Spirit in and through believers in Christ; these are the church and the Bible. The church existed before any of the New Testament was written. The Bible, and especially the New Testament to Christians, is an abiding and permanent book. Jesus said: "Heaven and earth shall pass away, but my words shall not pass away." (Matt. 24: 35.) The church is destined to remain as an institution until Christ shall make his second advent. Jesus declared of it: "The gates of Hades shall not prevail against it." (Matt. 16: 18.) "The gates of Hades" shall not prevail against the establishment of the church, neither shall it prevail against the perpetuity of it. The Bible and the church are among the permanences, among the things which cannot be shaken.

The Holy Spirit guided in the establishment of the church in the beginning; he filled it with his presence; he wrote letters of instruction and guidance to it. The Holy Spirit guided the pen in writing all of the New Testament letters. The Holy Spirit has a definite and vital relation to the church; it may be stated exactly and succinctly that the Holy Spirit bears the relation to the church as a creative force, resident in it, active and operative through it, and cooperant and concurrent with it. The Holy Spirit constituted the church, formed it, gave it being on the day of Pentecost, and preached the gospel of salvation through it. "Might be made known through the church the manifold wisdom of God, according to the eternal purpose which he purposed in Christ Jesus our Lord." (Eph. 3: 10, 11.) Christ is the authority *over* the church, and the Holy Spirit is the authority *within* the church.

I. RELATION OF HOLY SPIRIT TO THE CHURCH

The Holy Spirit sustained a very important and vital relation to the church in the early days of its existence. There have been stages of the history of the church—its early days, its apostolic days, and its present stage. The Holy Spirit came on the day of Pentecost and took the material that Jesus had prepared and created the church. The church did not have its existence until after the Holy Spirit came and gave it life. As the body of Adam was first formed, and then God "breathed into his nostrils the breath of life" (Gen. 2: 7), so the Holy Spirit gave to the church its life. The Holy Spirit was to teach the apostles all things, and bring to their remembrance all that Jesus said unto them. (John 14: 26.) As Jesus left his apostles on the day that he ascended he told them to "tarry ye in the city, until ye be clothed with power from on high." (Luke 24: 49.) The apostles patiently and prayerfully waited in Jerusalem until the Holy Spirit came, and then they began speaking, as the Spirit gave them utterance, the words of eternal life. They preached the gospel as God's power to save by the Holy Spirit; by the Holy Spirit they convinced and convicted sinners until they cried out: "Brethren, what shall we do?" The Holy Spirit guided Peter in telling them just what they should do; they promptly obeyed the commands of the Holy Spirit and "the Lord added" them to the church. So we have the beginning of the church on Pentecost.

Hence, we speak of Pentecost as "the birthday of the church." From this moment we have the church as an organism, an institution. It became an organism; that is, a living, growing institution like a human body or a tree. As Christ, when he came to this earth, needed a body through which to work, through which to obey, serve, suffer, die, and rise again, so the Holy Spirit needed a body through which to work out the redemption of man. The body which the Holy Spirit formed is the body in which he resides; this body is the church. (Eph. 1: 22, 23; Col. 1: 24.) Other apostles and Spirit-guided teachers preached the same gospel, and the Holy Spirit confirmed the words spoken by miraculous manifestations. "How shall we escape, if we neglect so great a salvation? which having at the first been spoken through the Lord, was confirmed unto us by them that heard; God also bearing witness with them, both by signs and wonders, and by manifold powers, and by gifts of the Holy Spirit, according to his own will." (Heb. 2: 3, 4.) These men of God continued to preach the gospel and reveal the will of God to lost man. The word spoken was finally recorded. The early church only knew "in part," but "when that which is perfect is come, that which is in part shall be done away. . . . For now we see in a mirror, darkly; but then face to face: now I know in part; but then shall I know fully even as also I was fully known." (1 Cor. 13: 9-12.)

The relation of the Holy Spirit today to the church differs somewhat to that relationship sustained in the early days of the church. All the miraculous manifestations which accompanied the spoken word to confirm it have ceased. We no longer need these extraordinary measures and gifts of the Holy Spirit to confirm the truth. Peter later in writing by the Holy Spirit expressed the apostolic method: "Which now have been announced unto you through them that preached the gospel unto you by the Holy Spirit sent forth from heaven." (1 Pet. 1: 12.) Paul states the apostolic method with this language: "How that our gospel came not unto you in word only, but also in power, and in the Holy Spirit." (1 Thess. 1: 5.) Those who heard and received the word had great "joy of the Holy Spirit." All the truth pertaining to man's redemption was spoken by these Spirit-guided men; it was confirmed, and today we have the perfect will of God. The church has been perfected in that it has the complete will of God today. (Eph. 4: 11-16.)

II. CHURCH THE BODY OF CHRIST

The church is frequently presented in the New Testament as the body of Christ. (Rom. 12: 4, 5; 1 Cor. 12: 14; Eph. 1: 22, 23; Col. 1: 24.) In the Ephesian letter the Holy Spirit depicts the church under these symbols: a building (Eph. 2: 20-22), a body (1: 22, 23), a bride (5: 25-32), and a brotherhood (2: 19). As a building the church has the foundation of the truth, "being

built upon the foundation of the apostles and prophets, Christ
Jesus himself being the chief corner stone." (Eph. 2: 20.)
Christians are the stones in this superstructure. This building is "a holy temple in the Lord, . . . a habitation of God in the
Spirit." (Eph. 2: 21, 22.) Blended with the idea of the church
as a building is the idea of it as a body. Great emphasis is put
upon the church as a body. In Ephesians the Holy Spirit uses
the figure of a body for the church to teach the relations of Christ
to Christians, Christians to each other, and the Holy Spirit to
Christians in their organic unity. Christ is the head of the body;
hence, the head of the church. (Eph. 5: 23; Col. 1: 18.) Christians are the individual members of the body of Christ; hence,
there is one body of Christ and but one church. (Eph. 4: 4.)
The concept of the church as a building and as a body is blended,
as the church is represented as "being built . . . *growth* . . .
builded together." (Eph. 2: 19-22.) The Holy Spirit further
writes of the body: "Unto the building up of the body of Christ
. . . may grow up in all things unto him, . . . maketh the increase
of the body unto the building up of itself in love." (Eph. 4:
12-16.) Christians are related to each other in being members of the one body, "and severally members one of another."
(Rom. 12: 5.)

The relation of the Holy Spirit to Christians in their organic
unity, that is, to the body of Christ, is expressed in this language:
"In whom ye also are builded together for a habitation of God
in the Spirit." "There is one body, and one Spirit." In the
Ephesian letter Paul states the relation of the Spirit to Christians
as individuals: the Holy Spirit seals them (1: 13; 4: 30), he
introduces them to the Father (2: 18), he gives them knowledge
(3: 5), he strengthens them with power in the inner man (3: 16),
he is the bond of their union (4: 3), he arms them with the
sword of the Spirit which is the word of God (6: 17), and he
inspires their prayers (6: 18). Another symbol of the church
is that of the bride; husbands are to love their wives as Christ
loves the church. "This mystery is great: but I speak in regard
of Christ and of the church." There seems to be progress in the
ascent of the symbols used here—building, body, bride. The
relation of the bridegroom to the bride is different from that of

building to foundation, or of body to head. The lesson of union is presented in all of the symbols. The fourth symbol is that of the brotherhood, and Christians have a fellowship that makes them one brotherhood; they are members of the one family of God, "of the household of God." (2: 19.) The Holy Spirit dwells in the body which is the church. "For as the body apart from the spirit is dead" (James 2: 26), even so a group or assembly apart from the Holy Spirit is dead.

III. CHURCH THE KINGDOM OF CHRIST

Christ while on earth teaching men frequently used the phrase "the kingdom of God," and the Holy Spirit in speaking of the church used the same phrase. (Matt. 6: 10; Acts 28: 23, 31; Rom. 14: 17; 1 Cor. 4: 20; 6: 9, 10; 15: 50; Gal. 5: 21; Col. 4: 11; 2 Thess. 1: 5.) Jesus only used the term "church" (Matt. 16: 18; 18: 17) twice so far as the record reveals; however, he used the term "kingdom" many times. The Holy Spirit used the term "church" more times than the phrase "kingdom of God." However, both Jesus and the Holy Spirit referred to the same institution. It is a spiritual kingdom; this is apparent from the titles which the Holy Spirit uses to describe the church. It is called "the kingdom of Christ and God" (Eph. 5: 5); "the kingdom of the Son of his love" (Col. 1: 13); God's "heavenly kingdom" (2 Tim. 4: 18); and "the eternal kingdom of our Lord and Saviour Jesus Christ" (2 Pet. 1: 11). All of these expressions indicate a spiritual relationship between Christ, the head of the church, and the king of the kingdom. Christ is not called "the king of the church," neither is he called "the head of the kingdom." But he is the king over his kingdom and the head of the church. He does not have two institutions, a kingdom and a church; these terms apply to one and the same thing. So long as the church remains on earth, Christ will be the head of it; so long as the kingdom continues among men, Christ will be the king of it. He continues to reign over his people. The citizens of the kingdom are admonished: "Sanctify in your hearts Christ as Lord." (1 Pet. 3: 15.) Every citizen in the kingdom of God acknowledges Christ as king; he is "the King of kings, and Lord of lords." (1 Tim. 6: 15.) He must rule in the hearts of his people. He will continue his reign until he delivers the kingdom back to God. "Then cometh the end, when he shall deliver up the kingdom to God, even the Father; when he shall have abolished all rule and all authority and power. For he must reign, till he hath put all his enemies under his feet. . . . And when all things have been subjected unto him, then shall the Son also himself be subjected to him that did subject all things unto him, that God may be all in all." (1 Cor. 15: 24-28.) We see the meaning of the term "kingdom" when we see what the kingdom is. The Holy Spirit describes the kingdom with this language: "For the kingdom of God is not eating and drinking, but righteousness and peace and joy in the Holy Spirit." (Rom. 14: 17.)

The church as a kingdom will continue so long as Christ reigns. This kingdom is a spiritual one and cannot be shaken. "Wherefore, receiving a kingdom that cannot be shaken, let us have grace, whereby we may offer service well-pleasing to God with reverence and awe: for our God is a consuming fire." (Heb. 12: 28, 29.) Christians constitute the kingdom of God on earth. The kingdom of Israel, or the Jewish theocracy, was removed and the church established; this kingdom which Christians have received cannot be shaken and removed as was the Jewish kingdom. This should give us courage and confidence.

IV. Church Temple of God

Under the patriarchal age God's people were permitted to worship at any place. The patriarch could erect his altar and make his sacrifice and worship God at that altar. Wherever the patriarch sojourned or wandered, he was permitted to build his altar and worship. Under the Jewish dispensation the tabernacle was constructed, and God called the worshiper to come to the altar at the tabernacle. The tent of meeting or tabernacle was made of cloth and other material suited to be moved from place to place. Finally Jerusalem was selected as a permanent place for the tabernacle, then David prepared some of the material to build a place of worship. He was not permitted to build this house of worship, but Solomon was permitted to build it. It was called the temple. The temple was the central and permanent place of worship for the Jews; the temple took the place of the tabernacle. God recorded his name and was supposed to dwell in the temple. The temple was to remain until the Christ should come and fulfill the law. The tabernacle may be called a type of the temple, and the temple a type of the church. As God dwelt in his tabernacle and temple, so through the Holy Spirit God dwells in the church. "Temple" became fixed in the mind and language of the Jews. Even after conversion in a symbolic way the term "temple" was used and has been applied to the church. The material temple has ceased to exist and a spiritual significance has been given to "temple." The interweaving of temple associations with Christian thought and life runs throughout the New Testament.

Jesus himself gave the germ of the idea of a spiritual temple when he spoke of his body as the temple. (John 2: 19, 21.) Paul by the Holy Spirit in his early writings spoke of "the Jerusalem that is above" as the "mother" of us all. (Gal. 4: 26.) Again the Holy Spirit speaks of the man of sin as sitting "in the temple of God." (2 Thess. 2: 4.) The middle wall of partition which separated Jew and Gentile has been broken down, and all Christians are now represented as "a holy temple in the Lord." (Eph. 2: 14, 21.) The church in the collective sense is spoken of as a temple, and individual Christians are represented as a temple. (1 Cor. 3: 16, 17; 6: 19.) Finally, in Revelation, the vision is that of the heavenly temple itself (Rev. 11: 19), and the climax is reached in the vision, "and the twelve gates were twelve pearls; each one of the several gates was of one pearl: and the street of the city was pure gold, as it were transparent glass. And I saw no temple therein: for the Lord God the Almighty, and the Lamb, are the temple thereof" (Rev. 21: 21, 22).

The church is called the house of God. (1 Tim. 3: 15.) It belongs to God and is the dwelling place of God through the Spirit. It is a spiritual house. (1 Pet. 2: 5.) Christians are "living stones" in this spiritual house, where God dwells through the Holy Spirit. (1 Cor. 3: 16, 17.) Christians are then called the temple of the Holy Spirit as he dwells in Christians.

V. CHRIST THE TRUE VINE

While Christ was on earth, and just before he left to go back to the Father, he spoke of himself as "the true vine." (John 15:

1-5.)   Christians are the branches of this vine, as they are members of the body of Christ and citizens of his kingdom. They must abide in Christ if they would bear fruit.   The fruit of the Spirit (Gal. 5: 22) can be borne only by abiding in Christ. Any branch separated from the vine is unfruitful; it is dead and must be destroyed.   Christians must have vital connection with the "true vine," which is Christ, before they can bear fruit.   They must have the Spirit of Christ in order to abide in him.   "But ye are not in the flesh but in the Spirit, if so be that the Spirit of God dwelleth in you.   But if any man hath not the Spirit of Christ, he is none of his.   And if Christ is in you, the body is dead because of sin; but the Spirit is life because of righteousness."   (Rom. 8: 9, 10.)   All life comes through Christ.   There is no such thing as a Christian out of Christ or not vitally connected with Christ.   As the branch must be connected with the vine in order to receive the life-giving fluid that it may bear fruit in the natural realm, so Christians must be connected with Christ in order that the life-giving Spirit may be in them and bear fruit to the glory of God.

The Holy Spirit is vitally connected with the church as our spirits are vitally connected with our bodies.   The church is the body of Christ, and the Spirit dwells in the body; it gives vitality to every member of the church; it gives life to the branches of the true vine.   On the day of Pentecost, the Holy Spirit came and took up his abode in the church; he continued to give direction to the church through the apostles.   The early days of the church were fruitful days as the Holy Spirit guided the leadership of the church. That the Holy Spirit continued to direct the activities of the church is manifest in the incidents recorded in the early chapters of Acts. Peter said to Ananias, "Why hath Satan filled thy heart to lie to the Holy Spirit, and to keep back part of the price of the land?" (Acts 5: 3.)   Peter then said, "Thou hast not lied unto men, but unto God."   (Verse 4.)   To lie to the Holy Spirit was to lie to God, as the Holy Spirit was guiding through the truth of the gospel the apostles in the activities of the church.   Later we find that the Holy Spirit guided in the activities of the church at Jerusalem when the question of circumcision was settled.   "For it seemed good to the Holy Spirit, and to us, to lay upon you no greater burden than these necessary things." (Acts 15: 28.) The Holy Spirit directed the leaders of the church at Antioch in sending out Paul and Barnabas. "And as they ministered to the Lord, and fasted, the Holy Spirit said, Separate me Barnabas and Saul for the work whereunto I have called them." (Acts 13: 2.) Verse four says, "So they, being sent forth by the Holy Spirit, went down to Seleucia." These men were members of the church; they were branches of the true vine and were thus guided by the Holy Spirit.

HOLY SPIRIT AND PRAYER

INTRODUCTION.

Prayer universal; man a praying being; a helpless and suffering being; looks up to a greater for help and relief.

I. MAN NEEDS TO KNOW HOW TO PRAY.

   1. New Testament teaches how to pray.

      a. Must pray in faith. (Matt. 21: 22; Mark 11: 24.)

      b. Pray according to God's will. (1 John 5: 14, 15.)

      c. In the name of Christ. (John 14: 13, 14.)

      d. Be obedient to God's will. (1 John 3: 22.)

   2. Examples of prayer.

      a. Jesus the perfect example. (Luke 11: 1.)

      b. Example for disciples. (Matt. 6: 9-15.)

   3. Persistence in prayer.

II. HOLY SPIRIT HELPS IN PRAYER. (Rom. 8: 26, 27.)

   1. Helps our infirmities.

   2. Teaches us how to pray.

   3. Makes intercession for us.

III. INFLUENCE OF THE HOLY SPIRIT.

   1. From *without* on sinners. (John 16: 7-11.)

      a. Through the gospel producing faith.

      b. Producing repentance.

      c. Leading to baptism.

   2. From *within* Christians.

      a. As Comforter. (John 14: 26; 15: 26.)

      b. As helper. (Rom. 8: 26, 27.)

IV. HOLY SPIRIT WITNESSETH WITH OUR SPIRIT. (Rom. 8: 16.)

   1. Holy Spirit given to believers. (Acts 5: 32; Gal. 3: 2, 3; 4: 6; 1 Thess. 4: 8.)

   2. Holy Spirit dwells in believers. (Rom. 8: 9; 1 Cor. 6: 19; Eph. 3: 17.)

   3. How Holy Spirit bears witness.

      a. Through word of God.

      b. Word must dwell in us. (Col. 3: 16.)

HOLY SPIRIT AND PRAYER

"And in like manner the Spirit also helpeth our infirmity: for we know not how to pray as we ought; but the Spirit himself maketh intercession for us with groanings which cannot be uttered; and he that searcheth the hearts knoweth what is the mind of the Spirit, because he maketh intercession for the saints according to the will of God." (Rom. 8: 26, 27.)

Man by nature is a religious being; man in every stage of development and every grade of civilization recognizes his helplessness and a need of a higher power to give him aid. Even savages looked to the Great Spirit for help; every heathen religion has a place for prayer. All nations and peoples have their gods, altars, and temples; a man without any system of worship is the exception and not the rule. This desire to call on some higher being grows out of the needs of man. With all of his superiority over other creatures, he is dependent on a being above himself. Prayer is universal with man. The subject of prayer is one of universal interest and of the greatest importance. Wherever man has gone, the practice of prayer has prevailed; sometimes it has been perverted by ignorance and prompted by superstition. Prayer becomes the cry of helplessness and suffering to one who is able, or thought to be able, to help and relieve the suffering. No one can restrain himself from uttering entreaties in prayer when he so deeply feels his necessities.

Prayer has a large place, as might be expected, in the Bible. The Bible recites constant examples of the practice of prayer as well as its prevalence. Abundant instructions are found in the Scriptures on the nature and obligations of prayer; the Scriptures provide for the observance of prayer in all of the relations of life— private, social, and public. It will be found that the revelations of Scripture are in complete accordance and agreement with the desires and necessities of man. At this time we are more concerned about the connection of the Holy Spirit and prayer, and especially with the connection of prayer with the work of the Holy Spirit. A thorough discussion of the Holy Spirit would be incomplete without the discussion of the part that the Holy Spirit has in the prayers of God's people today.

I. Man Needs to Know How to Pray

Since the New Testament is the guide to Christians, we find full and complete instructions in it concerning prayer. It teaches us how to pray, for what to pray, the duties of prayer. We learn that the Holy Spirit teaches us what to pray for, to enable us to pray aright, and to encourage us in the duty until we receive that for which we pray. There may be examples of prayer in the Old Testament which may be instructive to the Lord's people today, but the New Testament is the only book that can teach man how to be pleasing to God in all his acts of worship and service to God. When we collect or collate all the Scriptures in the New Testament concerning prayer, we find that there are certain essentials to acceptable prayer. Every Christian should know the conditions of acceptable prayer. It is not enough *just to pray,* neither is it enough to *recite* a prayer; we must know how to pray an *acceptable* prayer. Christians, to be pleasing to God, must pray *in faith.* Jesus said: "And all things, whatsoever ye shall ask in prayer, believing, ye shall receive." (Matt. 21: 22.) Mark records this instruction of Jesus as follows: "Therefore I say unto you, All things whatsoever ye pray and ask for, believe that ye receive them, and ye shall have them." (Mark 11: 24.) So we must *believe* our petitions and believe that God through Christ will give them. Furthermore, we must pray *according to God's will.* We pray to God, and he has expressed through the Holy Spirit his will concerning our prayers. The Holy Spirit said again through John: "And this is the boldness which we have toward him, that, if we ask anything according to his will, he heareth us: and if we know that he heareth us whatsoever we ask, we know that we have the petitions which we have asked of him." (1 John 5: 14, 15.) No one need think that God will hear and answer a prayer which is contrary to God's will. Moreover, an *acceptable prayer* must be *in the name of Christ.* Christ is our Mediator; he stands between us and God, and we can approach God only *through* Christ. (1 Tim. 2: 5; Heb. 12: 24.) Jesus said while on earth in anticipation of his leaving the earth: "Hitherto have ye asked nothing in my name: ask, and ye shall receive, that your joy may be made full." (John 16: 24.) Again he said: "And whatsoever ye shall ask in my name, that will I do, that the Father may be glorified in the Son. If ye shall ask anything in my name, that will I do." (John 14: 13, 14.) Therefore an *acceptable prayer* must be *in faith, according to the will of God, in the name of Christ, and in obedience to God's will.* The Holy Spirit again said: "And whatsover we ask we receive of him, because we keep his commandments and do the things that are pleasing in his sight." (1 John 3: 22.) The Holy Spirit warns Christians how to act that their "prayers be not hindered." (1 Pet. 3: 7.)

The New Testament records a number of prayers. Jesus is our perfect example; he prayed often to God. We have a record of many of these prayers; they become examples to his disciples. "And it came to pass, as he was praying in a certain place, that when he ceased, one of his disciples said unto him, Lord, teach us to pray, even as John also taught his disciples." (Luke 11: 1.) Upon this request Jesus then gave to his disciples a model prayer. This is familiar to all and is found in Matt. 6: 9-15 and Luke 11: 2-4. This model was given before the church was established; some modifications of it have been made by the Holy Spirit since the kingdom of God was established.

Christians are warned against using "vain repetitions" in prayer, and to avoid merely "forms of prayer" which have been written by others. However, the Savior and the Holy Spirit have taught the persistency in prayer. The answer to our prayers may be deferred in order that we may learn patience and trust in waiting for the answer. God uses his own time in answering our prayers, but in due season we know "we shall reap, if we faint not." Jesus said to the Canaanitish woman who importunately pleaded with him in prayer: "O woman, great is thy faith: be it done unto thee even as thou wilt." (Matt. 15: 28.) Again he said: "Unto them to the end that they ought always to pray, and not to faint." (Luke 18: 1.) We have a number of recorded examples of this type of prayers. Jacob wrestled all night with the angel and said: "I will not let thee go, except thou bless me." (Gen. 32: 26.) So prayed Moses, when he cried for Israel: "If thou wilt forgive their sin—; and if not, blot me, I pray thee, out of thy book which thou hast written." (Ex. 32: 32.) So prayed Joshua when he pleaded: "Oh, Lord, what shall I say, after that Israel hath turned their backs before their enemies!" (Josh. 7: 8.) So prayed the early disciples till "the place was shaken wherein they were gathered together; and they were all filled with the Holy Spirit, and they spake the word of God with boldness." (Acts 4: 31.) So prayed the church for Peter when he was in prison till an angel came and delivered him. (Acts 12: 5-11.) Then, truly, "the Spirit himself maketh intercession for us with groanings which cannot be uttered."

II. HOLY SPIRIT HELPS IN PRAYER (Rom. 8: 26, 27)

We may not understand all the work that the Holy Spirit does; we may not understand all his workings in our prayers; but there is one thing we can understand, and that is that the Holy Spirit *does have something to do in our prayers.* This is a declaration of the Holy Spirit through Paul: "And in like manner the Spirit also helpeth our infirmity: for we know not how to pray as we ought; but the Spirit himself maketh intercession for us with groanings which cannot be uttered; and he that searcheth the hearts knoweth what is the mind of the Spirit, because he maketh intercession for the saints according to the will of God." (Rom. 8: 26, 27.) We can understand this declaration to mean that the Holy Spirit helps us in praying. We have seen in the chapter "Indwelling of the Holy Spirit" that the Holy Spirit dwells in Christians; he dwells in the church. Since he dwells in Christians, he helps them in the act of prayer. Prayer is to God the Father in the name of Christ, and by the help of the Holy Spirit. Hence, each member of the Godhead is included in every *acceptable prayer.* The Holy Spirit through the word of God helps us to know what we should ask in prayer and how we should pray. The Holy Spirit inspires our prayers; we are not of ourselves sufficiently fervent; prayers languish on our tongues, but the Spirit pleads for us with unutterable groanings; hence, our intercession is not in vain or amiss. We do not know the will of God perfectly; many Christians are ignorant of many things that they ought to know, but the Holy Spirit knows the revealed will of God and the mind of God and helps us in our intercession to God. The Holy Spirit instructs us in the matter of our prayers, "for we know not how to pray as we ought." The Holy Spirit enables us to pray aright, while he instructs us in the matter of prayer through the New Testament teachings on prayer; again, "the Spirit himself maketh intercession for us with groanings which cannot be uttered." The Holy Spirit knows both what we need and how to pray for it; he therefore supplements our weakness; the mode in which the Spirit intercedes is by prayer; and the mode in which he prays is in groanings which cannot be framed into human speech, for they include things for which human speech has no names. They are the deep, real wants of human souls, both for time and eternity. The "groanings" are not the "groanings" of the Holy Spirit; they are our groanings; they are inarticulate expressions that the Holy Spirit makes for us. Words are faint signs or ideas of the desires of a humble soul; the agony of the heart oftentimes is beyond the cogency of language. The Holy Spirit is able to take the yearnings, longings, groanings of the soul and form them and direct them so as to make them express to God according to his will our true wants. Sometimes we feel a deep need of blessings from God; the thought may be too big for utterance in our language, but the Holy Spirit knows how to present this to God for us. How grateful we ought to be that we have this promise of the Holy Spirit in prayer!

III. INFLUENCE OF THE HOLY SPIRIT

The influence of the Holy Spirit in a general way takes two directions in his work for the redemption of man—his influence *from without* and his influence *from within*. The Holy Spirit wields an influence in the world *from without* through the gospel truth. Jesus said just before he left his disciples: "It is expedient for you that I go away; for if I go not away, the Comforter will not come unto you; but if I go, I will send him unto you. And he, when he is come, will convict the world in respect of sin, and of righteousness, and of judgment: of sin, because they believe not on me; of righteousness, because I go to the Father, and ye behold me no more; of judgment, because the prince of this world hath been judged." (John 16: 7-11.) The gospel is God's power to save. (Rom. 1: 16.) It is to be preached to the whole creation of lost men. (Mark 16: 15, 16.) The Holy Spirit uses the gospel in convicting the sinner; the sinner hears the gospel; he believes it; he obeys it. In this way the gospel *from without* is brought to bear upon the mind and heart of the sinner; in this way the Holy Spirit produces faith, repentance, and baptism. The Holy Spirit teaches the sinner to believe on Christ, to repent of his sins, and to be baptized into Christ.

The Holy Spirit, as he dwells in Christians, has an influence on them *from within*. The Holy Spirit was promised by Jesus to his apostles as a "Comforter." (John 14: 26; 15: 26.) Christians may "grieve the Spirit," or even "resist the Spirit"; Christians may also yield to the Spirit and pray in the Spirit. They may be influenced by the Holy Spirit as he helps them. We see no reason why the influence of the Spirit would be exerted *from without,* through the gospel, and not be active *from within* with the Christians. The Christian has been born of the Spirit; he is in a spiritual kingdom; he is a member of a spiritual body, the church; he is governed by spiritual laws; he has the indwelling of the Holy Spirit. Surely the influence of the Holy Spirit is active *from within* the Christian. This helps us to understand something of the work of the Holy Spirit in prayer.

IV. Holy Spirit Witnesseth with Our Spirit (Rom. 8: 16)

The New Testament frequently declares that the Holy Spirit is given to believers in Christ. Luke writes that Peter said: "We are witnesses of these things; and so is the Holy Spirit, whom God hath given to them that obey him." (Acts 5: 32.) Paul wrote: "This only would I learn from you, Received ye the Spirit by the works of the law, or by the hearing of faith? Are ye so foolish? having begun in the Spirit, are ye now perfected in the flesh? Did ye suffer so many things in vain? if it be indeed in vain. He therefore that supplieth to you the Spirit, and worketh miracles among you, doeth he it by the works of the law, or by the hearing of faith?" (Gal. 3: 2-5.) And again: "Because ye are sons, God sent forth the Spirit of his Son into our hearts, crying, Abba, Father." (Gal. 4: 6.) Again Paul wrote: "Therefore he that rejecteth, rejecteth not man, but God, who giveth his Holy Spirit unto you." (1 Thess. 4: 8.) So the Holy Spirit dwells only in the believers in Christ. (Rom. 8: 9; 1 Cor. 6: 19; Eph. 3: 17.)

"The Spirit himself beareth witness with our spirit, that we are children of God." (Rom. 8: 16.) How does the Holy Spirit bear witness with our Spirit? We have seen that the Holy Spirit dwells in the hearts of God's people in the same sense in which God and Christ dwell in them; that is, by the faith and love which he produces in the Christian heart through the word of God. "Let the word of Christ dwell in you richly" (Col. 3: 16) is the admonition of the Holy Spirit to Christians. No one ever has had a correct religious thought or a real Christian experience that the word of God has not prompted. This is the way that the Holy Spirit guides the Christian and bears witness "with our spirit" that we are the children of God. The Holy Spirit teaches what one must do to become a Christian. The spirit of man knows whether he has done that which the Holy Spirit teaches. "For who among men knoweth the things of a man, save the spirit of the man, which is in him? even so the things of God none knoweth, save the Spirit of God. But we received, not the spirit of the world, but the spirit which is from God; that we might know the things that were freely given to us of God." (1 Cor. 2: 11, 12.) The Holy Spirit teaches the alien sinner to hear the gospel; the sinner's spirit knows whether he has heard the gospel. The Holy Spirit teaches the sinner to believe in Christ; the Spirit of man can testify whether he believes in Christ. The Holy Spirit teaches one to repent of his sins; the spirit of man can testify that he has repented; the Holy Spirit teaches one to be baptized; the spirit of man can testify whether he has obeyed this command. If one has been baptized into Christ, that one is a new creature. (2 Cor. 5: 17.) He has been born of water and of the Spirit. (John 3: 5.) The Holy Spirit leads one to become a Christian, and "as many as are led by the Spirit of God, these are sons of God." (Rom. 8: 14.) The testimony of the Holy Spirit and the testimony of the Christian agree in that God's will has been done. Hence, as Christians we do not pray for the Holy Spirit to come. He is here. Neither do we pray for the baptism of the Holy Spirit; that promise has been accomplished. We let the word of Christ which dwells in us be the witness as to what we are to do, and our spirits testify that we have done this; hence, they agree that we are children of God.

Chapter XVIII

RESTRAINT AND CONSTRAINT OF HOLY SPIRIT

Introduction.

Many functions of the Holy Spirit; he both restrains and constrains; prohibition and permission.

I. Free Agency of Man.

1. God created man with volitional powers.

2. Man responsible for his acts.

3. God never forces man to serve him.

4. Christ respected the will power of man.

5. Holy Spirit acts in harmony with God and Christ.

II. Functions of Restraining.

1. Striving of the Holy Spirit. (Gen. 6: 3.)

2. Holy Spirit restrained Balaam. (Num. 22: 18, 35.)

3. Holy Spirit restrained Paul. (Acts 16: 6, 7.)

4. Elymas restrained by Holy Spirit. (Acts 13: 8-11.)

5. Seven sons of Sceva. (Acts 19: 13-20.)

III. Functions of Constraining.

1. Balaam constrained. (Num. 22: 20; 23: 12.)

2. Micaiah constrained. (1 Kings 22: 14.)

3. Apostles spoke by Holy Spirit. (Matt. 10: 20; Acts 2: 4.)

4. Paul constrained. (Acts 13: 2, 4; 16: 9, 10; 18: 5.)

5. Constrained to go to Jerusalem. (Acts 20: 22.)

6. Holy Spirit made bishops. (Acts 20: 28.)

IV. Various Functions of Holy Spirit.

1. Baptism of the apostles. (Acts 2: 1-4.)

2. Samaritans received the Holy Spirit. (Acts 8: 17.)

3. Household of Cornelius baptized. (Acts 10: 44-48.)

4. Disciples at Ephesus. (Acts 19: 6.)

RESTRAINT AND CONSTRAINT OF HOLY SPIRIT

"And they went through the region of Phrygia and Galatia, having been forbidden of the Holy Spirit to speak the word in Asia; and when they were come over against Mysia, they assayed to go into Bithynia; and the Spirit of Jesus suffered them not." (Acts 16: 6, 7.)

The work of God in the creation of the world and in ruling the universe requires many operations. The work that Christ did while in the flesh was manifold. He taught the will of God; trained his disciples; worked miracles and confirmed his claim to be the Son of God; refuted religious error; met the onslaughts of enemies; suffered in the flesh; prayed for his disciples; became obedient to the will of God; and was crucified for the sins of the world. The work of the Holy Spirit is as various as that of Christ. The Holy Spirit had a part in the material and spiritual creation; guided the writers of the Bible; came to earth in a miraculous manifestation on Pentecost; enabled different ones to speak with other tongues and other miraculous manifestations; takes part in the conversion of sinners; dwells in Christians; bears fruit to the glory of God; gives vitality to the church; helps God's people in prayer; restrains and constrains men upon the earth.

The Holy Spirit teaches man what not to do as well as giving him instructions as to what he should do. The teachings of the Holy Spirit are both exclusive and inclusive. He excludes everything that is not specifically taught and includes everything that is taught. Man has thus been given double instructions in the way of life and salvation; when he is forbidden to do certain things, this is one kind of instruction; when he is instructed what to do, it is another kind; so the Holy Spirit tells *what not to do* and then clearly instructs *what to do*. Man has no excuse for disobeying God. God's will has been so clearly revealed in so many different ways that intelligent man need not err. The prophet said that the way should be so plain that "the wayfaring men, yea fools, shall not err therein." (Isa. 35: 8.) The Holy Spirit has demonstrated and fulfilled this prophecy.

I. Free Agency of Man

Man has been created in the image of God. Whether we know the plenitude of this fact or not, we do know that man has the power, like God, to purpose, plan, and execute his plans. Man has been left free to direct his own course. It is true that man needed the revelation of God's will to *know* what is the best course to follow. The prophet said: "O Jehovah, I know that the way of man is not in himself; it is not in man that walketh to direct his steps." (Jer. 10: 23.) Furthermore, man has been warned against following that way which seems right to himself. "There is a way which seemeth right unto a man, but the end thereof are the ways of death." (Prov. 16: 25.) Yet with this warning, man is still left free to choose whether he will follow his own way or be guided by divine wisdom. When man was placed in the Garden of Eden, he was left free to choose whether he would obey God or whether he would obey Satan; man chose to eat of the fruit that God had forbidden. Man has been held responsible for his acts. There could be no condemnation of sin if man was not free to act. God would be unjust to condemn man for choosing a certain course if man was not free to make the choice. All the responsibilities that rest upon man emphasize the fact that man is free to act.

God has never forced man to serve him. In the long history from the first of Genesis to the close of the New Testament, not one instance do we find where God has refused to let man do as he pleased. All of the warnings in the Old Testament and the condemnation of disobedience in the New Testament emphasize the fact that God has left man free to exercise his own will. He has pointed out to man what is best and has encouraged him to do that which heaven instructs him to do, but leaves man free to choose whether he will do the will of God or follow 'his own course. God never compels man to serve him; he has never coerced or forced man to do his will. He has always left man free and has never used any coercion, nor has he used any coercive methods to force man to obey him. When Christ came and moved among men, he respected the will of man. At no time did he limit the power of man to choose whether he would obey or disobey. When he gave the commission for his gospel to be preached "to the whole creation," he said: "He that believeth and is baptized shall be saved; but he that disbelieveth shall be condemned." (Mark 16: 16.) This shows that he left man, as did God, free to believe or disbelieve, to obey or disobey, to follow him or to rebel against him.

The Holy Spirit acts in harmony with God and Christ. While we speak of the restraint and constraint of the Holy Spirit, yet we recognize that the Holy Spirit leaves man free to choose his own course in the work that he does. Man can turn a deaf ear to the words of the Holy Spirit, but the Holy Spirit will not force him to hear. The Holy Spirit can furnish evidence that Christ is the Son of God; this evidence can be accumulative and convincing, yet man is free to deny the evidence and disbelieve. The Holy Spirit may gently woo and influence Christians through the truth of God, but man is still left free to turn away from the influence of the Holy Spirit and follow his own will. The Holy Spirit may thunder his fearful warnings and pronounce the anathemas of God with the severity of the thunderbolts of heaven, still man is left free to defy God and take the consequences.

II. Function of Restraining

A study of the Holy Spirit would not be complete without taking some thought on the restraining power of the Holy Spirit. Early in the history of mankind God said: "My Spirit shall not strive with man for ever." (Gen. 6: 3.) This implies that the Spirit of God was seeking to restrain man in his wicked ways; in those early days through Noah and others, the Spirit of God would restrain the wicked. But those who willfully resisted and grieved the Spirit were left to the hardness of their own heart and the blindness of their own knowledge. God delights in extending mercy to fallen man; his mercy ever lingers longingly for man; his mercy graciously warns the wicked, but if man refuses to heed the warning, he must take the consequences. The earth at the time of Noah was ripe for destruction, yet God promised to give time for the repentance; if they should not repent, destruction by a flood was inevitable. "In which also he went and preached unto the spirits in prison, that aforetime were disobedient, when the longsuffering of God waited in the days of Noah, while the ark was a preparing, wherein few, that is, eight souls, were saved through water." (1 Pet. 3: 19, 20.) All of the good and righteous influence that Noah preached as a preacher of righteousness served as a restraining influence, but the wicked refused to heed the warning and yield to the instruction given by Noah.

We have another clear case where the Holy Spirit sought to restrain one. Balaam lived among the Midianites; he was a false prophet, or he was an unfaithful prophet. The children of Israel were in the wilderness and sought to pass through the territory of Balak, king of Moab. Balak did not want them to pass through his territory; he sent for Balaam to come and curse the people of God. Balaam entertained overnight the messengers of Balak. During the night God told Balaam: "Thou shalt not go with them; thou shalt not curse the people; for they are blessed." (Num. 22: 12.) Balaam next morning told the messengers that "Jehovah refuseth to give me leave to go with you." (Num. 22: 13.) The messengers returned to Balak and reported to him what Balaam had said. Balak then sent more honorable messengers with richer gifts to induce Balaam to come and curse Israel. This time Jehovah told him to go, but that he could not "go beyond the word of Jehovah" to do less or more. Balaam went and attempted three times to curse Israel, but each time "the Spirit of God came upon him" and he blessed Israel. He attempted to curse, but pronounced a blessing. We see here some of the restraining power of the Holy Spirit.

Another clear case of the restraining function of the Holy Spirit is seen in connection with Paul. Paul was on his second missionary tour; he had as his companions Silas and Timothy. "And they went through the region of Phrygia and Galatia, having been forbidden of the Holy Spirit to speak the word in Asia; and when they were come over against Mysia, they assayed to go into Bithynia; and the Spirit of Jesus suffered them not." (Acts 16: 6, 7.) This language is explicit; for some reason God's time had not come for the gospel to be preached in these provinces. Notwithstanding, Paul's purpose and endeavor was to go into these regions, but he and his company were "forbidden of the Holy Spirit" and "suffered" not to go. Here, in these verses, we are told twice that the restraint was of the Holy Spirit. We need not exercise an uninformed imagination and conjecture as to why the Holy Spirit restrained them. We simply have the fact that they were restrained from going into these regions by the Holy Spirit.

Furthermore, in the experience of Paul we have another clear case of the Holy Spirit's restraining one. This time Paul and Barnabas had come to Paphos on their first missionary tour. They had spoken the word of God to the people, and there "Elymas the sorcerer (for so is his name by interpretation) withstood them, seeking to turn aside the proconsul from the faith. But Saul, who is also called Paul, filled with the Holy Spirit, fastened his eyes on him, and said, O full of all guile and all villany, thou son of the devil, thou enemy of all righteousness, wilt thou not cease to pervert the right ways of the Lord?" (Acts 13: 8-10.) Then Paul smote him with blindness for a season; he was thus restrained by the Holy Spirit from further perverting the will of God or "the right ways of the Lord."

The case of the "seven sons" of Sceva is another illustration of the function of the Holy Spirit in restraining men. Paul had preached at Ephesus and had confirmed the preaching of the gospel with miracles. "And God wrought special miracles by the hands of Paul." There were "certain also of the strolling Jews, exorcists," who took it upon themselves "to name over them that had the evil spirits the name of the Lord Jesus, saying, I adjure you by Jesus whom Paul preacheth." "The evil spirit answered and said unto them, Jesus I know, and Paul I know; but who are ye?" The man who possessed the evil spirit leaped upon these seven sons of Sceva and "they fled out of that house naked and wounded." (Acts 19: 13-20.) The Holy Spirit in this manner restrained these wicked men from doing in the name of Jesus that which Paul was able to do.

III. Function of Constraining

The Holy Spirit has not only the power or function to restrain men from doing things, but he has the power of *constraining* them to do things. So another act of administration of the work of the Holy Spirit is seen in his constraining influence. Balaam was not only restrained from cursing Israel, but he was *constrained*

to bless Israel. When God told him that night that he should
go with the messengers of Balak, he also said to him: "But only
the word which I speak unto thee, that shalt thou do." (Num.
22: 20.) After Balaam had blessed Israel and Balak had com-
plained, Balaam answered: "Must I not take heed to speak that
which Jehovah putteth in my mouth?" (Num. 23: 12.) So
Balaam was constrained to speak the words which Jehovah had
given him to speak.

We have another example that illustrates the *constraining* influence of the Holy Spirit. Jehoshaphat had joined with Ahab
to fight against Ramoth-gilead. All the prophets of Ahab had
encouraged him to go against the king of Syria. However,
Jehoshaphat was not willing to be guided by what Ahab's false
prophets said; so he inquired if there was not another prophet of
Jehovah that they might inquire of him. Ahab replied that there
was one by the name of Micaiah, but "I hate him; for he doth
not prophesy good concerning me, but evil." However, Jehoshaphat had them to send for Micaiah. He came, and all the false
prophets of Ahab told him what they had prophesied and asked him
to voice their prophecy. Micaiah refused to do this, and said: "As
Jehovah liveth, what Jehovah saith unto me, that will I speak."
(1 Kings 22: 14.) Micaiah then predicted the fall of Ahab or
his defeat in battle. Because he would not join the false prophets,
Micaiah was put in prison. He pronounced the doom of Ahab;
he was constrained by the Holy Spirit to contradict the false
prophets of Ahab.

The apostles on the day of Pentecost were *constrained* to speak
the word of God. Jesus had told his apostles that "it is not ye
that speak, but the Spirit of your Father that speaketh in you."
(Matt. 10: 20.) So the Holy Spirit came on Pentecost and
baptized the apostles, "and they were all filled with the Holy
Spirit, and began to speak with other tongues, as the Spirit gave
them utterance." (Acts 2: 4.) This is a clear case where the
Holy Spirit constrained the apostles to speak. Paul, the apostle
to the Gentiles, was *constrained* by the Holy Spirit to leave Antioch
with Barnabas and preach the gospel to the Gentiles. (Acts 13:
2, 4.) Side by side with the act of restraining Paul from going
into Phrygia and Galatia and Bithynia, we have an example of

constraining him by a vision to go into Macedonia. "And when he had seen the vision, straightway we sought to go forth into Macedonia, concluding that God had called us to preach the gospel unto them." (Acts 16: 10.) So on the one hand, Paul and his companions are *prohibited and restrained,* and on the other they are *permitted and constrained* to go to another place. Another instance on record is "when Silas and Timothy came down from Macedonia, Paul was constrained by the word, testifying to the Jews that Jesus was the Christ." (Acts 18: 5.) This shows us how Paul was constrained by the Holy Spirit; he was *constrained by the word;* that is, the Holy Spirit taught him what he should do. Similar cases are when Paul was constrained to go to Jerusalem (Acts 20: 22), and when the Holy Spirit made bishops of certain men at Ephesus (Acts 20: 28).

IV. VARIOUS FUNCTIONS OF THE HOLY SPIRIT

There are various functions of the Holy Spirit in completing his work in the redemption of man. There were the miraculous manifestations of the work of the Holy Spirit. Sometimes the Holy Spirit is manifested in his work in a baptism. This occurred on the day of Pentecost to the apostles. (Acts 2: 1-4.) Again we have the apostles "filled with the Holy Spirit" (Acts 4: 8, 31); Saul was "filled with the Holy Spirit" (Acts 13: 9). The Samaritans received the Holy Spirit. Peter and John went down to Samaria and "then laid they their hands on them, and they received the Holy Spirit." (Acts 8: 17.) In each of these cases there were various manifestations of the work of the Holy Spirit.

The Gentiles received the baptismal form of the Holy Spirit. (Acts 10: 44-48.) Peter had gone to the household of Cornelius and began to speak the word of the Lord to them, and suddenly "the Holy Spirit fell on all them that heard the word." The Jewish Christians who were present "were amazed, as many as came with Peter, because that on the Gentiles also was poured out the gift of the Holy Spirit. For they heard them speak with tongues, and magnify God." Paul went to Ephesus and found certain ones there, and he asked them: "Did ye receive the Holy Spirit when ye believed? And they said unto him, Nay, we did not so much as hear whether the Holy Spirit was given." Paul then gave them further instruction, and when "they were baptized into the name of the Lord Jesus," Paul "laid his hands upon them, the Holy Spirit came on them; and they spake with tongues, and prophesied." (Acts 19: 6.) Many other examples could be cited showing the various functions of the Holy Spirit, both in restraining and constraining individuals.

The word of God as revealed in the Bible is the agent through which the Holy Spirit constrains and restrains Christians. God not only tells man what he should do, and often how he should do that, but he also tells what man should not do. God commands man to go forward at times, and again he forbids his doing things. There are two elements in the Christian doctrine—the positive and the negative. The positive element teaches what to do and the negative element restrains men from going beyond that which is written. The Holy Spirit said through James, "Pure religion and undefiled before our God and Father is this, to visit the fatherless and widows in their affliction, and to keep oneself unspotted from the world." (James 1: 27.) Here we see something that man must do and something that he must keep from doing. The Holy Spirit said, "Cease to do evil; learn to do well." (Isa. 1: 16, 17.) Here again we see the positive and the negative elements of Christianity—the constraining and the restraining influence of the Holy Spirit. Christians are taught not to take vengeance, but to do good to all. "Be not overcome of evil, but overcome evil with good." (Rom. 12: 21.) Again, Christians are taught to "put off the old man with his doings" and "put on the new man." (Col. 3: 9, 10.) Again, we see the positive and the negative elements. Jesus said, "If any man would come after me, let him deny himself, and take up his cross, and follow me." (Matt. 16: 24.) Here is the negative element expressed in restraining oneself, and the positive element in constraining one to follow Christ.

Preachers of the gospel are admonished not to go beyond "the things which are written." (1 Cor. 4: 6.) We have liberty but must not go beyond things that are written. We are to abide in Christ if we bear fruit, but if we do not abide in him, we are cut off as a dead branch and destroyed. (John 8: 31; 15: 10.) Moreover, the Holy Spirit said, "Whosoever goeth onward and abideth not in the teaching of Christ, hath not God: he that abideth in the teaching, the same hath both the Father and the Son." (2 John 9.) Only the gospel of Christ is to be preached; a curse is placed upon one who substitutes another gospel for that which has been preached. In all of these we see the constraining and restraining influence of the Holy Spirit through the truth of the gospel. In the wisdom and mercy of God his children have been constrained to go about doing good, and have been restrained from doing that which is evil. They are to learn to do good and to keep themselves unspotted from the world.

CHAPTER XIX

RECEPTION AND REJECTION OF HOLY SPIRIT

INTRODUCTION.

Another double subject; reception conditional; rejection possible; man has power to receive or reject Holy Spirit.

I. RECEPTION OF HOLY SPIRIT.

1. Who receives him. (1 John 4: 13.)
    a. Believers. (John 7: 39; Eph. 1: 13.)
    b. Those who obey God. (Acts 2: 38; 5: 32.)
    c. In answer to prayer. (Acts 8: 15.)
2. How receive him.
    a. As one receives God or Christ. (Matt. 10: 40, 41; John 12: 48.)
    b. By receiving his teaching.
3. He dwells in Christians. (Rom. 5: 5; 8: 9, 11, 15; 2 Tim. 1: 14; James 4: 5.)

II. RESULTS OF RECEIVING HOLY SPIRIT.

1. Able to call God Father. (Gal. 4: 6.)
2. Receive the blessings as a child of God.
3. A joint heir with Christ. (Rom. 8: 15-17.)
4. Entertain hope of heaven.

III. REJECTION OF HOLY SPIRIT.

1. Israel rejected God. (1 Sam. 8: 7; 10: 19.)
2. Saul rejected God. (1 Sam. 15: 23.)
3. Israel rejected word of Lord. (Jer. 8: 9.)
4. Rejected Christ. (Mark 8: 31; John 12: 48.)
5. Reject the Holy Spirit.
    a. By rejecting his teachings.
    b. By failing to obey God.

IV. RESULTS OF REJECTING HOLY SPIRIT.

1. God rejects those who reject him. (1 Sam. 15: 23.)
2. Christ rejects those who reject him.
3. Holy Spirit rejects those who reject him.
4. They have no hope. (Eph. 2: 12.)

RECEPTION AND REJECTION OF HOLY SPIRIT

"Receive ye the Holy Spirit." (John 20: 22.)
"Ye do always resist the Holy Spirit." (Acts 7: 51.)

It seems wise to treat here another double subject—the reception and the rejection of the Holy Spirit. These two acts may be treated as one theme. The reception of the Holy Spirit is conditional; those who receive him must comply with all the conditions involved. *The richest blessing that God can give and the most needed by man cannot be forced upon anyone.* The book of Acts, sometimes called Acts of Apostles, may appropriately be called "Acts of the Holy Spirit," since this book gives a record of many cases of the reception and the rejection of the Holy Spirit. On the day of Pentecost the obedient received the Holy Spirit; a little later Stephen's hearers rejected the Holy Spirit. Some of the Samaritans received the Holy Spirit (Acts 8: 15, 18), while others rejected him. Throughout the book many cases might be cited. The book closes with a record of "some believed the things which were spoken, and some disbelieved." (Acts 28: 24.)

All the references in Acts show the possibility on the part of man to reject the Holy Spirit; they also show that when man complied with the conditions, he received the Holy Spirit. It is a significant fact fraught with solemn significance that the book of Acts which opens with a reception of the Holy Spirit and is pervaded throughout with the presence and power of the Holy Spirit should close with a warning to those who rejected the Holy Spirit. "And when they agreed not among themselves, they departed after that Paul had spoken one word, Well spake the Holy Spirit through Isaiah the prophet unto your fathers." (Acts 28: 25.) The marvelous progress that the early church made is a history of the reception of the Holy Spirit; the many enemies of the church and the persecutors of Christians show a long list of those who rejected the Holy Spirit. The rare and rich blessings came to those who accepted him and the awful rebuke and condemnation of God rested upon those who rejected him. The sledge hammer of God's wrath fell heavily upon God's anvil of judgment to those who rejected the gospel of salvation. So it is possible for man to receive the Holy Spirit and for him to reject him.

I. RECEPTION OF HOLY SPIRIT

The Holy Spirit had been promised by the prophets (Joel 2: 28-32; Zech. 12: 10-13), by John the Baptist (Matt. 3: 11), by Christ (John 14: 26; 15: 26). Even after his resurrection and just before his ascension Christ promised the Holy Spirit to his disciples. (Acts 1: 8.) This promise was fulfilled, and we have a record of it in the Acts. We have many references to the fact that the Holy Spirit had come and dwelt among men. It is proper to raise the question as to who should receive the Holy Spirit. Jesus said: "But this spake he of the Spirit, which they that believed on him were to receive: for the Spirit was not yet given; because Jesus was not yet glorified." (John 7: 39.) Again in promising the Holy Spirit, Jesus said that he should be a Comforter, "even the Spirit of truth: whom the world cannot receive; for it beholdeth him not, neither knoweth him: ye know him; for he abideth with you, and shall be in you." (John 14: 17.) Paul said: "Having also believed, ye were sealed with the Holy Spirit of promise." (Eph. 1: 13.) The testimony is conclusive that only believers in Christ could receive the Holy Spirit in his plenitude of blessings. The evidence is clear, furthermore, that the believers who obeyed God should be the recipients of the Holy Spirit; only those who obey him should receive him. (Acts 2: 38.) "And we are witnesses of these things; and so is the Holy Spirit, whom God hath given to them that obey him." (Acts 5: 32.) The Holy Spirit in his miraculous measure was received through prayer and by the laying on of hands. (Acts 8: 14-18.)

It is needful to inquire further in our study: "How is the Holy Spirit received?" Since it is in the power of man to receive or reject the Holy Spirit, it may be in order to study this phase of the subject. Jesus said to his apostles after his resurrection and just before his ascension: "Receive ye the Holy Spirit." (John

20: 22.) The word "receive" is said to be in the imperative mood; it is not here a promise, not a suggestion, not a request, not an overture, but a positive command. The disciples could obey this command or disobey it. How could they obey this command? Jesus had said: "If ye love me, ye will keep my commandments." (John 14: 15.) Again: "No man can say, Jesus is Lord, but in the Holy Spirit." (1 Cor. 12: 3.) Among the last words that Jesus spoke to his disciples before his ascension were concerning the Holy Spirit. "And behold, I send forth the promise of my Father upon you: but tarry ye in the city, until ye be clothed with power from on high." (Luke 24: 49.) He charged his disciples that they should not "depart from Jerusalem, but to wait for the promise of the Father, which, said he, ye heard from me: for John indeed baptized with water; but ye shall be baptized in the Holy Spirit not many days hence." (Acts 1: 4, 5.) These express conditions of their receiving the Holy Spirit; they must not "depart from Jerusalem," but remain there until the promise was fulfilled.

One can receive God by receiving his teachings. One can receive Christ by receiving the teachings of Christ. Jesus said as he sent out his disciples: "He that receiveth you receiveth me, and he that receiveth me receiveth him that sent me. He that receiveth a prophet in the name of a prophet shall receive a prophet's reward: and he that receiveth a righteous man in the name of a righteous man shall receive a righteous man's reward." (Matt. 10: 40, 41.) "He that rejecteth me, and receiveth not my sayings, hath one that judgeth him: the word that I spake, the same shall judge him in the last day." (John 12: 48.) Here we have rejecting Christ as tantamount to "receiveth not my sayings." The only way by which one can receive Christ today is to receive his teachings; the only way to receive the Holy Spirit is to receive his teachings. No one can reject the teachings of the Holy Spirit and at the same time receive the Holy Spirit. The Holy Spirit dwells in Christians. (Rom. 5: 5; 8: 9, 11, 15; 2 Tim. 1: 14; James 4: 5.) However, the Holy Spirit dwells in Christians to the extent that they receive the teachings of the Spirit.

II. Results of Receiving Holy Spirit

The results of the reception of the Holy Spirit are too numerous to mention and too glorious to describe. The Acts record the progress of the church as it was guided by the Holy Spirit. Individuals and congregations can receive the Holy Spirit. The Spirit dwells in the body of Christ, which is the church, and if he is left free to work his own will, he will give vitality to the entire body. If members are filled with the Spirit of Christ, they will have a new care and love for one another, suffering and rejoicing together; there will be a holy jealousy for the welfare and happiness of all who belong to that group of Christians. If the Holy Spirit dwells in a group of God's children, all schisms and divisions, whether manifest in inward estrangements or in outward separation, become impossible where the Holy Spirit dwells; all heresies and speculations of human teachings become impossible where the spirit of truth prevails. All ignorance and superstition in worship are abandoned in the light of the Spirit of God. Where the Spirit dwells, God's people unite to purge the courts of God of all worldiness. Even the song service is directed by consecrated servants of God who are filled with the praise of God rather than artistic and esthetic music. The preaching of the gospel will be, not a display of human attainments, but the simple declaration of God's power to save; worldly men, however wealthy, cultured, influential, will be displaced in the congregations by men who love God and honor him through his church. All worldly methods of raising money for the Lord's work will be abandoned, and voluntary, freewill offerings, consecrated by devotion to God, will take their place. When the Spirit of God dwells in a Christian, the lost art of prayer in the closet will be put into practice, and the prayers of the assembly of the saints will be fervent in the name of Christ. Where the Holy Spirit is lacking in individuals or congregations, the church of our Lord may pass into eclipse behind the shadow of the world and lose its radiant glory.

Christians are able to call God Father as a result of receiving the Holy Spirit. "And because ye are sons, God sent forth the Spirit of his Son into our hearts, crying, Abba, Father." (Gal. 4: 6.) All the blessings that belong to a child of God come as the result of the reception of the Holy Spirit. The full and rich blessings cluster around the faithful life of Christians on earth because they have received the Holy Spirit and kept their bodies as temples of the Holy Spirit. "Or know ye not that your body is a temple of the Holy Spirit which is in you, which ye have from God? and ye are not your own; for ye were bought with a price: glorify God therefore in your body." (1 Cor. 6: 19.) Those who have received the Holy Spirit are "heirs of God, and joint-heirs with Christ; if so be that we suffer with him, that we may be also glorified with him." (Rom. 8: 17.) "We may have a strong encouragement, who have fled for refuge to lay hold of the hope set before us: which we have as an anchor of the soul, a hope both sure and stedfast and entering into that which is within the veil." (Heb. 6: 18, 19.) The hope of a Christian thus sustains him and helps him to endure patiently the persecutions of this life and brightens his way to eternal life. These are some of the results of receiving the Spirit through the teachings of the Spirit.

III. REJECTION OF HOLY SPIRIT

Man as a free agent may turn away from the offered mercy of God and, like Hymenaeus and Alexander, make "shipwreck concerning the faith," and finally be "delivered unto Satan." (1 Tim. 1: 19, 20.) Man has it in his power, like Adam and Eve, to disobey God and have the gates of Eden barred against him; he can hear the pleadings of mercy, spurn the gentle wooings of the Holy Spirit through the truth of God, judge himself unworthy of eternal life by stopping his ears to the truth of the gospel, and, like the rich young ruler, turn away from Christ with sorrow, and finally be "turned away" from the beautiful gate of the city "foursquare." Israel, God's chosen people, rejected him. Samuel was judge of Israel and the people asked for a king; this grieved the aged Samuel and he "prayed unto Jehovah," and God answered him and said: "Hearken unto the voice of the people in all that they say unto thee; for they have not rejected thee, but they have rejected me, that I should not be king over them." (1 Sam. 8: 7.) Samuel called the people together and said to them: "Ye have this day rejected your God, who himself saveth you out of all your calamities and your distresses; and ye have said unto him, Nay, but set a king over us." (1 Sam. 10: 19.) These people rejected God by rejecting God's way of ruling over them. No one can reject God's way without rejecting God. Saul, the first king over Israel, rejected God. He rejected God by disobeying the command of God. Samuel said to him: "Because thou hast rejected the word of Jehovah, he hath also rejected thee from being king." (1 Sam. 15: 23.)

Israel again rejected God by rejecting the word of God. The prophet said to Israel: "The wise men are put to shame, they are dismayed and taken: lo, they have rejected the word of Jehovah; and what manner of wisdom is in them?" (Jer. 8: 9.) By rejecting the word of God Israel rejected God. They could not reject his word without rejecting his wisdom, his way, his will—rejecting God himself. In the same way people rejected Christ while he was here upon earth. Jesus, after presenting his teachings while here among men, said: "Full well do ye reject the commandment of God, that ye may keep your tradition." (Mark 7: 9.) In failing to accept the teachings of Christ they rejected him; in rejecting the commandments of God they rejected Christ. Again Jesus said: "He that rejecteth me, and receiveth not my sayings, hath one that judgeth him; the word that I spake, the same shall judge him in the last day." (John 12: 48.) This shows clearly that they rejected Christ when they rejected his "sayings" or his teachings. Jesus was rejected by the "elders, and the chief priests, and the scribes." Mark records: "And he began to teach them, that the Son of man must suffer many things, and be rejected by the elders, and the chief priests, and the scribes, and be killed, and after three days rise again." (Mark 8: 31.) The only way they could reject Christ was to reject his teachings and crucify him. This they did. At the same time some accepted him by accepting his teachings.

So in like manner people reject the Holy Spirit by rejecting the teachings of the Holy Spirit. Every infidel has rejected the Holy Spirit by rejecting the New Testament teachings, which were given by the Holy Spirit. Stephen preached the same gospel by the Holy Spirit that Peter preached on the day of Pentecost; he preached the same Christ that Peter preached; he gave the same arguments that Peter gave; he pointed out the prophecies that the Christ fulfilled. About three thousand who heard Peter accepted his preaching and received "the gift of the Holy Spirit." The hearers of Stephen rejected his preaching and rejected the Holy Spirit. Stephen said to them at the conclusion of his sermon: "Ye stiffnecked and uncircumcised in heart and ears, ye do always resist the Holy Spirit: as your fathers did, so do ye." (Acts 7: 51.) Stephen was "full of the Holy Spirit" (Acts 6: 5; 7: 55) and spoke the words of the Holy Spirit. When they rejected his words, they rejected the words of the Holy Spirit. When one neglects or refuses to obey the teachings of the Holy Spirit, one is rejecting the Holy Spirit.

IV. RESULTS OF REJECTING HOLY SPIRIT

When the gospel is preached to alien sinners and they refuse to obey it, they are judging themselves unworthy of eternal life. "Seeing ye thrust it from you, and judge yourselves unworthy of eternal life, lo, we turn to the Gentiles," said Paul to the Jews who had heard the gospel. (Acts 13: 46.) King Saul rejected God by refusing to obey his command; as a result of his act God rejected him from being king over Israel. (1 Sam. 15: 23.) God rejected Israel when Israel rejected him; he withheld his blessings from Israel and punished them with severe penalties until they would repent and accept him. Christ rejected those who rejected him; they rejected him by refusing to accept his teachings. In like manner God rejected Israel; he cast Israel off and accepted the Gentiles when Israel rejected Christ. (Rom. 11: 1-24.)

The Holy Spirit is rejected when one refuses to hear the gospel, believe the gospel, and obey the gospel. No one can reject God and Christ and at the same time accept the Holy Spirit. To reject the Holy Spirit today is to reject the teachings of the Holy Spirit; to reject the Holy Spirit now is to reject Christ and God. One cannot reject one member of the Godhead without rejecting the other members, as one cannot accept today one member of the Godhead without receiving the other members. Since the Holy Spirit is the last member of the Godhead to sojourn among men, the one who rejects his teaching is in the world without God and without hope. Just as those who had not heard the gospel "were at that time separate from Christ, alienated from the commonwealth of Israel, and strangers from the covenants of the promise, having no hope and without God in the world" (Eph. 2: 12), so are all today who reject the teachings of the Holy Spirit.

The Bible is not only the will of God revealed to man, but it is the nature of man revealed to himself. In the Bible we have a long list of generations of man; every generation from Adam to Christ is replete with examples of those who rejected God and were destroyed. Adam and Eve rejected God in the Garden of Eden when they disobeyed him. Cain rejected God when he refused to worship according to the instruction of Jehovah. The generations of man before the flood rejected God; they turned from him in their disobedience. The great deluge visited upon the earth was a condemnation of the wickedness of man. God had said, "My Spirit shall not strive with man for ever." (Gen. 6: 3.) After the flood the children of men multiplied and became wicked; man showed his proneness to err by rejecting the teachings of God and turning away from him and following his own imaginations. Throughout the patriarchal age the punishment of sin and the condemnation of the wicked reveal the depravity of man when he turns from the teachings of God.

The law of Moses given upon Mount Sinai contained that which man needed for his guidance in that period of his history. Man was blessed when he received the teachings of God and was condemned when he turned aside from the law. The law had in it the blessings of obedience and the curses for disobedience. Israel as a nation was blessed when it was faithful to the law of God; it was cursed and made a curse unto nations when it rebelled against God. The nation reached the pinnacle of its glory when it was faithful to the law of Jehovah; it reached the depth of contempt among other nations when it failed to keep the law. A blessing and a curse awaited Israel, and Israel could determine or choose which it would receive.

The prophets warned the people against disobedience and encouraged them to obedience. Nearly every prophet was burdened with the task of condemning the sins of Israel and warning them against further sins. The captivity of the ten tribes came upon them because of their disobedience; they had been warned by the prophets against their wickedness. The captivity of the ten tribes was held up before the kingdom of Judah as a warning, yet Judah continued in its sins and was finally carried away into captivity. While in captivity the people suffered for their sins. They, like King Saul, had rejected Jehovah, and he had rejected them. To reject Jehovah was to cease to follow his teachings; to accept Jehovah was to become obedient to him. There is no hope held out to Israel when it continued in sin. The only hope was in turning from sin and following Jehovah.

The same principle holds under the Christian dispensation. Christ came and some rejected him; even those whom he came to save rejected him. They rejected Christ by refusing to receive his teachings; they turned away from him when they turned away from his teachings. The Holy Spirit came and guided the apostles in teaching the words of Christ. When people rejected the teachings of the apostles, they judged themselves unworthy of eternal life. "Seeing ye thrust it from you, and judge yourselves unworthy of eternal life, lo, we turn to the Gentiles." (Acts 13: 46.) These were the words of the Holy Spirit that they rejected; there was no hope for them so long as they remained in this state of rejection. The Holy Spirit through the truth revealed may thus be rejected or received. We receive him when we receive his words; we reject him when we reject his words.

CHAPTER XX

HOLY SPIRIT AND WORSHIP

INTRODUCTION.

Worship belongs to the Christian life; cannot worship God today out of Christ; a great lesson for Christians.

I. WHAT IS WORSHIP?

1. Word occurs in different forms about 190 times in the Bible.
2. It has the idea of "fall down"—found about 500 times in the Bible.
3. To humble oneself before another. (Psalms 95: 6; Rev. 22: 8, 9.)
4. To manifest one's faith; to do honor to another.

II. KINDS OF WORSHIP.

1. First class.
   a. True worship.
   b. False worship.
2. Second class.
   a. Public worship.
   b. Private worship.

III. TWO ESSENTIAL ELEMENTS OF WORSHIP.

1. In spirit. (John 4: 23.)
   a. God a Spirit, or spiritual being.
   b. Must have an object of worship. (2 Cor. 3: 17; Phil. 3: 3.)
   c. This object a spiritual being. (Acts 17: 25.)
   d. Can be worshiped anywhere. (John 4: 21.)
   e. Worshiper becomes like the object. (Psalm 135: 15-18.)
2. In truth.
   a. According to the truth.
   b. Not scientific, philosophical, or historical.
   c. God's truth revealed in the Bible.
   d. The idea of reality and accuracy.

IV. HOLY SPIRIT IN WORSHIP.

1. He teaches us *whom* to worship. (Matt. 4: 10.)
2. He teaches *how* to worship God.
3. Guides in the acts of worship. (John 4: 24.)
4. Helps the worshiper.

HOLY SPIRIT AND WORSHIP

"God is a Spirit: and they that worship him must worship in spirit and truth." (John 4: 24.)

There are two classes of responsible people on earth—the unconverted and the converted. The unconverted class is the unsaved, unredeemed, alien sinner. This class cannot worship God acceptably. The second class, the converted, includes those who have been redeemed and who have entered into Christ; they have become members of his body, citizens of his kingdom, children of God. This class can worship God acceptably. So when we discuss the theme of this chapter we have in mind those who have been adopted into the family of God and who are living faithful to God. It is true that many who never have been converted *worship* something in some way; many of them may be even devout, like Cornelius, but their worship is not *acceptable to God*. There may be some benefit or reaction of the spirit of the worshiper, but he has no assurance that God blesses such worship.

The New Testament teaches clearly that *acceptable* worship today must be in Christ. The true spirit of worship is found only in Christ, and God blesses only those who are in him and worship "as it is written." It is important that people learn this so that they may know where their worship will be acceptable, and where they can receive the fullest and richest blessings in the act of worship. The Holy Spirit has an important part in every act of acceptable worship; he has no part in the worship of those who are out of Christ. The highest and noblest impulse of a human soul may find expression in true worship. The Spirit of acceptable worship lifts one into the higher realms of spiritual activities. The deepest yearnings of the soul can be satisfied only in true worship to God. It is sad to find so many "mere church members" who never experience the "joy of the Holy Spirit" (1 Thess. 1: 6) in the worship of God our Father. This worship is adorned with simplicity so that the humblest and lowliest of earth can engage in it with assurance that God will bless them. Much comfort and encouragement comes to the faith-

ful saints of God in their worship to God.   Christians need to
learn the value of worship; they need to go to the spiritual feast
with joy and return strengthened in their spiritual lives.   They
miss so much when they fail to worship God.

I. What Is Worship?

It is well to inquire into the nature of worship as we meditate
upon it. What is meant by *worship?* By actual count we find
that "worship" occurs in its different forms about one hundred
ninety times in the Bible. It is found one hundred thirteen times
in the Old Testament and seventy-eight times in the New Testament. It carries with it a variety of meanings, which range from
a simple act of courtesy to a fellow being to the true worship
of the living God. Not every time that the word is used does it
imply *acceptable* worship. There is another word which is closely
allied with worship; it is "fall down" or to prostrate oneself on
the ground or floor in the presence of another. This form is
found about five hundred times in the Bible. There is the act
of humiliating oneself in the presence of a superior in the "falling
down." Balaam, when he saw "the angel of Jehovah standing
in the way, with his sword drawn in his hand; and he bowed
his head, and fell on his face." (Num. 22: 31.) Again we find
that when Saul had the witch of Endor to call up Samuel, when
Saul saw him, "then Saul fell straightway his full length upon
the earth, and was sore afraid." (1 Sam. 28: 20.) Similar
examples may be cited to show that there is the act of prostrating
oneself in the act of worship.

The element of humility is included in the act of worship.
There is an effort to bring onself into a state of worthiness in
the act of worship. To humble oneself before another is to
attempt to bring oneself into the state of worthiness to be permitted to dwell in the presence of a superior. "Oh come, let us
worship and bow down; let us kneel before Jehovah our Maker:
for he is our God, and we are the people of his pasture, and the
sheep of his hand." (Psalm 95: 6, 7.) When John was permitted in his vision to see some of the spiritual raptures, he said:
"And when I heard and saw, I fell down to worship before the
feet of the angel that showed me these things. And he saith

unto me, See thou do it not: I am a fellow-servant with thee and with thy brethren the prophets, and with them that keep the words of this book: worship God." (Rev. 22: 8, 9.) In the act of worship one manifests one's faith in doing honor to a superior. It would be sham and hypocrisy for one to pay the act of honor to another when that one did not believe in the superior characteristics of another. Man needs the Holy Spirit to teach him all these things. In the true act of worship the one who "stoops the lowest may reach the highest."

II. Kinds of Worship

There may be many classifications of the acts of worship; it depends upon the viewpoint of the one who makes the classification. Broadly speaking, there are two great classes—true worship and false. The Holy Spirit is not concerned with any of the acts of false worship except to condemn them. He is deeply concerned about every act of true worship. The essentials of true worship will be discussed further in this chapter. Suffice it to say here that true worship must be *right* in principle. Practice is what one *does*—right or wrong. *Principle* is the foundation upon which the practice rests. It is important to know these things. True worship is divinely prescribed and spiritually followed. It is sinful to introduce anything *good* or *bad* in nature which the Holy Spirit has not ordained. Under the old covenant God called upon Israel to make a distinction between *common matters* and the *worship*. The priests were instructed and warned to make a distinction between that which God had required in the worship and that which he had not. "That ye may make a distinction between the holy and the common, and between the unclean and the clean." (Lev. 10: 10.) A condemnation was pronounced upon the priests because they did not make this distinction. "Her priests have done violence to my law, and have profaned my holy things: they have made no distinction between the holy and the common, neither have they caused men to discern between the unclean and the clean." (Ezek. 22: 26.)

It stands to reason that the items of worship must be *limited* or *unlimited*. The Holy Spirit has settled this question. If the worship is unlimited, nothing can be rejected; man can bring into the worship anything that he may desire and receive a blessing in his act of worship; but if the worship is *limited,* then nothing can be added to or subtracted from that which the Holy Spirit has prescribed as true worship. The "worship" is one thing and the "place" of worship is another thing. The places of worship, houses, seats, heating apparatus, ventilating devices have something to do with the comfort and convenience of the worshiper, but *they have nothing to do with the worship.* Neither is a thing right in the worship of God because it is right in the home; nor is a thing wrong in the home simply because it is wrong to use it in the worship. That which makes it wrong in the worship is that the Holy Spirit did not put it as an item of worship.

There is such a thing as false or vain worship. Jesus said: "But in vain do they worship me, teaching as their doctrines the precepts of men." (Matt. 15: 9.) The same is recorded in Mark 7: 7-9. Vain worship leads to a vain religion. (James 1: 26.) The Holy Spirit does not sanction, neither does he instruct, anyone in a vain worship. All human systems and human objects of worship are included in the class of vain worship. Even the observance of the system as given by the Holy Spirit is vain worship if it is not done as the Holy Spirit directs. The erroneous observance of a divine command may become vain. Hence, when the Holy Spirit teaches *how* to do a thing, then its *manner* becomes a part of the command. Will-worship, self-devised worship is condemned. (Col. 2: 20-23.) God, Christ, and the Holy Spirit are exacting—one must do exactly what is commanded in order to receive the blessings of God.

Viewing worship from another angle, it is divided into two classes—public worship and private. Public worship is that worship to which the public is invited or may attend; it is the worship of a group of worshipers. Public worship requires some leader; this leader guides the group in the different acts of worship. There is opportunity for those who worship only in the public assembly to neglect the all-important acts of worship; the individual may lose himself in the group and fail to worship. The general items of public worship are prayers, praises, meditations or reading the Scripture, exhortations, teaching or preaching, the fellowship in giving, and eating the Lord's Supper. It is easy to see how one in a large group could neglect to worship in any of these public acts. If one is guided by the Holy Spirit, that one will engage in all of the acts which are required by the Holy Spirit. While some of God's people are singing his praises, others may be silent; while some of them may give liberally, others may not give at all. They do not worship.

We mean by "private worship" that worship which is done in private. This is an act of worship where the individual is alone; it is the opposite of public worship. There is no opportunity for one to play the part of a hypocrite in private worship. He is alone with God; he goes into the closet and gets away from all others; he shuts the door, thus shutting the world out and shutting himself in with God. This is a solemn and sweet act of worship. No pretense or hypocrisy, sham or make-believe, is practiced in the solemn presence of God. The soul appears there stripped of all things and stands naked before God with all of its defects in the gaze of the all-seeing eye of God. The spiritual growth may be measured by the amount of time spent in private worship. Of course, there are items that belong to the public worship which are not included in the acts of private worship.

III. Two Essential Elements of Worship

Jesus outlined worship which is acceptable to God in his conversation with the Samaritan woman. The law of Moses had required certain things in the worship, and had designated a specific place for the worship. However, as Jesus fulfilled the law and took it out of the way, nailing it to the cross (Col. 2: 14), he gave another form of worship. The Holy Spirit has taken this and instructed the Lord's people how to worship him. There are at least two essential elements of true worship. Jesus said: "But the hour cometh, and now is, when the true worshippers shall worship the Father in spirit and truth: for such doth the Father seek to be his worshippers. God is a Spirit: and they that worship him must worship in spirit and truth." (John 4: 23, 24.) "God is a Spirit"; that is, God is Spirit; he is a spiritual being. This is why we must worship him "in spirit." The act of worship demands an object of worship; hence, the Holy Spirit teaches that God who is spiritual is the true object of worship. "Now the Lord is the Spirit: and where the Spirit of the Lord is, there is liberty." (2 Cor. 3: 17.) "For we are the circumcision, who worship by the Spirit of God, and glory in Christ Jesus, and have no confidence in the flesh." (Phil. 3: 3.) The object of the worship of Christians is a spiritual being. Christians do not worship material things such as idols (Acts 17: 25), neither do they worship a material force, nor any blind impersonal energy. Such objects would localize God and degrade him. God fills the universe and can be worshiped anywhere. (John 4: 21.) It is an important fact to know that the worshiper becomes like the object he worships. Not only does the worshiper become like the object that he worships, but *he becomes like his conception of the object that he worships.* "The idols of the nations are silver and gold, the work of men's hands. They have mouths, but they speak not; eyes have they, but they see not; they have ears, but they hear not; neither is there any breath in their mouths. They that make them shall be like unto them; yea, every one that trusteth in them." (Psalm 135: 15-18.) The Holy Spirit thus teaches that we become like our conception of our God; hence, the importance attached to following the Holy Spirit in every act of worship. To worship "in spirit" one must worship sincerely; that is, with all the spirit that is within him. The spirit of man responds in worship to the Spirit of God, and by the Holy Spirit we can cry, "Abba, Father." We have in this spiritual worship "deep calling deep." (Gal. 4: 6.)

Another essential element outlined by our Lord and emphasized by the Holy Spirit in true worship is "in truth." We must worship according to the truth of God. We are not guided by scientific, philosophical, or historical truth; we are guided by the truth which the Holy Spirit has revealed in the New Testament. The formal rule or law by which God through the Holy Spirit has outlined is called worshiping "in truth." There is a certain form or ceremonial part in true worship. The Holy Spirit has given the pattern, and guides through the teachings of the New Testament the true worshipers today. "In truth" may cover two ideas—reality and accuracy. There is the idea of reality, not symbolical, in worshiping "in truth." Again, there is the idea of accuracy, not deviating from the instruction given by the Holy Spirit in worship.

IV. HOLY SPIRIT IN WORSHIP

No one should ever lose sight of the part that the Holy Spirit has in worship. Not only does he teach us the general outline of acceptable worship, but we find instruction to guide us in every detail of true worship. It is useless to worship in vain or according to a false system of worship. Everyone ought to diligently search for the instructions given by the Holy Spirit to guide him in both public and private worship. The Holy Spirit teaches clearly the object of our worship. Christ said: "Thou shalt worship the Lord thy God, and him only shalt thou serve." (Matt. 4: 10.) The angel said to John: "Worship God." (Rev. 22: 9.) Hence, we know *whom* we are to worship. Those who have not the teachings of the Bible as given by the Holy Spirit do not know *whom* to worship. When Paul went to Athens, he "found also an altar with this inscription, TO AN UNKNOWN GOD." (Acts 17: 23.) These were worshiping in ignorance of the true God.

Furthermore, the Holy Spirit teaches *how* to worship this one God. He must be worshiped "in spirit and truth." Every item that belongs to the worship of God has been named by the Holy Spirit. No one can add an item to the act of true worship, neither can he take anything from what the Holy Spirit has given except at the peril of his own soul. The moment that he adds something to the teachings of the Holy Spirit or subtracts anything from it, that moment his act of worship becomes vain and is condemned in the sight of God. Furthermore, the Holy Spirit which dwells in Christians and in the church guides in the acts of true worship. This makes the worship spiritual. As we saw in the chapter of the "Holy Spirit and Prayer" that the Holy Spirit helps our infirmities and makes intercessions for us in prayer, and since prayer is one of the items of worship, we have the Holy Spirit helping us in the acts of true worship. It is a blessed thought to know that we have the third member of the Godhead to help us in our acts of worship. No one can afford to miss a single act of worship, either in public or private; to do so would be to rob one's life of spiritual blessings.

CHAPTER XXI

UNITY OF THE SPIRIT

INTRODUCTION.

Difference between *unity* and *union;* a neglected distinction should be emphasized; abundantly taught in New Testament.

I. WHAT IS "UNITY OF THE SPIRIT"?

    1. Unity in all of God's work.
    2. Unity in work of Christ.
    3. Unity in the work of Holy Spirit.
    4. Unity in the Godhead.
    5. Unity in the temple of Holy Spirit.
      a. The Jerusalem church.
      b. Members one of another. (Rom. 12: 5.)

II. "KEEP THE UNITY OF THE SPIRIT." (Eph. 4: 3.)

    1. This requires effort.
    2. Duty enjoined on unity.
    3. Must be kept "in the bond of peace."
    4. How it is to be kept.
      a. "With all lowliness."
      b. "Meekness."
      c. "With longsuffering."
      d. "Forbearing one another in love."

III. THE SEVEN "ONES." (Eph. 4: 4-6.)

    1. "There is one body."
    2. "One Spirit."
    3. "One hope."
    4. "One Lord."
    5. "One faith."
    6. "One baptism."
    7. "One God and Father."

IV. CHRISTIAN UNITY.

    1. All born of one Spirit. (John 3: 5.)
    2. All partake of same divine nature. (2 Pet. 1: 4.)
    3. Christ the pattern of each life. (1 Pet. 2: 21-25.)
    4. New Testament the guide of each one. (2 Tim. 3: 16, 17.)
    5. Each one has the same mediator. (1 Tim. 2: 5.)
    6. Each wears the same name. (James 2: 7.)
    7. All have a common Father. (Matt. 6: 9.)

UNITY OF THE SPIRIT

"Giving diligence to keep the unity of the Spirit in the bond of peace."
(Eph. 4: 3.)

No doctrine is more often pronounced and greater stressed in the New Testament than the unity of the Lord's people, their *oneness*. There is a wide and emphatic distinction made in the New Testament between *unity* and *union*. It seems strange that this distinction has been neglected and even ignored. We are not surprised that the world has not discovered this distinction, but it is astounding that Christians who claim to be guided by the New Testament have failed to differentiate between these two terms. *Union* is always present where there is *unity*, but *unity* may not be in all *unions*. "Unity" means oneness in the divine substance; it carries with it, not only the harmonious adjustment of constituent elements, but the sameness of character. It is illustrated by the oneness of all the members of the body; it means that oneness in Christ that exists in the Godhead. *Union* may include only a combination or assembly of similar parts and persons. It may mean only loosely joined or assembled. Religious denominations do not understand the *unity* of New Testament teachings; many of them think that a federation of all the denominations into one large group is "unity"; there can be no *unity* between such heterogeneous groups as the present-day denominations present. They differ too widely in their faiths, practices, and organizations; they are too loosely connected in their separate memberships to form a close *union* between all of them. For instance, in one group some of the members practice sprinkling and pouring for baptism, while others in the same denomination refuse to practice anything but immersion; in another group some of the members believe that they cannot "fall away from grace," while in the same group others believe and practice "falling from grace"; some in one group believe in infant membership in the group, while others of the same group will not let their infants belong to the church; and so the divisions within the same group prevent their being anything but a *union*.

It is hopeless and impossible for all of the denominations to form the *unity* of the New Testament. The moment this *unity* is formed that abolishes all division, denominationalism will cease.

I. What Is "Unity of the Spirit"?

It is well to inquire what is the "unity of the Spirit." It is that unity which the Spirit produces and requires in the church of our Lord. God is one; all of his works are united; they constitute the *universe*. It has been said that there is a connection and relation between everything in the universe; to know one thing fully and absolutely is to know everything in the universe; it is to be omniscient; this thought grows out of the unity of God's work. There is an apparent difference in the work of God; but fundamentally there is a close relation between all of his work. There is unity of matter, law, and force; light, heat, and gravitation are the same throughout the universe. The animal and the vegetable kingdoms meet and harmonize with each other; all the highways of science in the earth and in the heavens lead in upon the central throne and bring us into the presence of the one God because of their unity. The races of man may differ in color, habits, and character, yet there is unity in the human family. God "made of one every nation of men to dwell on all the face of the earth." (Acts 17: 26.) The stars and planets may seem to be sown broadcast in the heavens, but a closer study of them reveals that fact that they are arranged in mathematical order and move in their orbits with precision. This is due to the unity of all of God's work.

We can see the same unity in the work of Christ. He was the agent in the material creation; all things were made through him; hence, the pattern of unity for his work is from eternity. God had through his prophets foretold of the coming of Christ; a program was announced in the prophets for the work of Christ. He came and fulfilled all the prophecies and all the types of Old Testament Scripture. Unity is seen in all of these works. Moreover, when he began his public ministry, he gradually unfolded the will of the Father in his teachings. All of his teachings constitute one body of teachings with a consistent harmony in all of its details. The miracles of our Lord fit uniquely into the teachings and confirm the word of God. The teachings, parables, miracles, and the life of Christ all harmonize into one consistent system. The line of the priests were fulfilled in Christ; the prophets were fulfilled in him; the royal seed of the house of David was fulfilled in Christ—priest, prophet, and king all converge in Christ and blend harmoniously in his functions as the redeemer of man.

The work of the Holy Spirit bears the stamp of the pattern of unity which God and Christ have manifested. The Holy Spirit took the words and work of Christ and continued them on to completion. Jesus said of the Holy Spirit: "Howbeit when he, the Spirit of truth, is come, he shall guide you into all the truth: for he shall not speak from himself; but what things soever he shall hear, these shall he speak: and he shall declare unto you the things that are to come. He shall glorify me: for he shall take of mine, and shall declare it unto you." (John 16: 13, 14.) So the unity of the Christian system which was begun with Christ was completed by the Holy Spirit. The unity of the work of the Holy Spirit is manifest in all of its details. The same gospel is preached to every creature; the requirements of obedience are the same for everyone; there is but one law of pardon to the alien sinner. In the church God is no respecter of persons; the Holy Spirit teaches every member of the church the same things; the requirements of living the Christian life are uniform. There is unity in living the Christian life because the same instruction is given to each. Every congregation is molded after the same pattern; the congregations have the same organization, the same faith, the same ordinances, the same work, and the same mission. This emphasizes the unity of the Holy Spirit in his work. The Holy Spirit dwells in the faithful congregation; he does not dwell in one kind of body in one section and another kind in another section; the body in which he dwells is the same for every generation.

There is the closest concord in the members of the Godhead; the unity is so complete that they constitute one. The Holy Spirit dwells in the church, and thus it is called the temple. The first congregation established on the day of Pentecost in Jerusalem formed one church. A description of it says that "all that

believed were together, and had all things common. . . . Continuing
stedfastly with one accord in the temple, and breaking bread at
home, they took their food with gladness and singleness of heart."
(Acts 2: 44-46.)   We read further that the Jerusalem church
"lifted up their voice to God with one accord" in prayer (Acts
4: 24), "and the multitude of them that believed were of one
heart and soul" (Acts 4: 32).   These describe the unity of the
work of the Holy Spirit.   This unity was so complete that the
members are declared to be "severally members one of another."
(Rom. 12: 5.)

II. "Keep the Unity of the Spirit" (Eph. 4: 3)

Every Christian has been given the instruction to give "diligence
to keep the unity of the Spirit in the bond of peace."   (Eph. 4:
3.)   This admonition implies that an effort needs to be made to
keep the unity of the Spirit; it also implies that the unity of the
Spirit ought to be maintained.   Division, distractions, and con-
fusions have no place in the plan of the Holy Spirit.   The duty is
enjoined upon every member of every congregation to give "diligence" toward keeping the unity of the Spirit.   Another phrase
which emphasizes the unity of the Spirit is "in the bond of peace."
There have been so many unholy disputes about holiness, unlovely
quarrels about love, so many unjust contentions about justice,
so many unchristian debates about Christ, and so many discordant
arguments about unity that "the bond of peace" has been broken
and "the unity of the Spirit" destroyed in so many places.

It is wise to raise the question, "How can the unity of peace
be kept?"   The Holy Spirit has answered this question.   There
are unfolded in the teachings of the Holy Spirit four graces, by
the exercise of which the unity of the Spirit may be maintained.
Christians are exhorted "to walk worthily" of their calling, prac-
ticing these four graces which adorn the Christian life.   The first
is "with all lowliness."   This is properly laid as the foundation
of all.   It means humility.   A lack of humility is the chief cause
of contentions that arise among the followers of Christ.   "Make
full my joy, that ye be of the same mind, having the same love,
being of one accord, of one mind; doing nothing through faction
or through vainglory, but in lowliness of mind each counting

other better than himself." (Phil. 2: 2, 3.) "Be of the same mind one toward another. Set not your mind on high things, but condescend to things that are lowly. Be not wise in your own conceits." (Rom. 12: 16.) "Yea, all of you gird yourselves with humility, to serve one another: for God resisteth the proud, but giveth grace to the humble." (1 Pet. 5: 5.) It is easy to see the operation of pride and its tendency to contention. The Holy Spirit teaches it as a solemn duty to Christians to cultivate humility. "Meekness" is allied with lowliness; it is the opposite of self-will. Meekness is compatible with firmness and zeal. "And the Lord's servant must not strive, but be gentle towards all, apt to teach, forbearing, in meekness correcting them that oppose themselves; if peradventure God may give them repentance unto the knowledge of the truth." (2 Tim. 2: 24, 25.)

The third grace to be practiced in keeping "the unity of the Spirit in the bond of peace" is "with longsuffering." It is not enough that we do not give offense as God's people, but we must not take offense. The Holy Spirit teaches that Christians must not only keep themselves from injuring or wounding others, but they must bear patiently the injuries which others inflict upon them. Enemies may speak evil of Christians, but they must do no evil to others; they must endure with forbearance or long-suffering all persecutions. In thus suffering they are keeping the unity of the Spirit in the bond of peace. Christians will reach the highest dignity on earth by forbearing with long-suffering whatever may be imposed upon them. "Forbearing one another in love" is the crowning grace which enables Christians to keep the unity of the Spirit in the bond of peace. Love is the fountain out of which forbearance must be drawn. These are the graces that the Holy Spirit teaches as the basis for keeping the unity of the Spirit. When we ask, "How can we keep the unity of the Spirit in the bond of peace?" the answer is by humility, meekness, long-suffering and forbearance in love.

III. The Seven "Ones" (Eph. 4: 4-6)

The Holy Spirit gives a very minute description of the unity of Christianity. These grow out of the admonition to keep the unity of the Spirit in the bond of peace; they are the basic and fundamental principles, upon which the unity of God's people rests. "There is one body." Frequently the Holy Spirit has referred to the church as a "body." "For as the body is one, and hath many members, and all the members of the body, being many, are one body; so also is Christ." (1 Cor. 12: 12.) "Now ye are the body of Christ, and severally members thereof." (1 Cor. 12: 27.) All are united under a common head which is Christ, and are members one of another. "But now they are many members, but one body." (1 Cor. 12: 20.) "And whether one member suffereth, all the members suffer with it; or one member is honored, all the members rejoice with it." (1 Cor. 12: 26.) There is just "one Spirit," which dwells in this "one body." This is the Holy Spirit; as one spirit animates, guides, and governs the body, so does the Holy Spirit the church. The entire church or body must be subject to the Holy Spirit, as every member of the fleshly body must be to our spirits. "Know ye not that ye are a temple of God, and that the Spirit of God dwelleth in you?" (1 Cor. 3: 16.)

"One hope," which belongs to all Christians. Christians are called in one hope of their calling. This is also described as "Christ in you, the hope of glory." (Col. 1: 27.) Christians have all been raised with Christ and are seeking "the things that are above, where Christ is, seated on the right hand of God." (Col. 3: 1.) Christians are all looking for the happy home of the soul, and hope someday to enjoy the blessed union in heaven. There is "one Lord" who is the Lord Jesus Christ. "For one is your master, even the Christ." (Matt. 23: 10.) His authority is paramount with each and all; whatever he commands they must do; whatever he forbids they must refrain from doing; whatever he appoints they hold themselves ready to observe. Christians acknowledge no other master; Christ only has authority to command, or forbid, or institute. He is supreme and absolute. "All authority hath been given unto me in heaven and on earth," said Jesus. (Matt. 28: 18.)

"One faith," which is the faith of the gospel. The unity of the Spirit enjoins this one faith; there is one set of evidences upon which to base that faith; this faith comes by hearing "the word of Christ." (Rom. 10: 17.) This "one faith" leads one to submit to the "one baptism." This "one baptism" is that which is commanded by Christ and is performed into "the name of the Father and of the Son and of the Holy Spirit." (Matt. 28: 19.) It is the one baptism which puts one into Christ. (Rom. 6: 3, 4; Gal. 3: 27.) The Holy Spirit teaches but the "one baptism" which is a burial. (Col. 2: 12.) The last of the "seven ones" is the "one God and Father of all, who is over all, and through all, and in all." The church is God's family; its members have all been born of the water and the Spirit. This one God and Father of all "is over all" in that he is the supreme and ever-lasting Father; he is "through all" in that his Son dwells in Christians; and he is "in all" through the Holy Spirit who abides in his people as his own chosen temple.

IV. CHRISTIAN UNITY

The unity of God's people is called "Christian unity." The unity of the Spirit is seen in that all who are members of the body of Christ, or citizens of his kingdom, have been born of water and the Spirit. (John 3: 5.) They are related to the family of God by virtue of this birth; they are united with each other in that they have experienced a common birth. Moreover, they are all partakers of the divine nature. (2 Pet. 1: 4.) They are the children of God and are brethren in Christ; they all follow Christ and fashion their lives after him as the one pattern; he is our example. (1 Pet. 2: 21-25.) The New Testament is the guide of each one, and thus all live the same kind of lives. (2 Tim. 3: 16, 17.) Each one approaches God the Father through the one and same mediator, which is Christ. (1 Tim. 2: 5.) Each of them wear the same name (James 2: 7) and other names given by the Holy Spirit. They have one common Father, which is God. They are taught to address him as "our Father who art in heaven." (Matt. 6: 9.) All these and other things emphasize the unity of the Holy Spirit. God's people are to dwell together and always give "diligence to keep the unity of the Spirit in the bond of peace." "Behold, how good and how pleasant it is for brethren to dwell together in unity! It is like the precious oil upon the head, that ran down upon the beard, even Aaron's beard; that came down upon the skirt of his garments; like the

dew of Hermon, that cometh down upon the mountains of Zion:
for there Jehovah commanded the blessing, even life for evermore."
(Psalm 133.)

God has taught unity among his people in every dispensation.
Those who love truth and righteousness love God and love each
other. When people love God and love each other, they are united.
No one can love God without loving that which God loves. "Whosoever believeth that Jeseus is the Christ is begotten of God: and
whosoever loveth him that begat loveth him also that is begotten
of him. Hereby we know that we love the children of God, when
we love God and do his commandments. For this is the love of
God, that we keep his commandments: and his commandments
are not grievous." (1 John 5: 1-3.) It is clear that we must love
God by keeping his commandments; it is also evident that we love
God when we love the children of God. They are so related, God
and his children, that one cannot love one without loving the other;
hence, God and his people are united; this is the unity that the Holy
Spirit teaches.

The unity that the Holy Spirit teaches is based upon the
eternal truth of God; this truth has been expressed by the Holy
Spirit in many ways. The only "organic" unity is that which is
taught by the Holy Spirit. What the New Testament says to one
it says to all; what it commands one alien sinner to do it commands everyone to do. In this way everyone becomes a Christian
in the same way; they are united in Christ as they obey the gospel;
the Lord adds them to his church. He adds everyone who obeys
the gospel to his church; in adding them to the church they are
united with each other. So as they continue faithful to the Lord
they continue in the unity of the Spirit; this unity is taught in the
New Testament and no resolution, convention, or federation is
necessary to keep God's people united. They are kept in the unity
of the Spirit by their faithfulness to the Lord.

There is congregational unity in the sense that each Christian
that worships at the same place forms a congregation. All of the
Lord's people cannot meet at the same place; some of them are
on one continent, and others on another continent; some of them
live in one state or city and others live in other states and cities;
they must have a convenient place of worship; they come together

for this worship in this convenient place. However, this does not unite them; they are already in spirit united, and they come together and express themselves in worship to God after the same pattern. This unity is not brought about by some of them agreeing to be united; they are united if they are the people of God. It is not the unity taught in the New Testament merely for different groups of religious people *agreeing* to say nothing about their differences. The unity taught in the New Testament is basic in their relation to God and to each other; this unity is maintained only when they are faithful to God.

The unity of Christians who have been cleansed and sanctified by the blood of Christ can be maintained only by all doing the will of God. "If we walk in the light, as he is in the light, we have fellowship one with another, and the blood of Jesus his Son cleanseth us from all sin." (1 John 1: 7.) We can be united with Christ only by keeping his words. Jesus prayed for his disciples that they might be one even as he and his Father were one; this unity can be maintained only by doing the will of God. It is true that those in error can be united in error; this is not the unity of the Spirit. The unity of the Spirit is the unity on the truth expressed by the Spirit. This is the teaching of the New Testament; it is plain and simple and should be respected by man.

CHAPTER XXII

HOLY SPIRIT AND FIRE

Introduction.

Confusion about "Holy Spirit and fire"; need of clear thinking and prayerful study; "fire" mentioned many times in Bible.

I. Symbolic Use of Fire in Bible.

    1. In the Old Testament.

        a. Used to represent God. (Ex. 3: 2.)

        b. Used to represent protection of God. (Ex. 13: 21; Neh. 9: 12, 19; Zech. 2: 5.)

        c. Purification. (Zech. 13: 9; Mal. 3: 2, 3.)

        d. Denotes destruction. (Ex. 27: 17; Deut. 9: 3; Isa. 30: 27.)

        e. Represents God's judgment. (Gen. 19: 24; Ex. 9: 23, 24; Deut. 32: 22; Psalm 21: 9; Isa. 29: 6.)

    2. In the New Testament.

        a. Symbol of proving or testing. (1 Cor. 3: 13, 15; 1 Pet. 1: 7.)

        b. God a consuming fire. (Heb. 12: 29.)

        c. Tongues of fire. (Acts 2: 3, 19.)

        d. Tongue is a fire. (James 3: 5, 6.)

        e. Ministers of God represented by fire. (Heb. 1: 7.)

        f. Fire of God's vengeance. (Matt. 13: 40-42; Mark 9: 43, Luke 17: 29.)

        g. Destruction of the world. (2 Pet. 3: 12.)

        h. Eternal punishment. (Rev. 14:10.)

        i. Christ's coming in fire. (2 Thess. 1: 7, 8.)

II. Double Function of Symbol.

    1. Destroys and purifies.

        a. Destroys evil and wickedness. (1 Cor. 3: 10-15.)

        b. Purifies the obedient and righteous. (John 16: 8, 13; Eph. 6: 17.)

    2. Fire a symbol of Holy Spirit.

III. Baptism in Fire.

    1. Connected with Holy Spirit baptism. (Matt. 3: 9-12; Luke 3: 15-17.)

        a. The two contrasted.

        b. They are for two classes.

    2. Jesus came to judge as well as save. (John 3: 17; 9: 39; 12: 47.)

    3. Baptism of suffering in fire. (Matt. 10: 34; Luke 12: 49, 50.)

    4. Judgment of the wicked. (Matt. 3: 12.)

    5. Punishment in hell.

HOLY SPIRIT AND FIRE

"John answered, saying unto them all, I indeed baptize you with water; . . . he shall baptize you in the Holy Spirit and in fire." (Luke 3: 16.)

Someone has counted the number of times the Holy Spirit is mentioned in the Bible, and has discovered that he is mentioned more than four hundred times under forty-one different names and titles; he or his works are mentioned in one verse out of every twenty-six verses in the Bible. Yet there is much confusion about "the Holy Spirit and fire." "Fire" is mentioned many, many times in the Bible in various ways; fire is connected with the Holy Spirit both in the Old Testament and in the New. There is great need for some clear thinking and prayerful study on this subject. It seems wise to give treatment on this theme in connection with a discussion of the Holy Spirit. As the Holy Spirit in the life of Jesus and the Holy Spirit in the teachings of Jesus are two distinct themes, though closely related, and require separate considerations, so the Holy Spirit in his baptismal form and the baptism "in fire" are two entirely different themes, but are closely connected in the study of the Holy Spirit.

References to the place and work of the Holy Spirit in the life and teachings of Jesus are not very numerous; likewise reference to the "baptism in fire" find a smaller place in the teachings of Jesus. No distinction is to be drawn between the use of the term "Holy Spirit" with and without the articles "a, an, and the." The Holy Spirit is regarded in this treatment as a divine person; he is a member of the Godhead. "Fire" is about as old as the history of man; we find it mentioned early in the Bible. God, Christ, and the Holy Spirit each have made frequent reference to fire, and have used the term in various ways. We need to look at it or take the view that the Bible presents in revealing God's will to man.

I. SYMBOLIC USE OF FIRE IN BIBLE

The Bible contains many symbols; none is used more frequently than that of fire. In the New Testament the personal work of the Holy Spirit is frequently represented by means of symbols or emblems. It seems that man can grasp divine thought more fully when the nature and character of the work of the Holy Spirit is represented by physical symbols. These symbols are then God's chosen illustrations from natural things to help us to understand the work of the Holy Spirit and to get a clearer conception of all of his functioning. Early in the history of Moses we have the symbol of fire to represent God. The attention of Moses was drawn to a "flame of fire out of the midst of a bush." "The bush burned with fire, and the bush was not consumed." When Moses came near to it, "God called unto him out of the midst of the bush" and commanded him to put off his shoes, "for the place whereon thou standest is holy ground." (Ex. 3: 2-5.) Again it seems that the protection of God over Israel was represented by the symbol of fire. "And Jehovah went before them by day in a pillar of cloud, to lead them the way, and by night in a pillar of fire, to give them light; that they might go by day and by night: the pillar of cloud by day, and the pillar of fire by night, departed not from before the people." (Ex. 13: 21, 22.) See also Neh. 9: 12, 19. Again, Jehovah said: "For I . . . will be unto her a wall of fire round about, and I will be the glory in the midst of her." (Zech. 2: 5.)

Moreover the symbolic use of fire is used to represent purification. "And I will bring the third part into the fire, and will refine them as silver is refined, and will try them as gold is tried." (Zech. 13: 9.) God is represented as a refiner through one of his servants; "for he is like a refiner's fire, and like fullers' soap: and he will sit as a refiner and purifier of silver." (Mal. 3: 2, 3.) The dross will be destroyed and the gold will be purified. Again, fire is used in the Old Testament to denote destruction. (Ex. 27: 17; Deut. 9: 3; Isa. 30: 27.) Sometimes it is used to represent the severe judgment of God. Fire was rained down upon Sodom and Gomorrah and these cities were destroyed for their wickedness. (Gen. 19: 24.) Jehovah "sent thunder and hail, and fire ran down unto the earth," and Egypt was punished; "so there was hail, and fire mingled with the hail, very grievous, such as had not been in all the land of Egypt since it became a nation." (Ex. 9: 23, 24.) See also Deut. 32: 22; Psalm 21: 9; Isa. 29: 6.

There are too many references to "fire" in the Old Testament to mention them all here.

The New Testament abounds in the symbolic use of the term "fire." Jesus frequently uses the term as also does the Holy Spirit. Fire is used to prove or test the works of man. "Each man's work shall be made manifest: for the day shall declare it, because it is revealed in fire; and the fire itself shall prove each man's work of what sort it is." (1 Cor. 3: 13.) "That the proof of your faith, being more precious than gold that perisheth though it is proved by fire." (1 Pet. 1: 7.) God is represented both in the Old Testament and the New as "a consuming fire." (Heb. 12: 29.) In his jealousy for righteousness and his power to destroy the wicked, he will consume them as fire destroys the stubble. One manifestation of the presence of the Holy Spirit on the day of Pentecost was the presence of "tongues parting asunder, like as of fire." (Acts 2: 3.) The manifestation of the presence of the Holy Spirit was represented as "blood, and fire, and vapor of smoke." (Acts 2: 19.) It will be noted that these "tongues" were *not fire,* but "like as of fire."

James represents the tongue as a fire. "So the tongue also is a little member, and boasteth great things. Behold, how much wood is kindled by how small a fire! And the tongue is a fire: the world of iniquity among our members is the tongue; which defileth the whole body, and setteth on fire the wheel of nature, and is set on fire by hell." (James 3: 5, 6.) The ministers of God are represented as "a flame of fire" (Heb. 1: 7), and fire is used to represent the vengeance of God (Matt. 13: 40-42; Mark 9: 43; Luke 17: 29). Again, the next destruction of the world will be with fire; the first destruction was by a flood of water, but the last will be with fire. "But the day of the Lord will come as a thief; in the which the heavens shall pass away with a great noise, and the elements shall be desolved with fervent heat, and the earth and the works that are therein shall be burned up . . . looking for and earnestly desiring the coming of the day of God, by reason of which the heavens being on fire shall be dissolved, and the elements shall melt with fervent heat." (2 Pet. 3: 10-12.) Eternal punishment is represented by fire. (Rev. 14: 10.) Jesus said of those wicked ones who would come before him in judgment: "Depart from me, ye cursed, into the eternal fire which is prepared for the devil and his angels. . . . And these shall go away into eternal punishment." (Matt. 25: 41-46.) Furthermore, Jesus is represented as coming the second time "from heaven with the angels of his power in flaming fire, rendering vengeance to them that know not God, and to them that obey not the gospel of our Lord Jesus: who shall suffer punishment, even eternal destruction from the face of the Lord and from the glory of his might." (2 Thess. 1: 7-9.)

II. DOUBLE FUNCTION OF SYMBOL

A general study of the use of the symbol of fire in the Bible reveals a double function of it. "Fire" is made to serve in this double office, and we need to observe the context in order to get the meaning of the symbol. This double office of the symbol of fire is clearly indicated by Paul in his picture of the judgment of the works of Christians; they are represented as being built on the foundation "which is Jesus Christ." Some works are compared to "gold, silver, costly stones, wood, hay, stubble." Here are two classes of works; one is represented by "gold, silver, costly stones," and the other class by "wood, hay, stubble." Each man's work shall be made manifest: for the day shall declare it, because it is revealed in fire; and the fire itself shall prove each man's work of what sort it is. If any man's work shall abide which he built thereon, he shall receive a reward. If any man's work shall be burned, he shall suffer loss: but he himself shall be saved; yet so as through fire." (1 Cor. 3: 11-15.) Here we have the use of the symbol of fire for the testing and purifying one class of works, and burning and destroying the other class—the one symbol with a double function.

The sanctifying power of the Holy Spirit of necessity involves destruction; there is the saving influence of the Holy Spirit and the destructive power as experienced by the wicked. The individual is purified by cleansing of sin when forgiveness is extended; at the same time, people are purified by the destruction of the wicked and the forgiveness of sins. It is like precious metal that is purged of its dross. The wicked were destroyed by the flood in the days of Noah; yet Noah and his family were saved;

here was a double function of water—destruction and salvation.
Sodom and Gomorrah were destroyed, but Lot was saved. "Thou
puttest away all the wicked of the earth like dross; therefore I
love thy testimonies." (Psalm 119: 119.) "Take away the
dross from the silver, and there cometh forth a vessel for the
refiner: take away the wicked from before the king, and his throne
shall be established in righteousness." (Prov. 25: 4, 5.) Ezekiel
said of the wickedness of Israel that it had "become dross" and
needed to be cast into "the midst of the furnace," and "because
ye are all become dross, therefore, behold, I will gather you into
the midst of Jerusalem. As they gather silver and brass and
iron and lead and tin into the midst of the furnace, to blow the
fire upon it, to melt it; so will I gather you in mine anger and
in my wrath, and I will lay you there, and melt you. Yea, I
will gather you, and blow upon you with the fire of my wrath, and
ye shall be melted in the midst thereof. As silver is melted in
the midst of the furnace, so shall ye be melted in the midst thereof." (Ezek. 22: 18-22.) The double work of fire in purifying
and destroying is similar to the double office of the Spirit. "For
the word of God is living, and active, and sharper than any two-
edged sword, and piercing even to the dividing of soul and spirit,
of both joints and marrow, and quick to discern the thoughts and
intents of the heart." (Heb. 4: 12.) This word of God which
is "sharper than any two-edged sword" is the "sword of the
Spirit." (Eph. 6: 17.) The double function is further seen in
that "the Spirit searcheth all things, yea, the deep things of God"
(1 Cor. 2: 10), and exposes and condemns the wickedness that
is in man and blesses the obedient and righteous things of man.
Spirit and fire then are not in every instance antithetical and
mutually exclusive conceptions, but fire represents one phase of
the work of the Holy Spirit. However, there are antithetical uses
of the symbol of the baptism of fire and the baptism of the Holy
Spirit.

III. Baptism in Fire

John the Baptist created such a sensation among the Jews that
many of them "reasoned in their hearts concerning John, whether
haply he were the Christ." (Luke 3: 15.) However, John

answered them and said: "I indeed baptize you with water; but there cometh he that is mightier than I, the latchet of whose shoes I am not worthy to unloose: he shall baptize you in the Holy Spirit and in fire: whose fan is in his hand, thoroughly to cleanse his threshing-floor, and to gather the wheat into his garner; but the chaff he will burn up with unquenchable fire." (Luke 3: 16, 17.) Matt. 3: 9-12 gives a record of the same event. There has been much discussion in the religious world as to the meaning of John's statement: "He shall baptize you in the Holy Spirit and in fire." Mark omits the phrase "in fire." Matthew and Luke in this record are the only writers that add "in fire." Does John refer to two baptisms—the Holy Spirit baptism and baptism in fire? Or does he refer only to one baptism of the two elements? Does the term "fire" signify here purification or destruction? Does it represent one aspect of the work of the Holy Spirit, or something entirely distinct from it? Are there two classes in view here—one to receive the baptism of the Holy Spirit, and the other to receive the baptism in fire? Much confusion exists in the minds of Bible students on this subject.

It is evident that the penal use of the term "fire" is here to be recognized. The following verses teach clearly that there are two classes in view. "Whose fan is in his hand, and he will thoroughly cleanse his threshing-floor; and he will gather his wheat into the garner, but the chaff he will burn up with unquenchable fire." (Matt. 3: 12.) Luke also in his record presents two classes— one represented by the wheat, the other by the chaff. One class, the "wheat," is to be gathered "into his garner," while the other class, "the chaff," he will "burn up with unquenchable fire." There are three successive verses in Matthew treating of the ministry of Christ. Is it credible that "fire" should have one meaning in the first and third verses, and an entirely different meaning in the second? We must conclude that "fire" has the same meaning in verses ten, eleven, and twelve. With this conclusion, we must believe that two baptisms are mentioned here, and that two classes are to receive the baptisms; that one class is to receive the baptism of the Holy Spirit and the other class the baptism in fire. "Fire" as used here cannot be taken as a symbol of the Holy Spirit; this would be a confusion to say that Christ would "baptize in the Holy Spirit and in the Holy Spirit." Where fire is used in a literal sense in the Bible, it invariably sets forth God's divine judgment upon sin; where it is used in a figurative sense it represents the process by which evil is removed, and destruction. No sound principle of interpretation admits of representing the same truth under a literal and a figurative form in the same connection. This shows that the Holy Spirit and fire are used in the passage quoted *not as synonyms, but as opposites*—the one, the baptism of the blessings of life, and the other, the baptism to the condemnation of death. The baptism of the Holy Spirit culminating for the believer in heaven and eternal glory, and the baptism in fire culminating to the unbeliever in hell and eternal destruction. So then to the ungodly "our God is a consuming fire," but to the believer he is "the God of our salvation." It is recognized as true that the fire of judgment and condemnation is from God, and also that holiness and salvation are from him; but they are distinct and separate.

Jesus came to judge the world as well as to save it. In one sense he came to save the world; that is, all who would accept him; in another sense he came to condemn the world; that is those who would reject him. "For God sent not the Son into the world to judge the world; but that the world should be saved through him." (John 3: 17.) This expresses one phase of the mission of Christ to earth. "And Jesus said, For judgment came I into this world, that they that see not may see; and they that see may become blind." (John 9: 39.) This expresses another phase of his mission. Other Scriptures teach the two phases of the mission of Christ. "Think not that I came to send peace on the earth: I came not to send peace, but a sword." (Matt. 10: 34.) Again Jesus said: "I came to cast fire upon the earth; and what do I desire, if it is already kindled?" He then speaks of a baptism which we call the baptism of suffering. (Luke 12: 49, 50.) Here baptism and fire are joined, but the baptism relates to Christ's own personal experience, and the fire to his ministry among men.

There is abundant proof in the context of Matt. 3: 9-12 and Luke 3: 15-17 and in the general tenor of Bible teaching, alike in the Old Testament and the New, to interpret fire as signifying

judgment upon the wicked and the eternal blessings of the Holy
Spirit upon the righteous.   By these two baptisms—the Holy
Spirit baptism and the baptism in fire—the processes of the work
of separating good from evil will go on until the world has been
redeemed from sin, and the new heavens and a new earth have
come from God.   And God shall dwell with them forever and be
their God, and the wicked "shall go away into eternal punishment"
—the baptism in fire.

BIBLE REFERENCES TO THE HOLY SPIRIT

"THE SPIRIT"

Num. 11: 26; 27: 18.
1 Chron. 12: 18.
Ezek. 2: 2; 3: 12, 14, 24; 3: 3; 43:
5.
Matt. 10: 20; 22: 43.
Mark 1: 10, 12.
Luke 2: 27; 4: 1.
John 1: 32, 33; 3: 5, 8, 34; 4: 24.
Acts 2: 4; 6: 10; 8: 29; 10: 19;
11: 12; 16: 7; 21: 4.
Rom. 8: 4, 5, 9, 10, 11, 15, 16, 26.
1 Cor. 2: 10, 11; 12: 8.
2 Cor. 3: 17.
Gal. 3: 2, 3, 5; 4: 6, 29; 5: 5, 17;
6: 8.
Eph. 2: 22; 3: 5; 6: 18.
Col. 1: 8; 2: 5.
1 Thess. 5: 19.
1 Tim. 4: 1.
Heb. 9: 14, 10: 29.
James 4: 5.
1 Pet. 1: 11; 4: 14.
1 John 5: 7, 8.
Rev. 1: 10; 2: 7; 4: 2; 14: 13; 22:
17.

"BY THE SPIRIT"

1 Chron. 28: 12.
Acts 11: 28.
Rom. 8: 13.
Gal. 5: 16, 18, 25.
1 John 3: 24.

"SPIRIT OF GOD"

Gen. 1: 2; 41: 38.
Ex. 31: 3; 35: 31.
Num. 24: 2.
1 Sam. 10: 10; 11: 6; 19: 20, 23.
2 Chron. 15: 1; 24: 20.
Job 27: 3; 33: 4.
Ezek. 11: 24.
Matt. 3: 16; 12: 28.

Rom. 8: 9, 14.
1 Cor. 2: 11, 14; 3: 16; 6: 11; 7:
40; 12: 3.
2 Cor. 3: 3.
Eph. 4: 30.
Phil. 3: 3.
1 Pet. 4: 14.
1 John 4: 2.

"HIS SPIRIT"

Num. 11: 29.
Job 26: 13.
Psalm 106: 33.
Isa. 34: 16; 48: 16.
Dan. 2: 1.
Zech. 7: 12.
Mark 2: 8; 8: 12.
John 19: 30.
Rom. 8: 11.
Eph. 3: 16.
1 John 4: 13.

"HOLY SPIRIT"

Psalm 51: 11.
Isa. 63: 10, 11.
Matt. 1: 18, 20; 3: 11; 12: 32;
28: 19.
Mark 1: 8; 3: 20; 12: 36; 13: 11.
Luke 1: 15, 35, 41, 67; 2: 25, 26,
3: 16, 22; 4: 1; 10: 21; 11: 13;
12: 10, 12.
John 1: 33; 14: 26; 20: 22.
Acts 1: 2, 5, 8, 16; 2: 4, 33, 38;
4: 8; 5: 3, 32; 6: 5; 7: 51, 55;
8: 15, 17, 18, 19; 9: 17, 31; 10:
38, 44, 45, 47; 11: 15, 16, 24; 13:
2, 3.
Acts 13: 9, 52; 15: 8, 28; 16: 6;
19: 2, 6; 20: 23, 28; 21: 11; 28:
25.
Rom. 5: 5; 9: 1; 14: 17; 15: 13,
16, 19.
1 Cor. 6: 19; 12: 3.

2 Cor. 6: 6; 13: 14.
Eph. 1: 13; 4: 30.
1 Thess. 1: 5, 6; 4: 8.
2 Tim. 1: 14.
Tit. 3: 5.
Heb. 2: 4; 3: 7; 6: 4; 9: 8; 10: 15.
1 Pet. 1: 12.
2 Pet. 1: 21.
Jude 20.

"Spirit of Jehovah"

Judges 3: 10; 6: 34; 11: 29; 13: 25; 14: 6.
1 Sam. 10: 6; 16: 13, 14.
2 Sam. 23: 2.
1 Kings 18: 12; 22: 24.
2 Kings 2: 16.
2 Chron. 18: 23; 20: 14.
Isa. 11: 2; 40: 13; 59: 19; 63: 14.
Ezek. 11: 5; 37: 1.
Mic. 2: 7; 3: 8.

"Spirit of the Lord"

Isa. 61: 1.
Luke 4: 18.
Acts 5: 9; 8: 39.
2 Cor. 3: 17, 18.

"My Spirit"

Gen. 6: 3; Isa. 30: 1; 42: 1; 44: 3; 59: 21.
Ezek. 36: 27; 37: 14; 39: 29.
Joel 2: 28, 29.
Hag. 2: 5.
Zech. 4: 6.
Matt. 12: 18.
Acts 2: 17, 18.

"Of the Spirit"

Num. 11: 17, 25.
Prov. 15: 4.
Mal. 2: 15.
Matt. 5: 1.
Luke 4: 14.
John 3: 6, 8; 7: 39.
Rom. 8: 2, 5, 6, 23; 15: 30.
1 Cor. 2: 4; 12: 7.
2 Cor. 1: 22; 5: 5.
Gal. 3: 14; 5: 22; 6: 8.
Eph. 6: 17.
Phil. 1: 19; 2: 1.
2 Thess. 2: 13.
1 Pet. 1: 2.

"One Spirit"

1 Cor. 6: 17; 12: 9, 13.
Eph. 2: 18; 4: 4.
Phil. 1: 27.

"Same Spirit"

1 Cor. 12: 4, 8, 9, 11.

"Thy Spirit"

Neh. 9: 20, 30.
Job 15: 13.
Psalms 104: 30; 139: 7; 143: 10.
2 Tim. 4: 22.

"Spirit of Truth"

John 14: 17; 15: 26; 16: 13.
1 John 4: 6.

"With the Spirit"

1 Cor. 14: 14.
Eph. 5: 18.

BIBLIOGRAPHY

The following books were found helpful in the preparation of this book, and due acknowledgment is hereby made:

Acts of the Holy Spirit, A. T. PIERSON.

Acts of the Apostles, H. LEO BOLES.

Administration of the Holy Spirit, GEORGE MOBERLY.

Baptist Quarterly, Vol. V.

Baptism of the Holy Ghost, ASA MAHAN.

Baptismal Controversy, J. HARTZEL.

Debate, CAMPBELL-RICE.

Debate, Influence of Holy Spirit in Conversion, SLEETH-RANDALL.

Divine Demonstration, H. W. EVEREST.

Encyclopedia of Religious Knowledge, Vol. II, SCHAFF-HERZOG.

Encyclopedia, International Standard Bible, Vol. III.

Fullness of the Spirit, A. McMILLAN.

Gift of Tongues, DAWSON WALKER.

Gospel Plan of Salvation, T. W. BRENTS.

He That Is Spiritual, L. S. CHAFER.

Holy Spirit Resisted, CALEB KIMBALL.

Indwelling Spirit, W. T. DAVISON.

Internal Evidence of Inspiration, HARRY RIMMER.

Inspiration of Holy Scripture, WILLIAM LEE.

Inspiration, W. SANDAY.

Inspiration of the Old Testament, ALFRED CAVE.

Lard's Quarterly, Vols. II and III.

Luke, Commentary, H. LEO BOLES.

Matthew, Commentary, H. LEO BOLES.

New Christian Quarterly, Vol. I.

Office of the Holy Spirit, R. RICHARDSON.

Operation of the Holy Spirit, F. C. EWER.

Personality of the Holy Spirit, E. R. HENDRIX.

Power of Pentecost, THOMAS WAUGH.

Queries and Answers, LIPSCOMB AND SEWELL.

Queries and Answers, D. LIPSCOMB.

Reason and Revelation, R. MILLIGAN.

Revelation and Inspiration, JAMES ORR.

Salvation from Sin, D. LIPSCOMB.

Scheme of Redemption, R. MILLIGAN.
Scripture Testimony to the Holy Spirit, JAMES MORGAN.
Sermons and Addresses, J. B. BRINEY.
Studies in the Holy Spirit, JAMES B. GREEN.
The Holy Spirit, W. T. ROUSE.
The Holy Spirit, "A PASTOR."
The Holy Spirit, R. C. ZARTMAN.
The Holy Spirit, RAYMOND CALKINS.
The Holy Spirit, T. REES.
The Holy Spirit, I. J. ROSENBERGER.
The Holy Spirit, J. C. MASSEE.
The Holy Spirit in the Gospels, J. RITCHIE SMITH.
The Spirit and the Word, Z. T. SWEENEY.
The Work of the Holy Spirit, AUSTIN PHELPS.
The Witness of the Spirit, JAMES W. ZACHARY.
The Triune God, C. NORMAN BARTLETT.
Who Is the Holy Spirit? HENRY W. FROST.
Vox Dei, The Doctrine of the Spirit, R. A. REDFORD.

INDEX

CPSIA information can be obtained at www.ICGtesting.com
Printed in the USA
BVOW080800080513

320181BV00002B/391/A